Synthetic Markets

Using Generative AI to Stress-Test Trading Strategies

Victor Trex

Published by NobleTrex Press

For permissions and other inquiries, write to:
P.O. Box 3132, Framingham, MA 01701, USA

Contents

Introduction

Financial markets are adaptive, path-dependent systems whose most consequential behaviors often occur in the tails. Yet most strategy development still leans on a thin sliver of realized history and a handful of crisis episodes. Backtests that look rigorous on paper can fail at the first sign of regime change, liquidity drought, or execution friction. This book advances a complementary paradigm: synthetic markets-data, scenarios, and simulators produced by principled statistical and generative techniques that respect empirical regularities and market mechanics. Our goal is to stress-test trading strategies against a much wider, controllable, and auditable universe of possibilities, exposing fragility before capital is at risk.

Synthetic markets are not about fabricating convenient worlds. They are instruments for falsification. By fusing probabilistic modeling with deep generative learning, microstructure-aware simulation, and rigorous evaluation, we create environments where strategies confront adverse yet plausible conditions: clustered volatility, regime breaks, liquidity withdrawals, queue dynamics in limit order books, and cross-asset contagion. The emphasis is on reproducibility and governance as much as on creativity: every scenario has lineage; every experiment is tracked; every conclusion is traceable.

The text is organized to build this capability end to end. We begin with quantitative foundations-probability, statistical inference, time-series analysis, stochastic simulation, linear algebra, and optimization-laying the mathematical scaffolding for both classic resampling methods and modern neural generators. These fundamentals anchor the stylized facts of markets: heavy tails, volatility clustering, leverage effects, and the constraints implied by no-arbitrage approximations. We then turn to market structure and microstructure. Instruments are only as tradable as the venues, order types, and frictions that mediate them; synthetic scenarios must therefore encode limit order book mechanics, liquidity and impact, transaction costs, and execution algorithms from TWAP/VWAP to Almgren-Chriss. Alongside these domain elements, we establish data engineering practices-versioned datasets, lineage-preserving pipelines, and GPU-accelerated experiment tracking-so that results remain both scalable and auditable.

With this context in place, we develop the generative foundations for financial time series and order flow. The book connects latent-variable modeling and neural training dynamics to the demands of controlled scenario generation. We treat evaluation as a first-class citizen, defining fidelity and utility metrics, two-sample tests, and conditioning mechanisms that steer generation toward factors, regimes, or liquidity states of interest. Baselines matter: block bootstraps and copulas provide transparent dependence structures against which GANs, VAEs and normalizing flows, diffusion models, and sequence/event architectures (transformers and Hawkes processes) can be judged for stability, likelihood control, and tail coverage.

Simulation and stress-testing methodologies integrate these models with calibrated agent-based and order-book simulators. We formalize empirical targets and constraints, couple learned generators to market simulators that preserve impact and queue dynamics, and design stress programs that include historical replay, hypothetical "what-if" shocks, and reverse stress testing that works backward from failure thresholds. Adversarial and tail-focused techniques-combining latent-space search with extreme value theory and Monte Carlo-yield extreme-yet-plausible market paths. Throughout, backtesting is re-architected to be execution-aware and unbiased via walk-forward design and purged cross-validation, ensuring that synthetic streams integrate cleanly with evaluation engines.

Stress insights only matter when they inform decisions. We therefore link scenario outputs to risk measures (VaR, CVaR, drawdown distributions) and to allocation frameworks spanning mean-variance, risk parity, and Kelly-style sizing with capacity and turnover constraints. Scenario-based decision playbooks translate diagnostics into concrete hedges, sizing adjustments, and governance sign-offs across the trade lifecycle. Finally, we address validation, governance, and MLOps: model-risk inventories, robustness envelopes, documentation standards, privacy-utility trade-offs for synthetic data (including defenses against membership inference), benchmark harnesses, deployment orchestration, drift monitoring, and incident response. The closing case studies demonstrate how these elements combine in practice for equities order-book strategies and options portfolios under volatility spikes, and they distill lessons for production adoption.

This book is written for quantitative researchers, traders, risk managers, data scientists, and students who seek to elevate strategy evaluation beyond historical happenstance. Readers comfortable with undergraduate probability, linear algebra, and programming can follow the foundations; later chapters offer depth for specialists. Throughout, the guiding principles are empirical fidelity, controllability, and accountability. Synthetic markets, used responsibly, do not replace history-they enlarge it, enabling us to test what we could have seen as rigorously as what we did see. In an era defined by structural breaks and machine-mediated liquidity, that enlargement is not a luxury; it is a prerequisite for robust decision making.

Chapter 1

Quantitative Foundations for Synthetic Markets

In synthetic markets, every price path you generate is a compact opinion about how the world might unfold-and whether your trading strategy survives it. This chapter equips you with the quantitative language to express and manipulate those opinions: how to think in probabilities instead of anecdotes, how to separate noise from signal in historical data, how to use linear algebra and optimization to shape risk, and how to model market dynamics over time. The goal is not academic rigor for its own sake, but a sharp, practical foundation: by the end, you'll be able to read market data the way a generative model does-and deliberately bend it into stress scenarios that expose the true fragility of your strategies.

1.1 Probability and Statistical Inference

Synthetic markets are, at their core, probability machines. They generate possible futures for prices, returns, and risk factors. To design, calibrate, and evaluate these machines, we need a precise probabilistic vocabulary. In this section we develop that vocabulary: random variables, expectations, distributions, and the basic tools of statistical inference. Throughout, we keep the link to trading concrete: every definition will be tied to returns, *P&L*, and performance metrics such as drawdowns and Sharpe ratios.

From Uncertain Markets to Random Variables

When you place a trade today, tomorrow's *P&L* is uncertain. You might say "I think I'll make around 0.5%," but you cannot list the exact outcome in advance. Probability theory formalizes this uncertainty.

- **Outcome (scenario).** A complete specification of what happens in the market over some horizon (e.g., all end-of-day prices for your universe over the next month).
- **Probability.** A numerical degree of belief assigned to sets of outcomes, respecting the usual rules (probabilities are between 0 and 1, and the probability of all possible outcomes is 1).
- **Random variable.** A numerical quantity defined on outcomes, such as the one-day return on an asset, or the maximum drawdown of a strategy over a year.

Formally, we imagine an abstract probability space $(\Omega, \mathcal{F}, \mathbb{P})$, where:

- Ω is the set of all possible market scenarios (paths of prices, volatilities, macro variables, ...),
- $\mathcal{F}$ is a collection of sets of scenarios (the events we can reason about),
- $\mathbb{P}$ assigns probabilities to these events.

A *random variable* is then a function

$$X : \Omega \to \mathbb{R},$$

such as

$$X(\omega) = \text{next-day log-return of SPX in scenario } \omega,$$

or

$$Y(\omega) = \text{12-month maximum drawdown of strategy S in scenario } \omega.$$

For synthetic markets, this perspective is operational: each simulated path ω is one synthetic scenario, and every portfolio or risk metric you compute on that path is a random variable.

Distributions: How Random Variables Behave

The distribution of a random variable tells you which values are more or less likely. For an asset daily log-return R, the distribution captures properties you care about in backtesting and stress testing.

Discrete and continuous distributions

A random variable can be:

- **Discrete**, taking values on a countable set (e.g., default/no-default, or a state indicator like bull/bear regime).
- **Continuous**, taking values on an interval of the real line (e.g., a continuously distributed return).

For discrete X, we specify probabilities directly:

$$\mathbb{P}(X = x_i) = p_i, \qquad \sum_i p_i = 1.$$

For continuous X, we typically specify a probability density function (pdf) f_X such that for any interval $[a, b]$,

$$\mathbb{P}(a \le X \le b) = \int_a^b f_X(x)\, dx.$$

In trading, we often start by assuming returns are continuous and approximately Gaussian, then relax that assumption to capture heavy tails and skew.

Distribution functions and quantiles

The cumulative distribution function (cdf) of X is

$$F_X(x) = \mathbb{P}(X \leq x).$$

The cdf provides a complete picture of the distribution. From it we can define:

- **Quantiles.** The α-quantile q_α solves $F_X(q_\alpha) = \alpha$. For example, the 1% quantile of portfolio return is the loss level exceeded only 1% of the time under the model; this is closely related to Value-at-Risk.
- **Tail probabilities.** $\mathbb{P}(X \leq q_\alpha)$ gives the likelihood of extreme losses, which is central to stress testing.

Synthetic market generators implicitly specify a distribution (or family of distributions) for returns, volatilities, and other quantities of interest. When you calibrate such a generator, you are trying to match salient features of the empirical distribution: mean, variance, skewness, kurtosis, tail probabilities, and so on.

Expectations and Moments: Summarizing Risk and Reward

The expectation of a random variable is its long-run average over repeated draws from the distribution. If R is daily return, $\mathbb{E}[R]$ is the expected daily return assumed by your synthetic market. This quantity connects single-scenario outcomes to aggregate performance.

Definition of expectation

For discrete X with values x_i and probabilities p_i,

$$\mathbb{E}[X] = \sum_i x_i p_i.$$

For continuous X with density f_X,

$$\mathbb{E}[X] = \int_{-\infty}^{\infty} x f_X(x)\, dx,$$

provided the integral exists.

If R is a portfolio return, $\mathbb{E}[R]$ is the expected return; if $L = -R$ is loss, $\mathbb{E}[L]$ is the expected loss. For a synthetic generator, the law of large numbers tells us that if we simulate many independent scenarios $\{R^{(1)}, \ldots, R^{(M)}\}$, their average

$$\bar{R}_M = \frac{1}{M} \sum_{m=1}^{M} R^{(m)}$$

will be close to $\mathbb{E}[R]$ when M is large.

Variance, covariance, and higher moments

The **variance** of X measures the dispersion of outcomes:

$$\text{Var}(X) = \mathbb{E}\big[(X - \mathbb{E}[X])^2\big].$$

The **standard deviation** $\sigma_X = \sqrt{\text{Var}(X)}$ is often used as a volatility measure for returns.

For two random variables X and Y, the **covariance** is

$$\text{Cov}(X, Y) = \mathbb{E}\big[(X - \mathbb{E}[X])(Y - \mathbb{E}[Y])\big],$$

and the **correlation** is

$$\rho_{X,Y} = \frac{\text{Cov}(X, Y)}{\sigma_X \sigma_Y}.$$

In a multi-asset setting, the covariance matrix of returns encodes how risks co-move and thus how portfolios diversify. Synthetic markets must reproduce realistic covariance and correlation structures; otherwise, simulated stress scenarios will misrepresent diversification benefits or contagion effects.

Higher moments like skewness and kurtosis capture asymmetry and tail heaviness:

$$\text{skew}(X) = \frac{\mathbb{E}[(X - \mathbb{E}[X])^3]}{\sigma_X^3}, \qquad \text{kurt}(X) = \frac{\mathbb{E}[(X - \mathbb{E}[X])^4]}{\sigma_X^4}.$$

Negative skewness (frequent small gains, occasional big losses) is common in option-writing strategies. Fat tails (high kurtosis) are typical in returns and must be captured if synthetic markets are to stress-test drawdowns credibly.

Expected performance metrics

Many performance metrics are themselves functions of random variables, and we care about their expectations.

Sharpe ratio. For returns R_t over $t = 1, \dots, T$, the sample Sharpe ratio is

$$\hat{S} = \frac{\bar{R}}{\hat{\sigma}_R},$$

where $\bar{R}$ is the sample mean and $\hat{\sigma}_R$ the sample standard deviation (possibly annualized). In a synthetic market, each simulated time series of returns yields a random Sharpe ratio $\hat{S}^{(m)}$; the distribution of $\hat{S}$ under your model describes how stable apparent performance might be.

Drawdown. Maximum drawdown over a horizon T is defined as

$$\text{MDD} = \max_{1 \le t \le T} \left(\max_{1 \le s \le t} P_s - P_t \right),$$

where P_t is portfolio value at time t. Under a synthetic generator, MDD is a random variable; its expectation and quantiles tell you about typical and extreme capital losses.

Thus, even complex objects like Sharpe ratios and drawdowns can be thought of as random variables with distributions, expectations, and tail risks.

Conditional Expectation: Updating Beliefs with Information

In trading, information arrives over time: yesterday's returns, today's macro announcement, or an observed volatility regime. We often want expectations *conditional* on such information. Conditional expectations formalize this.

Definition and intuition

Given random variables X and Y, the **conditional expectation** $\mathbb{E}[Y \mid X]$ is the expected value of Y when X is known (or fixed). Intuitively, it is a function of X that tells you:

$$x \mapsto \mathbb{E}[Y \mid X = x].$$

Examples in a trading context:

- $\mathbb{E}[R_{t+1} \mid R_t]$: expected next-day return given today's return (useful for mean-reversion or momentum models).
- $\mathbb{E}[\text{future volatility} \mid \text{current volatility}]$: foundational in GARCH-type volatility models used to drive synthetic scenarios.
- $\mathbb{E}[\text{future P\&L} \mid \text{regime indicator}]$: expected performance conditioned on being in a bull vs. bear regime.

For discrete variables, conditional expectation reduces to a weighted average over the conditional distribution. For continuous variables, it involves conditional densities, but the intuition is the same: we average outcomes using probabilities updated by observed information.

Conditional expectation as a building block

Conditional expectation underlies:

- **Forecasting models** (e.g., linear regressions, time-series models) where the model output is $\mathbb{E}[Y \mid X]$.

- **Risk measures** conditional on states (e.g., conditional Value-at-Risk given current volatility).
- **Scenario generation** where synthetic paths are evolved by taking expectations conditional on past simulated values.

In synthetic markets, you repeatedly apply conditional expectations and random shocks to propagate paths forward in time.

Concept Map: Probability to Inference in Finance

Right after establishing random variables, distributions, and expectations, it is helpful to see how these concepts connect to the inference tools we will use to calibrate and evaluate synthetic markets.

This concept map emphasizes two clusters:

- *Probability objects*: random variables, distributions, and expectations, which describe how returns and risk metrics behave under a model.
- *Inference tools*: estimators, confidence intervals, and hypothesis tests, which learn about and challenge the model using observed data or synthetic runs.

In synthetic markets, you move constantly between these clusters: from model distributions to estimators based on realized or simulated data, and back again to refine the model.

Estimators: Learning Distributions from Data

So far, we have treated quantities like $\mathbb{E}[R]$ or $\mathrm{Var}(R)$ as known. In practice, they are unknown and must be estimated from data, whether historical or synthetic. This is the role of **estimators**.

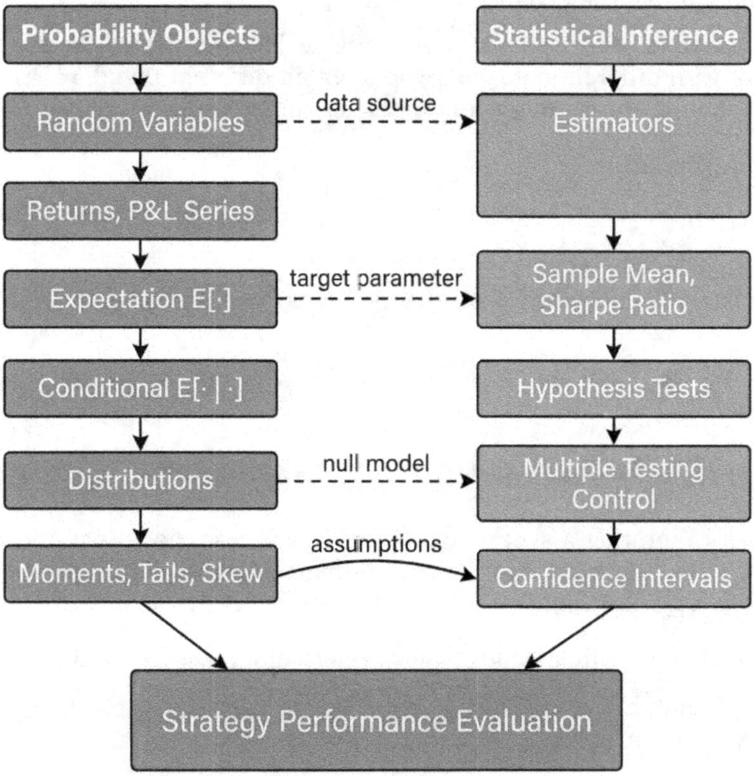

Point estimation

Suppose we observe returns $R_1, \ldots, R_T$ from a strategy. The sample mean

$$\hat{\mu} = \frac{1}{T} \sum_{t=1}^{T} R_t$$

is an estimator of the true expected return $\mu = \mathbb{E}[R_t]$. The sample variance

$$\hat{\sigma}^2 = \frac{1}{T-1} \sum_{t=1}^{T} (R_t - \hat{\mu})^2$$

estimates the true variance $\sigma^2 = \mathrm{Var}(R_t)$.

Each estimator is itself a random variable: if you repeated the experiment with different data, you would obtain different $\hat{\mu}$ and $\hat{\sigma}^2$. Their distributions under the model characterize:

- **Bias**: $\mathbb{E}[\hat{\mu}] - \mu$.
- **Variance of the estimator**: $\mathrm{Var}(\hat{\mu})$, a measure of estimation noise.

For large T, the central limit theorem often implies that $\hat{\mu}$ is approximately normal:

$$\hat{\mu} \approx \mathcal{N}\left(\mu, \frac{\sigma^2}{T}\right).$$

Calibration via estimation

When calibrating a synthetic market, you choose model parameters (e.g., drift, volatility, correlation) so that certain model expectations match empirical estimates:

- Match the model mean and variance of returns to $\hat{\mu}$ and $\hat{\sigma}^2$.
- Match higher-order moments or risk measures (e.g., skewness, kurtosis, tail quantiles) to their empirical counterparts.
- For time-series models, match autocorrelation or conditional volatility patterns.

Understanding the sampling variability of these estimators is crucial. Otherwise, you might overtune your model to noise in a particular sample, leading to synthetic markets that are overconfident or misrepresent risk.

Confidence Intervals: Quantifying Uncertainty About Parameters

Point estimates give a single "best guess" for a parameter, but they hide uncertainty. **Confidence intervals** (CIs) quantify the range of plausible values for the parameter given the data.

Example: CI for the mean return

Assume returns R_t are i.i.d. with unknown mean μ and variance σ^2, and that T is large enough for approximate normality of $\hat{\mu}$. Then an approximate $100(1-\alpha)\%$ confidence interval for μ is

$$\hat{\mu} \pm z_{1-\alpha/2} \cdot \frac{\hat{\sigma}}{\sqrt{T}},$$

where $z_{1-\alpha/2}$ is the corresponding normal quantile.

Interpretation:

- If we repeated the data-generating process many times, and constructed such an interval each time, about $100(1-\alpha)\%$ of these intervals would contain the true μ.
- For your particular data set, the CI describes the range of values for μ that are consistent with the data under the model.

In strategy evaluation, a narrow CI for μ indicates that your long-run mean return is estimated precisely; a wide CI indicates substantial uncertainty. Synthetic markets can help here: by simulating many alternative histories under a candidate model, you can examine the distribution of CIs and understand how much variation to expect.

Hypothesis Testing: Is There Really an Edge?

Hypothesis testing formalizes questions of the form: "Is this strategy's apparent alpha real, or just noise?" A test consists of:

- A **null hypothesis** H_0 (e.g., no alpha: $\mu = 0$).
- An **alternative hypothesis** H_1 (e.g., positive alpha: $\mu > 0$).
- A **test statistic** (e.g., a t-statistic for $\hat{\mu}$).
- A **decision rule** based on a critical value or p-value.

For example, the one-sample t-test for mean return uses

$$t = \frac{\hat{\mu} - 0}{\hat{\sigma}/\sqrt{T}},$$

which, under certain assumptions, has approximately a Student-t distribution under H_0. Large positive values of t provide evidence against H_0 in favor of $H_1 : \mu > 0$.

While detailed testing theory appears later in the chapter, two points are essential for synthetic markets:

1. The distribution of the test statistic is defined under a probabilistic model. If your synthetic market is misspecified, the test may misstate evidence for or against alpha.
2. You can *use* synthetic markets to study test behavior: simulate data under H_0 and H_1, compute test statistics, and empirically estimate false-positive and false-negative rates.

Multiple Testing and Overfitting in Strategy Search

In modern quantitative research, you rarely test a single strategy. Instead, you explore many variations: different signals, lookback windows, stop-loss rules, parameter grids, and model architectures. Each is a separate hypothesis test. If you run hundreds or thousands of tests, some will look good purely by chance even if no true edge exists.

This is the **multiple testing** problem:

- Naive p-values understate the chance that at least one strategy will pass your threshold by luck.
- Sharpe ratios from the "best" strategy in a large search are biased upward; you have selected them based on noise.

Classical multiple-testing corrections, such as Bonferroni or false discovery rate (FDR) procedures, adjust thresholds or p-values to account for the number of tests. In the context of synthetic markets, you can go further:

- Use synthetic data under a "no-edge" generator to estimate the distribution of the maximum Sharpe ratio across your search space; this tells you how impressive your best Sharpe really is.

- Adjust your selection criteria (e.g., require that a candidate strategy's performance exceed the synthetic "best Sharpe under no edge") to control false discoveries.

These techniques rely again on our probabilistic foundations: we treat performance statistics as random variables, characterize their distributions, and design decision rules calibrated to those distributions.

Bringing It Together for Synthetic Markets

This section has built a chain of ideas:

- Market quantities (returns, P&L, drawdowns, Sharpe ratios) are modeled as random variables living on a probability space.
- Distributions, expectations, and moments summarize their behavior, including risk (variance, tails) and reward (mean).
- Conditional expectations and dependence structures describe how information and co-movements shape dynamics.
- Estimators and confidence intervals allow us to learn about these underlying distributions from finite samples of data.
- Hypothesis tests and multiple-testing corrections help us separate genuine edges from artifacts of noise, especially in large-scale strategy or model searches.

For synthetic markets, these tools are indispensable. Scenario generators are essentially engines that produce random variables with specified distributions and dependence. Calibration aligns those distributions with empirical estimates and their uncertainty. Performance evaluation interprets realized or simulated outcomes through the lens of sampling variability and multiple testing.

In the following sections, we will add the linear algebra and optimization machinery needed to represent portfolios, risk factors, and model parameters, and to solve the constrained problems that arise when training sophisticated generative models and constructing stress-aware portfolios.

1.2 Linear Algebra and Optimization

The probabilistic language of the previous section tells us *what* we are modeling: random returns, risk factors, and performance statistics. Linear algebra and optimization tell us *how* to organize these objects and *how* to act on them. In synthetic markets, almost every practical task—from describing a portfolio to training a generative model—can be written as manipulating vectors and matrices and then solving an optimization problem.

This section develops the linear algebra and optimization machinery needed to:

- represent portfolios, risk factors, and model parameters compactly,
- map between risk factors and asset returns,
- encode risk and constraints in matrix form, and
- solve constrained optimization problems for both portfolios and models.

We build gradually, starting from vectors and matrices, moving to covariance and factor structures, and then to optimization and numerical issues.

Vectors as Portfolios and Risk Factors

At a basic level, a portfolio is a list of position sizes. Linear algebra turns that list into a vector and gives us powerful operations "for free."

Portfolio vectors

Consider N tradable assets (stocks, futures, options, ...). A portfolio is represented by a weight vector

$$w = \begin{bmatrix} w_1 \\ w_2 \\ \vdots \\ w_N \end{bmatrix},$$

where w_i is the dollar or fraction-of-capital weight in asset i. A return vector

$$r = \begin{bmatrix} r_1 \\ r_2 \\ \vdots \\ r_N \end{bmatrix}$$

collects the asset returns over one period.

The portfolio return is then simply the *inner product*

$$R_p = w^\top r = \sum_{i=1}^{N} w_i r_i.$$

This is a key pattern: many quantities of interest are linear in positions or parameters, and thus can be written as inner products or matrix–vector products.

Risk factor vectors

Similarly, we can represent a set of K risk factors (e.g., market, value, momentum, carry, volatility) as a vector

$$f = \begin{bmatrix} f_1 \\ f_2 \\ \vdots \\ f_K \end{bmatrix}.$$

Assets load on these factors via a matrix of *factor loadings* (betas) $B \in \mathbb{R}^{N\times K}$:

$$B = \begin{bmatrix} \beta_{11} & \beta_{12} & \cdots & \beta_{1K} \\ \beta_{21} & \beta_{22} & \cdots & \beta_{2K} \\ \vdots & \vdots & \ddots & \vdots \\ \beta_{N1} & \beta_{N2} & \cdots & \beta_{NK} \end{bmatrix}.$$

A simple linear factor model for asset returns is

$$r = Bf + \epsilon,$$

where ϵ is an N-vector of idiosyncratic (asset-specific) returns.

From the portfolio perspective, the portfolio's factor exposure is

$$x = B^\top w \in \mathbb{R}^K,$$

because

$$R_p = w^\top r = w^\top (Bf + \epsilon) = (B^\top w)^\top f + w^\top \epsilon = x^\top f + w^\top \epsilon.$$

Thus:

- w: positions in assets,
- $x = B^\top w$: implied positions in factors.

Designing portfolios with desired factor exposures or stress-testing portfolios with respect to factor shocks reduces to manipulating these vectors and matrices.

Matrices as Covariance and Transformation Operators

Matrices allow us to represent more complex relationships: not just single inner products, but entire systems of linear equations and transformations.

Covariance matrices

If $r \in \mathbb{R}^N$ is the random return vector, the covariance matrix is

$$\Sigma = \mathbb{E}\big[(r-\mu)(r-\mu)^\top\big] \in \mathbb{R}^{N\times N},$$

where $\mu = \mathbb{E}[r]$ is the mean vector. The (i,j) entry Σ_{ij} is $\mathrm{Cov}(r_i, r_j)$.

Portfolio variance is then

$$\mathrm{Var}(R_p) = \mathrm{Var}(w^\top r) = w^\top \Sigma w.$$

This compact quadratic form is central to modern portfolio theory and risk modeling. In synthetic markets, we often aim to:

- match an empirical covariance matrix with a model covariance $\Sigma(\theta)$,

- generate return vectors whose sample covariance approximates a target Σ,
- compute risk measures and constraints based on $w^\top \Sigma w$.

Factor model covariance

Under a linear factor model $r = Bf + \epsilon$ with

- factor covariance $\Sigma_f = \mathrm{Cov}(f)$,
- idiosyncratic covariance $\Sigma_\epsilon = \mathrm{Cov}(\epsilon)$ (often diagonal),

we have

$$\Sigma = B\Sigma_f B^\top + \Sigma_\epsilon.$$

This decomposition is crucial in practice:

- It reduces the dimensionality of the risk description from $N(N+1)/2$ parameters to those in Σ_f, B, and Σ_ϵ.
- It gives a clear interpretation of systemic vs. idiosyncratic risk.
- It provides a natural way to stress-test: shocking factors f in synthetic scenarios while keeping ϵ unchanged (or vice versa).

Matrix notation for multi-period data

Suppose we have returns for N assets over T days. We can organize them in a data matrix

$$R = \begin{bmatrix} r_{11} & r_{12} & \cdots & r_{1N} \\ r_{21} & r_{22} & \cdots & r_{2N} \\ \vdots & \vdots & \ddots & \vdots \\ r_{T1} & r_{T2} & \cdots & r_{TN} \end{bmatrix} \in \mathbb{R}^{T\times N},$$

where row t is the vector of asset returns at time t. The sample covariance matrix is then

$$\hat{\Sigma} = \frac{1}{T-1}(R - \mathbf{1}\hat{\mu}^\top)^\top (R - \mathbf{1}\hat{\mu}^\top),$$

where $\hat{\mu} \in \mathbb{R}^N$ is the sample mean vector and $\mathbf{1}$ is a T-vector of ones.

Writing things in matrix form makes both implementation and analysis more transparent. Many operations in synthetic data generation—such as applying a linear factor model to many simulated factor paths—are just matrix multiplications.

Inner Products, Norms, and Geometry of Risk

Linear algebra is not just about notation; it gives us a geometric view of portfolios and risks that is extremely useful.

Inner products

The standard inner product on $\mathbb{R}^N$ is

$$\langle u, v \rangle = u^\top v.$$

We already saw that portfolio return $R_p = w^\top r$ is the inner product between positions and returns. More generally:

- Exposure of portfolio w to a signal s is $\langle w, s \rangle$.
- The contribution of factor k to a portfolio can be expressed as an inner product between the factor loadings and the portfolio weights.

Norms as size and risk

A norm measures the "size" of a vector. The ℓ_2 norm is

$$\|w\|_2 = \sqrt{w^\top w}.$$

It is often used to penalize large positions (L2 regularization) or to measure overall exposure.

Risk naturally induces another inner product:

$$\langle u, v \rangle_\Sigma = u^\top \Sigma v,$$

with induced norm

$$\|w\|_\Sigma = \sqrt{w^\top \Sigma w}.$$

This is precisely the portfolio volatility if Σ is the return covariance. Thus, the risk of a portfolio is the "length" of its weight vector in the risk geometry defined by Σ.

In synthetic markets, we frequently:

- constrain $\|w\|_\Sigma$ (risk budget),
- penalize it in objective functions (risk-adjusted return),
- study how different vectors w sit in this risk geometry.

Eigenvalues, Eigenvectors, and Risk Modes

Eigen-decomposition reveals the dominant *modes* of variability in the data.

Eigen-decomposition of covariance

For a symmetric positive semi-definite covariance matrix Σ, we can write

$$\Sigma = Q\Lambda Q^\top,$$

where:

- Q is an orthogonal matrix whose columns $q_1, \ldots, q_N$ are eigenvectors,
- $\Lambda = \text{diag}(\lambda_1, \ldots, \lambda_N)$ contains the eigenvalues, typically ordered $\lambda_1 \geq \lambda_2 \geq \cdots \geq \lambda_N \geq 0$.

Each eigenvector q_i is a *principal component* or risk mode, and λ_i is the variance explained along that direction. In practice:

- q_1 often resembles a "market" direction (all assets moving together).
- Subsequent eigenvectors correspond to sectoral or style-like modes.

A portfolio's exposure to mode i is $q_i^\top w$. Its contribution to portfolio variance is approximately

$$(q_i^\top w)^2 \lambda_i.$$

Eigen-decomposition is used to:

- reduce dimension by keeping only the top k eigenvectors (principal component analysis),
- construct synthetic factors that explain most of the variance,
- regularize covariance estimates by shrinking small or noisy eigenvalues.

In synthetic markets, eigen-structures guide how we:

- generate correlated shocks (via Cholesky or eigen-decomposition),
- stress specific risk modes (e.g., amplifying shocks along the first principal component),
- compress high-dimensional universes into a manageable factor space for generative modeling.

Optimization: Objectives, Constraints, and Feasible Sets

With our geometric view in place, we now turn to optimization problems. An optimization problem consists of:

- an **objective function** to minimize or maximize,
- a set of **constraints** defining which solutions are allowed.

Portfolio optimization as a quadratic program

The classical mean–variance portfolio problem is:

$$\begin{aligned} \max_{w} \quad & w^\top \mu - \frac{\lambda}{2} w^\top \Sigma w \\ \text{s.t.} \quad & \mathbf{1}^\top w = 1, \\ & w_{\text{min}} \le w \le w_{\text{max}}, \end{aligned}$$

where:

- μ is the expected return vector,

- Σ is the covariance matrix,
- $\lambda > 0$ is a risk-aversion parameter,
- $\mathbf{1}^\top w = 1$ enforces full investment,
- box constraints $w_{\text{min}}, w_{\text{max}}$ encode leverage and concentration limits.

This is a *quadratic program* (QP): the objective is quadratic in w, the constraints are linear. Under standard conditions (e.g., Σ positive definite), it is a *convex* problem with a unique global solution.

In stress-aware portfolios, we often modify the objective or constraints to include:

- factor risk budgets: $\|B^\top w\|_2 \leq \kappa$,
- stress-scenario losses: $s_j^\top w \geq -L_j$ for specific shock vectors s_j,
- transaction costs or turnover penalties.

All of these can be written compactly with vectors and matrices.

Optimization for synthetic generators

Generative models—from simple parametric simulators to deep generative networks—are trained by minimizing a loss function over parameters θ. Abstractly,

$$\min_{\theta} \mathcal{L}(\theta),$$

where $\mathcal{L}$ might measure:

- distance between model-generated statistics and empirical statistics (e.g., means, covariances, autocorrelations),
- divergence between model and empirical distributions (e.g., likelihood, adversarial losses),
- penalties for violating risk or realism constraints.

Even when the model is highly nonlinear, linear-algebra operations appear at every layer: matrix–vector products, convolutions (which are matrix multiplications in disguise), and so on. Understanding these operations helps in diagnosing issues like ill-conditioning and overfitting.

Convexity, Gradients, and Gradient-Based Methods

Most optimization problems we solve in finance and machine learning rely on gradients.

Convex vs. non-convex problems

A function $f : \mathbb{R}^n \to \mathbb{R}$ is *convex* if

$$f(\alpha x + (1-\alpha)y) \leq \alpha f(x) + (1-\alpha)f(y), \quad \forall x, y, \, \alpha \in [0,1].$$

Convex problems are attractive because:

- any local minimum is a global minimum;
- efficient algorithms with convergence guarantees exist (e.g., interior-point methods, projected gradient descent).

Quadratic programs with positive semidefinite quadratic terms and linear constraints are convex. Many portfolio optimization problems fall in this class or can be approximated as such.

Non-convex problems (e.g., deep neural network training) may have many local minima and saddle points. Still, gradient-based methods work well in practice and are the workhorse of modern generative models.

Gradients and matrix calculus

For an objective $f(w)$, the gradient $\nabla f(w)$ is the vector of partial derivatives. For linear and quadratic functions:

- If $f(w) = a^\top w$, then $\nabla f(w) = a$.
- If $f(w) = \frac{1}{2} w^\top Q w$ for symmetric Q, then $\nabla f(w) = Qw$.

These simple formulas are heavily used. For example, the gradient of the mean–variance objective

$$f(w) = -w^\top \mu + \frac{\lambda}{2} w^\top \Sigma w$$

is

$$\nabla f(w) = -\mu + \lambda \Sigma w.$$

In model training, we compute gradients of losses with respect to parameters θ. Modern frameworks automate this (automatic differentiation), but the underlying operations are the same: chains of matrix–vector products, elementwise nonlinearities, and their derivatives.

Gradient descent and variants

Gradient descent updates parameters iteratively:

$$\theta^{(k+1)} = \theta^{(k)} - \eta_k \nabla \mathcal{L}(\theta^{(k)}),$$

where η_k is a step size (learning rate). In constrained problems, we project back onto the feasible set after each step.

Variants include:

- **Stochastic gradient descent (SGD)**: using minibatches of data to approximate the gradient, crucial for large-scale training.
- **Momentum methods**: incorporating past gradients to accelerate convergence.
- **Adaptive methods** (Adam, RMSProp, ...): adjusting learning rates per parameter.

In the context of synthetic markets:

- Portfolio optimizers for large universes may use gradient-based solvers instead of closed-form solutions.
- Training generative models (e.g., VAEs, GANs, diffusion models for returns) is almost always done via gradient-based methods on high-dimensional parameter vectors.

Constraints as Linear and Convex Sets

Real portfolios and models are subject to constraints beyond simple budget and leverage. Linear algebra provides a language for these restrictions.

Linear constraints

Many natural constraints are linear:

- Budget: $\mathbf{1}^\top w = 1$.
- Net exposure: $c^\top w = 0$ (e.g., dollar-neutral or beta-neutral).
- Sector or group bounds: $Aw \leq b$, where rows of A aggregate weights within sectors.

In synthetic markets, we may also constrain parameters:

- Factor risk limits: $F\theta \leq g$, where θ are model parameters that control factor volatilities or correlations.
- Calibration constraints: match certain empirical moments within tolerances, expressed as linear inequalities.

Convex constraints and regularization

Some constraints are naturally expressed as norms:

- Position size limit via $\|w\|_1 \leq C$ (sparsity or gross exposure).
- Risk budget via $\|w\|_\Sigma \leq \sigma_{\max}$.

These sets are convex, enabling efficient optimization. Closely related are *regularization* terms added to the objective:

- L2 regularization: add $\gamma\|w\|_2^2$ or $\gamma\|\theta\|_2^2$ to penalize large weights or parameters.
- L1 regularization: add $\gamma\|w\|_1$ to encourage sparse portfolios or feature selection, important in high-dimensional factor models.

For synthetic generators, regularization combats overfitting to limited historical data and improves stability when extrapolating into stressed regimes.

Numerical Stability and Conditioning

Linear algebra is also where numerical issues surface. Poorly conditioned matrices and ill-posed problems can make optimization unstable or misleading.

Conditioning of covariance matrices

A covariance matrix Σ with eigenvalues spread across many orders of magnitude is *ill-conditioned.* Inverting such a matrix (needed in many optimizers) amplifies estimation noise and numerical errors.

Common remedies include:

- **Shrinkage**: blend $\hat{\Sigma}$ with a simpler, well-conditioned target such as a scaled identity:

$$\Sigma_{shrunk} = (1 - \alpha)\hat{\Sigma} + \alpha\sigma^2 I.$$

- **Factor modeling**: approximate Σ as $B\Sigma_f B^\top + \Sigma_\epsilon$ with fewer effective dimensions.
- **Eigenvalue clipping**: replace very small eigenvalues with a floor value.

These techniques are vital when using covariance matrices in both portfolio construction and synthetic scenario generation (e.g., drawing correlated shocks via Cholesky decomposition).

Scaling and preconditioning

Optimization algorithms often benefit from rescaling variables:

- Standardize features or factors to comparable scales before model training.
- Precondition gradient steps by approximate inverse Hessians or diagonal scalings to reduce ill-conditioning.

In practice, this means mapping raw financial data (returns, volumes, signals) into normalized vectors and matrices before feeding them to an optimizer or generative model.

From Linear Algebra to Synthetic Market Design

We can now see how linear algebra and optimization support synthetic markets end-to-end:

- **Representation.** Vectors and matrices encode portfolios, factor structures, covariances, and model parameters in a unified language.
- **Risk geometry.** Inner products, norms, and eigen-decompositions illuminate the structure of risk and diversification, guiding what synthetic shocks and scenarios to generate.
- **Optimization.** Portfolio construction and model training are expressed as optimization problems with linear and convex constraints, solvable with gradient-based methods.
- **Regularization and stability.** Norm-based penalties and matrix conditioning techniques ensure robustness and realism in both optimized portfolios and synthetic generators.

In the next section, we will bring time explicitly into the picture, using time-series analysis and stochastic processes to model the dynamics of returns and risk factors. Combined with the linear algebra and optimization tools developed here, those dynamic models will allow us to build and train generative systems capable of producing rich, stress-aware synthetic markets.

1.3 Time-Series Analysis and Stochastic Processes

Up to this point, we have treated returns and risk factors as random variables with distributions and covariance structures, and we have used linear algebra and optimization to organize and act on them. Time is implicit in those constructions, but not yet modeled. In real markets, however, *the way uncertainty unfolds over time* is as important as its one-period distribution.

This section introduces the basic tools for describing the dynamics of financial time series and for turning those descriptions into Monte Carlo engines for synthetic markets. We focus on four recurring empirical features:

- serial dependence in levels and returns (autocorrelation),
- time-varying, clustered volatility,
- regimes and structural breaks, and
- continuous-time and discrete-time stochastic processes that model these features.

We then connect these to simulation: how to generate synthetic paths that exhibit realistic temporal behavior and properly stress path-dependent risk measures such as drawdowns, time-under-water, and hitting times.

What Is a Financial Time Series?

A *time series* is a sequence of observations ordered in time. For a single asset, examples include:

- price levels $P_0, P_1, \dots, P_T$,
- simple returns $R_t = \frac{P_t - P_{t-1}}{P_{t-1}}$,
- log-returns $r_t = \log P_t - \log P_{t-1}$,
- realized volatility or volume.

From the perspective of probability, a time series is a collection of random variables indexed by time:

$$\{X_t\}_{t=0}^{T}.$$

For financial markets, $\{X_t\}$ is usually not a sequence of independent draws. Instead, it exhibits *dependence*: current observations carry information about the likely distribution of future ones.

Our goal is twofold:

- **Description:** summarize and model this dependence structure,
- **Generation:** simulate new paths $\{X_t^{(m)}\}$ from those models to form synthetic markets.

Autocorrelation: When the Past Predicts the Future

A central question in time-series analysis is: to what extent does history predict the next realization?

Autocovariance and autocorrelation functions

Consider a (weakly) stationary time series $\{X_t\}$, meaning that its mean and covariance structure do not change over time:

$$\mathbb{E}[X_t] = \mu, \qquad \text{Cov}(X_t, X_{t+k}) = \gamma(k)$$

depends only on the lag k, not on t.

The function $\gamma(k)$ is the *autocovariance function*. The corresponding *autocorrelation function* (ACF) is

$$\rho(k) = \frac{\gamma(k)}{\gamma(0)} = \frac{\text{Cov}(X_t, X_{t+k})}{\text{Var}(X_t)}.$$

For daily returns of liquid equity indices, $\rho(k)$ is often close to zero except at very short lags; this is roughly consistent with weak-form market efficiency. But for many signals used in trading—such as moving-average filters, value spreads, or volatility measures—$\rho(k)$ exhibits clear persistence.

Estimating autocorrelation

Given data $\{x_t\}_{t=1}^{T}$, we estimate the sample autocorrelation at lag k as

$$\hat{\rho}(k) = \frac{\sum_{t=k+1}^{T} (x_t - \bar{x})(x_{t-k} - \bar{x})}{\sum_{t=1}^{T} (x_t - \bar{x})^2},$$

where $\bar{x}$ is the sample mean. Plotting $\hat{\rho}(k)$ against k produces the empirical ACF, a basic diagnostic for time-series models.

In synthetic markets, we want generated data to reproduce key features of the empirical ACF:

- For *returns*, near-zero autocorrelation is appropriate in many cases.
- For *signals* or *volatility*, persistent positive autocorrelation is characteristic.

AR and MA models for mean dynamics

Autoregressive (AR) and moving-average (MA) models are simple yet powerful descriptions of mean dynamics.

The AR(1) model is

$$X_t = \phi X_{t-1} + \epsilon_t,$$

with $|\phi| < 1$ for stationarity and $\{\epsilon_t\}$ white noise. Here:

- $\phi > 0$ implies *momentum*: positive shocks tend to be followed by positives.
- $\phi < 0$ implies *mean-reversion*: a positive shock is likely followed by a negative move.

An MA(1) model is

$$X_t = \epsilon_t + \theta\epsilon_{t-1}.$$

ARMA models combine both:

$$X_t = \phi_1 X_{t-1} + \cdots + \phi_p X_{t-p} + \epsilon_t + \theta_1\epsilon_{t-1} + \cdots + \theta_q\epsilon_{t-q}.$$

In trading:

- AR components capture predictable drifts in signals or spreads.
- MA components often arise from microstructure noise (e.g., bid-ask bounce).

In synthetic markets, fitting ARMA models to historical series and then simulating from them is a baseline way to preserve realistic autocorrelation in generated paths.

Volatility Clustering and Conditional Heteroskedasticity

While raw returns often have weak autocorrelation, their *magnitudes* or *squares* display strong persistence: periods of high volatility cluster, as do tranquil periods. This is volatility clustering.

Stylized facts of returns

Across many assets and markets, daily or intraday returns share several empirical features:

- **Heavy tails:** large moves occur more often than predicted by a normal distribution.
- **Volatility clustering:** high-volatility days tend to be followed by high-volatility days.
- **Leverage effect:** for equities, large negative returns tend to increase future volatility more than large positive returns.

Any synthetic market that ignores volatility clustering and heavy tails will understate drawdowns and misrepresent the path-dependent risk that strategies face in reality.

GARCH-type models

A widely used family of models for time-varying volatility is GARCH (Generalized Autoregressive Conditional Heteroskedasticity). The simplest GARCH(1,1) model for a zero-mean return r_t is

$$\begin{aligned} r_t &= \sigma_t z_t, \\ \sigma_t^2 &= \omega + \alpha r_{t-1}^2 + \beta \sigma_{t-1}^2, \end{aligned}$$

where $\{z_t\}$ are i.i.d. with mean 0 and variance 1 (often taken as Gaussian or Student-t).

Interpretation:

- σ_t^2 is the *conditional variance* at time t, i.e., $\mathbb{E}[r_t^2 \mid \mathcal{F}_{t-1}]$.
- A large squared return r_{t-1}^2 boosts σ_t^2, creating volatility clusters.
- The persistence parameter $\alpha + \beta$ controls how long volatility shocks last.

Extensions add asymmetry to capture the leverage effect (e.g., EGARCH, GJR-GARCH). In a synthetic market engine, a GARCH-type volatility process can:

- generate realistic bursts of volatility,
- propagate shocks from one day to the next,
- serve as a state variable conditioning future returns.

Regimes and Structural Breaks

Market behavior is not stationary forever. Structural breaks and regime shifts occur: periods of low volatility and tight spreads alternate with crises; bull and bear markets differ in drift, volatility, and cross-asset correlations.

Regime-switching models

One way to capture this is via *regime-switching* models. Suppose $S_t \in \{1, \dots, K\}$ is a latent (or observable) regime indicator following a Markov chain with transition matrix P. Conditional on regime $S_t = k$, returns follow regime-specific parameters:

$$r_t \mid (S_t = k) \sim \text{Distribution}(\mu_k, \Sigma_k, \dots).$$

This structure implies:

- piecewise-stationary behavior within regimes,
- occasional shifts between regimes governed by P,

- different means, variances, and even factor structures across regimes.

In synthetic markets, using regime-switching models allows you to:

- generate realistic clusters of crises (e.g., a "high-vol, high-correlation" regime),
- stress-test strategies for regime transitions (e.g., bull-to-bear, low-vol-to-high-vol),
- model the probability and duration of stress episodes explicitly.

Structural breaks and re-calibration

Even without explicit regimes, time-series parameters estimated over one historical window may not hold in another. Synthetic markets can acknowledge this by:

- re-estimating models on rolling windows and sampling parameters from a distribution reflecting that variability,
- explicitly incorporating parameter uncertainty into the simulation.

In all cases, the message is the same: dynamic risk modeling should not assume that the world is unchanged over decades; realistic synthetic scenarios must reflect the possibility of breaks and shifts.

Stochastic Processes for Prices and Returns

So far we have discussed discrete-time models indexed by trading days. It is often useful to embed these in continuous-time stochastic processes, both for conceptual clarity and for certain applications (e.g., options pricing, high-frequency modeling).

Random walks and discrete-time diffusion

A baseline discrete-time model for log-price $X_t = \log P_t$ is the random walk with drift:

$$X_{t+1} = X_t + \mu + \sigma \epsilon_{t+1},$$

where $\{\epsilon_t\}$ are i.i.d. standard normal. Then

$$r_{t+1} = X_{t+1} - X_t = \mu + \sigma \epsilon_{t+1}$$

are i.i.d. Gaussian log-returns. This corresponds to a simple, homoskedastic world: no autocorrelation, no volatility clustering, no regimes. It is too simplistic as a full description of markets, but remains a useful benchmark and a building block for more complex models.

Brownian motion and geometric Brownian motion

In continuous time, the canonical building block is Brownian motion $\{W_t\}_{t \geq 0}$, which has:

- $W_0 = 0$,
- independent increments, with $W_t - W_s \sim \mathcal{N}(0, t - s)$ for $t > s$,
- continuous paths almost surely.

A standard model for asset prices is geometric Brownian motion (GBM):

$$dP_t = \mu P_t \, dt + \sigma P_t \, dW_t.$$

Its solution is

$$P_t = P_0 \exp\left(\left(\mu - \frac{1}{2}\sigma^2\right) t + \sigma W_t\right),$$

so that log-returns over $[0, t]$ are normally distributed with mean $\left(\mu - \frac{1}{2}\sigma^2\right) t$ and variance $\sigma^2 t$.

For synthetic markets, GBM is rarely sufficient on its own because it lacks time-varying volatility and fat tails. But:

- it provides a tractable baseline for understanding continuous-time dynamics,
- many more sophisticated models are perturbations or extensions of GBM (e.g., stochastic volatility models, jump-diffusions).

Mean-reverting processes

Some quantities, such as interest rates or spreads, display mean-reversion. The continuous-time Ornstein–Uhlenbeck (OU) process models this:

$$dX_t = \kappa(\theta - X_t)\,dt + \sigma\,dW_t,$$

where $\kappa > 0$ is the speed of mean-reversion and θ the long-run mean. The process tends to drift back towards θ over time, with random fluctuations around it.

OU dynamics are often used for:

- modeling short rates in fixed income,
- describing stationary spreads for pairs trading or statistical arbitrage,
- generating synthetic mean-reverting factors.

Jump processes

Large, sudden moves in prices are not well described by continuous diffusions. Jump-diffusion models add Poisson-driven jumps:

$$dP_t = \mu P_t\,dt + \sigma P_t\,dW_t + P_{t-} dJ_t,$$

where J_t is a jump process that occasionally shifts the price by a random multiple. In synthetic markets, including jumps can:

- generate realistic gap moves,
- stress options and stop-loss rules that are sensitive to discontinuities,
- interact with volatility processes to create extreme but plausible scenarios.

Monte Carlo Simulation of Synthetic Paths

With models of dynamics in hand, we now turn to simulation: generating synthetic paths that reflect autocorrelation, volatility clustering, and regimes.

Discretization and path generation

For discrete-time models (AR, GARCH, regime-switching), simulation is straightforward:

- Initialize the state (e.g., X_0, σ_0, regime S_0).
- For $t = 1$ to T:
  - draw new shocks (e.g., ϵ_t, z_t, regime transitions),
  - update the state via the model's recursion,
  - record the new prices/returns and any derived quantities.

For continuous-time processes, we discretize time with step Δt and use schemes like Euler–Maruyama:

$$X_{t+\Delta t} \approx X_t + a(X_t, t)\Delta t + b(X_t, t)\sqrt{\Delta t}\, Z_{t+\Delta t},$$

where $Z_{t+\Delta t}$ are i.i.d. standard normals and a, b are drift and diffusion functions from the SDE.

Encoding autocorrelation and volatility clustering

To generate returns with both autocorrelation and volatility clustering, we can combine components:

- A mean process (e.g., AR(1)) for the conditional expected return:

$$\mu_t = \phi\mu_{t-1} + \eta_t,$$

- A volatility process (e.g., GARCH(1,1)) for σ_t,

- Returns given by

$$r_t = \mu_t + \sigma_t z_t.$$

By calibrating $(\phi, \omega, \alpha, \beta)$ and the distribution of z_t to historical data, we build a synthetic generator that reproduces:

- low linear autocorrelation in raw returns (if ϕ is modest),
- strong persistence in volatility (if $\alpha + \beta$ is near 1),
- heavy tails (if z_t is heavy-tailed).

Simulating regimes

For regime-switching models:

- Initialize regime S_0 (e.g., sample from stationary distribution of the Markov chain).
- At each step, transition to a new regime S_t according to P, then draw returns conditional on S_t:

$$r_t \mid (S_t = k) \sim \mathcal{D}(\mu_k, \Sigma_k, \dots).$$

Regime-specific parameters may include:

- different drifts and volatilities,
- different factor structures and correlations,
- different levels of jump intensity.

By varying the transition matrix P, we can create scenarios with more or fewer and longer or shorter stress episodes, enabling targeted stress testing.

Path-dependent risk measures

Once synthetic paths are generated, we can compute path-dependent risk measures for each:

- **Maximum drawdown** over horizon T,
- **Time-under-water**: the duration spent below a previous peak,
- **Hitting times**: the first time the process crosses a barrier (e.g., breach of a risk limit).

The distribution of these measures across simulated paths is the core output of a synthetic market engine: it tells us how often and how severely strategies may be stressed under modeled dynamics.

Visualizing Dynamics: From Historical Features to Synthetic Paths

After discussing volatility clustering and stochastic processes, it is useful to see these ideas in a concrete, visual form. The following multi-panel chart contrasts:

- a price series and its returns,
- volatility clustering and autocorrelation in returns,
- several Monte Carlo-simulated paths from a simple stochastic process, with drawdowns and regimes highlighted.

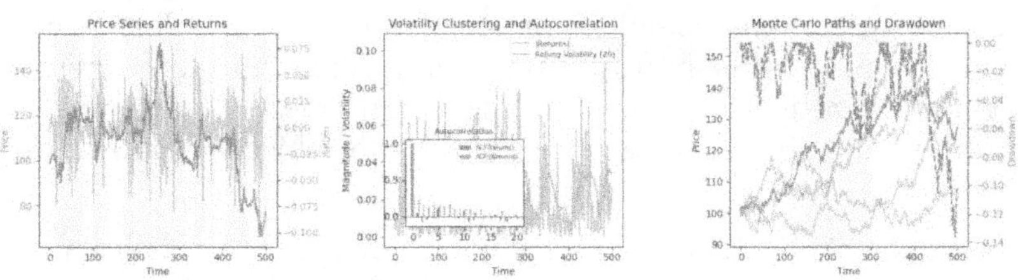

This figure emphasizes three key messages:

- Price paths and returns display clear volatility clusters and regime-like segments.
- Autocorrelation in raw returns may be weak, yet autocorrelation in absolute returns is strong.
- Monte Carlo paths, even from simple models, can produce a rich distribution of drawdowns and path shapes; adding time-varying volatility or regimes only increases that richness.

From Time-Series Models to Synthetic Markets

Time-series analysis and stochastic processes transform our probabilistic and linear-algebraic foundations into dynamic engines. In practice, building a synthetic market involves:

- **Selecting models** (ARMA, GARCH, regime-switching, jump-diffusions, etc.) that capture salient features of your asset class and horizon.
- **Estimating parameters** from historical data, with awareness of sampling variability and structural breaks.
- **Generating paths** via Monte Carlo simulation, possibly including parameter uncertainty.
- **Evaluating** path-dependent risk measures and strategy performance across those paths.

Modern generative models (VAEs, GANs, diffusion models) often embed or extend these classical structures: they may learn nonlinear conditional expectations, complex volatility surfaces, or high-dimensional factor dynamics directly from data. Yet, at their core, they are still engines generating time-indexed random variables with dependence, volatility clustering, and regimes—precisely the objects we have developed in this section.

In subsequent chapters, we will see how to marry these classical time-series tools with generative AI architectures to produce synthetic markets that are both statistically faithful to history and rich enough to expose trading strategies to genuinely challenging future scenarios.

Chapter 2

Market Structure, Microstructure, and Data Context

Synthetic markets only become useful when they behave like the noisy, constrained, politically incorrect reality of live trading. In this chapter we step away from models and code to dissect that reality: how instruments are quoted and risked, how orders collide inside a limit order book, how liquidity vanishes when you most need it, and how data engineering either preserves or destroys the subtle signals you hope to learn. By the end, you will see precisely which microstructure and data features your generative models must honor if their synthetic scenarios are to matter for real money.

2.1 Asset Classes, Derivatives, and Risk Metrics

In earlier chapters we treated prices and returns somewhat abstractly, as time series produced by a market. To use generative models for stress-testing actual trading strategies, we now have to be much more concrete about *what* is trading, *how* it is quoted and margined, and *which* risk and performance measures matter.

A synthetic scenario that looks plausible in terms of price paths but violates basic conventions of contract design, payoff structure, or factor exposure is not just unrealistic; it is unusable for serious portfolio or execution analysis. This section builds the bridge between financial instruments and the statistical objects that a synthetic market generator must reproduce.

We proceed in four steps:

- Introduce major asset classes and their quoting conventions.
- Add key derivative instruments and their payoff shapes.
- Define core return and risk metrics at the instrument and portfolio level.
- Link these to factor models and explain what "realistic enough" means in this context.

Core Asset Classes and Quoting Conventions

At the base of any synthetic market are the primary asset classes. Each carries its own conventions that directly shape how data should be represented and how strategies interact with it.

Equities. Common and preferred stocks represent ownership claims on a firm. They are:

- **Quoted** in units of currency per share (e.g., USD/share), typically as a continuous price tick grid (e.g., $0.01 increments).
- **Subject to corporate actions**: dividends, stock splits, rights issues, mergers. These actions change the economic meaning of the raw price series.

For synthetic markets, it is critical to distinguish:

- *Price-only* series (no dividend reinvestment).

- *Total-return* series, which assume all cash flows are reinvested.

Backtests on synthetic data must align with the convention of the benchmarks and risk models they are compared to.

Fixed income. Bonds, notes, and bills are debt instruments with specified coupons and maturities.

Key conventions include:

- **Clean price** vs. **dirty price**. The clean price excludes accrued interest; the dirty price adds accrued interest:

$$P_{dirty} = P_{clean} + \text{accrued coupon}.$$

- **Yield-to-maturity** quotation: a scalar rate summarizing the present value of all remaining cash flows.
- **Day-count conventions** (e.g., 30/360 vs. Actual/Actual) that affect how interest accrues.

A synthetic yield curve scenario must respect these structures: shifts, twists, and curvature changes must map consistently into bond prices and returns.

Foreign exchange (FX). FX involves exchange rates between currency pairs, such as EUR/USD.

- **Quoted** as the amount of quote currency per unit of base currency (e.g., 1.10 USD per EUR).
- **Spot** vs. **forward**:

Spot is typically T+2 settlement.

Forward price reflects interest rate differentials between the two currencies:

$$F_{t,T} \approx S_t \frac{(1 + r_T^{dom})}{(1 + r_T^{for})}.$$

Because FX returns are essentially pure relative price changes between economies, synthetic FX data are an important testbed for cross-sectional factor models.

Commodities. These include energy (oil, gas), metals, and agricultural products. The economically relevant variables include:

- **Spot prices** and physical storage/transport costs.
- **Futures curves** across delivery months, capturing expectations about supply, demand, and convenience yield.

Synthetic commodity curves must plausibly exhibit backwardation and contango regimes, since carry and roll yields are central to commodity strategies.

Cryptoassets. Cryptocurrencies and tokens share some equity- or commodity-like features, but often with:

- 24/7 trading and high volatility.
- Fragmented venues and varying contract conventions (e.g., perpetual futures with funding rates instead of fixed maturities).

For synthetic markets, crypto is a useful stress case for liquidity, volatility clustering, and regime shifts.

Derivatives and Payoff Structures

Derivatives derive their value from underlying assets. For synthetic markets, derivatives are essential because they introduce nonlinearity and path dependence into portfolios.

Futures and Forwards

A forward or futures contract is an agreement to buy or sell an asset at a future date T for a pre-agreed price K.

- **Linear payoff**: At maturity, the long position receives

  $$\Pi_{long}(T) = S_T - K,$$

  where S_T is the underlying price at T. The short receives the negative of this.
- **No initial premium** (ignoring margin): entry price is zero in value terms.

Margining. In practice, exchange-traded futures are marked to market daily. Each day:

- The change in futures price ΔF_t generates a cash flow.
- Variation margin credits or debits the trader's margin account.

Synthetic futures scenarios must therefore produce plausible paths for both F_t and associated margin calls, especially under stress, since these govern liquidity risk and potential forced unwinds.

Options

A (European) call option gives the holder the right, but not the obligation, to buy the underlying at strike K on date T; a put gives the right to sell.

- **Call payoff**:
$$\Pi_{call}(T) = \max(S_T - K, 0).$$
- **Put payoff**:
$$\Pi_{put}(T) = \max(K - S_T, 0).$$

Unlike futures, options have:

- **Upfront premium** at inception, paid by the option buyer.
- **Convex payoffs**, generating nonlinear exposure to the underlying.

Greeks and implied structure. The sensitivity measures (delta, gamma, vega, theta) describe how option values respond to changes in underlying price, volatility, and time. From a synthetic-data perspective:

- The joint distribution of S_t and its volatility must be such that simulated option prices exhibit realistic *volatility smile and skew.*
- The *term structure* of implied volatility across maturities should be consistent with the dynamics of the underlying.

Generating synthetic paths for S_t but ignoring how these paths map into plausible implied vol surfaces will break any analysis that depends on option portfolios.

Swaps

Swaps exchange one stream of cash flows for another. The canonical example is an interest rate swap:

- One leg pays a fixed rate on a notional principal.
- The other leg pays a floating rate (e.g., overnight benchmark) reset periodically.

The swap's value depends on the evolution of the relevant yield curve.

Margin and collateral. Post-crisis practice has moved most standardized swaps into central clearing with variation margin similar to futures. Synthetic yield curve and funding scenarios must be coherent with these margining conventions, as funding and collateral costs are integral strategies for many fixed-income and macro funds.

From Prices to Returns

Once instruments and payoffs are clear, we can discuss returns. Synthetic markets typically generate *returns* rather than prices, because returns have more stable statistical properties.

Arithmetic vs. Log Returns

For a price series P_t observed at discrete times, the one-period arithmetic return is

$$R_t = \frac{P_t - P_{t-1}}{P_{t-1}},$$

and the log return is

$$r_t = \ln\left(\frac{P_t}{P_{t-1}}\right).$$

Important relationships:

- For small moves, $r_t \approx R_t$.

- Over multiple periods, log returns *add*:

$$r_{t,t+n} = \sum_{k=t+1}^{t+n} r_k,$$

whereas arithmetic returns compound multiplicatively.

For stress-testing, log returns are often more convenient for modeling and simulation, while arithmetic returns are more intuitive for P&L. A synthetic generator should be explicit about which convention it preserves.

Total Returns and Cash Flows

For assets with cash flows (dividends, coupons), the return should incorporate both price change and cash income. For a single period,

$$R_t^{tot} = \frac{P_t - P_{t-1} + C_t}{P_{t-1}},$$

where C_t is the cash flow between $t-1$ and t.

Synthetic scenarios that omit cash flows will misstate the level and variability of returns, particularly for income-heavy assets like bonds and high-dividend equities.

Risk Metrics: Volatility, Drawdowns, and Tails

Risk metrics translate return paths into digestible summaries. For synthetic data, they serve two roles:

- As *targets* or constraints during model training (e.g., match historical volatility).
- As *evaluation* criteria for generated scenarios (e.g., are tail risks realistic?).

Volatility

Given a series of returns $r_1, \ldots, r_T$, empirical volatility over the period is typically computed as

$$\hat{\sigma} = \sqrt{\frac{1}{T-1}\sum_{t=1}^{T}(r_t - \bar{r})^2},$$

where $\bar{r}$ is the sample mean.

For higher-frequency returns, we often work with:

- **Annualized volatility**: scaling by $\sqrt{N}$ where N is the number of periods per year (e.g., 252 for daily).
- **Realized volatility**: aggregating squared intraday returns over shorter intervals.

A realistic synthetic generator should match not only long-run volatility levels but also volatility clustering and regime shifts (calm vs. turbulent periods).

Drawdowns

Drawdowns capture path-dependent downside risk. For a cumulative return process V_t (e.g., portfolio value), the running maximum is

$$M_t = \max_{1 \le s \le t} V_s,$$

and the drawdown at time t is

$$D_t = \frac{M_t - V_t}{M_t}.$$

Key measures:

- **Maximum drawdown** (MDD): $\max_t D_t$.
- **Drawdown duration**: the length of time between a peak and full recovery.

Synthetic scenarios must produce not only plausible MDD magnitudes but also durations, since long drawdowns materially affect investor behavior and funding constraints.

Tail Risk: VaR and Expected Shortfall

Value-at-Risk (VaR). For a given confidence level α (e.g., 95% or 99%) and horizon, VaR is the threshold loss such that the probability of exceeding it is $1 - \alpha$. Formally, if L is the loss distribution, then VaR is

$$\mathrm{VaR}_\alpha = \inf\{\ell : \mathbb{P}(L \leq \ell) \geq \alpha\}.$$

Expected Shortfall (ES). Also known as Conditional VaR, ES is the expected loss given that the loss exceeds VaR:

$$\mathrm{ES}_\alpha = \mathbb{E}[L \mid L \geq \mathrm{VaR}_\alpha].$$

VaR and ES are highly sensitive to the shape of the return distribution's tails. A synthetic generator that matches mean and variance but underestimates tail thickness will dramatically understate these metrics, leading to over-optimistic stress tests.

Path-Dependent Measures for Trading Strategies

Execution and trading strategies often care about the *path* of prices, not just the distribution of terminal outcomes. Two useful measures are:

Maximum Adverse Excursion (MAE). For a given trade, MAE is the worst price move against the position between entry and exit. For a long trade, this is the minimum unrealized P&L during the trade.

Maximum Favorable Excursion (MFE). Conversely, MFE is the best price move in favor of the position during the trade.

Synthetic order paths should produce realistic MAE/MFE distributions conditioned on trade horizon, volatility regime, and liquidity conditions. Otherwise, backtests of stop-loss or take-profit rules on synthetic data will be misleading.

Performance Ratios: Sharpe, Sortino, and Beyond

Risk-adjusted performance metrics summarize the trade-off between return and volatility/tail risk.

Sharpe Ratio

For a portfolio with average excess return $\bar{r}_p$ over a risk-free rate r_f, and volatility σ_p,

$$\text{Sharpe} = \frac{\bar{r}_p - r_f}{\sigma_p}.$$

Sharpe assumes returns are symmetrically distributed around the mean. It penalizes upside and downside volatility equally.

Sortino Ratio

The Sortino ratio focuses on downside deviations. Let σ_{down} be the standard deviation of returns below a target (often r_f or 0). Then

$$\text{Sortino} = \frac{\bar{r}_p - r_f}{\sigma_{down}}.$$

If synthetic scenarios under-generate downside volatility relative to upside, they will inflate Sortino ratios and understate the risk of drawdowns.

From Instruments to Factors

Most institutional risk management organizes portfolios in terms of *factors* rather than individual positions. A factor model expresses asset returns as

$$r_{i,t} = \alpha_i + \sum_{k=1}^{K} \beta_{i,k} f_{k,t} + \epsilon_{i,t},$$

where:

- $f_{k,t}$ are factor returns (e.g., market, size, value, momentum, carry, quality, volatility).
- $\beta_{i,k}$ are factor loadings for asset i.
- $\epsilon_{i,t}$ is idiosyncratic noise.

Key Equity and Cross-Asset Factors

Commonly used factors include:

- **Market** (Mkt): broad equity market return.
- **Size**: small vs. large capitalization.
- **Value**: cheap vs. expensive on valuation metrics.
- **Momentum**: recent winners vs. losers.
- **Carry**: high vs. low yield, across bonds, FX, and commodities.
- **Quality**: profitability, leverage, earnings stability.
- **Volatility**: low-vol vs. high-vol portfolios.

Cross-Sectional Structure

For a synthetic equity universe to be "realistic enough," it must preserve:

- The distribution of factor returns $f_{k,t}$ (means, volatilities, autocorrelations).
- The cross-sectional distribution of loadings $\beta_{i,k}$ (e.g., value stocks actually loading on the value factor).
- The residual structure $\epsilon_{i,t}$, including its correlation patterns (e.g., sector-specific shocks).

Simply generating independent price paths for each stock will not reproduce realistic cross-sectional clustering of returns, nor will it capture that diversification benefits shrink during stress (correlations rise). Synthetic data must encode that in bad scenarios, factor correlations and volatilities typically increase.

What "Realistic Enough" Means for Synthetic Scenarios

We can now articulate a working definition of realism for synthetic markets, grounded in instruments and metrics:

- **Instrument realism**: Generated price and return series respect contract conventions (e.g., futures margining, option convexity, bond coupon schedules) and cash flows.
- **Distributional realism**: Marginal return distributions match key statistics (means, volatilities, skewness, kurtosis, VaR, ES) over relevant horizons.
- **Path realism**: Temporal features such as volatility clustering, autocorrelations, and drawdown profiles resemble those seen in real markets.
- **Cross-sectional realism**: Correlation matrices, factor structures, and co-movements across asset classes behave plausibly, especially in stress.
- **Scenario richness**: The synthetic set includes both "typical" regimes and rare but economically coherent extremes (e.g., yield curve inversions, liquidity crunches, volatility spikes), while still respecting the above constraints.

Subsequent chapters will design generative models that target these criteria explicitly. This section provides the financial foundation: once we know how real instruments behave and how risk is measured, we can specify exactly what our synthetic markets must preserve in order for backtests, stress tests, and execution analyses to be credible.

2.2 Limit Order Books, Liquidity, and Impact

In the previous section we described *what* trades in financial markets: asset classes, derivative contracts, and the risk metrics that describe their payoffs. We now move one level down, into the mechanism that turns trading intentions into actual executions. This is the domain of *market microstructure*.

For synthetic markets, microstructure matters because:

- It determines the price you actually obtain when you trade, not just the "mid" price in a time series.

- It controls how your own orders disturb prices (market impact).
- It shapes the realized distribution of P&L for execution strategies, especially in stressed conditions.

A generative model that produces plausible daily returns but ignores these details cannot reliably stress-test intraday or execution-sensitive strategies. This section therefore dissects how orders become trades in a modern electronic limit order market and identifies the key invariants that synthetic scenarios must preserve.

Anatomy of a Limit Order Book

Most electronic trading venues (equities, futures, many crypto venues) use a *central limit order book* (LOB). The LOB is a dynamic data structure that stores outstanding buy and sell orders, ranked by price and arrival time.

Bids, Asks, and the Spread

At any instant:

- A **bid** is an order to buy a given quantity at a specified maximum price.
- An **ask** (or offer) is an order to sell a given quantity at a specified minimum price.

The book is usually represented as two ladders:

- The *bid side*: sorted from highest to lowest price.
- The *ask side*: sorted from lowest to highest price.

We define:

- **Best bid** b_1: the highest bid price currently in the book.
- **Best ask** a_1: the lowest ask price currently in the book.

- **Bid–ask spread**:

$$\text{spread}_t = a_1(t) - b_1(t).$$

- **Mid-price**:

$$m_t = \frac{a_1(t) + b_1(t)}{2}.$$

The spread is the instantaneous cost of trading one "infinitesimal" unit of the asset if you cross the spread (buy at the ask or sell at the bid). The mid-price is a convenient reference level, but in reality no infinitesimal trades exist: every real order has a finite size and therefore interacts with the *depth* of the book.

Depth and Price Levels

Each price level p on either side of the book has an associated **depth**, the total quantity available to buy or sell at that price. We denote:

- Q_k^{bid}: total bid quantity at the k-th best bid price b_k.
- Q_k^{ask}: total ask quantity at the k-th best ask price a_k.

Conceptually, the book is a step function of available liquidity as you move away from the mid-price. For a trader wanting to buy a large quantity, depth at and above the best ask determines how much the trade will move the price.

Queueing Rules: Price–Time Priority

Modern order books typically follow *price–time priority*:

- Orders at better prices are always filled before orders at worse prices (price priority).
- Among orders at the same price, earlier arrivals are filled first (time priority).

Thus, a limit order joining a crowded price level is placed at the back of that price level's queue. This simple rule has deep implications:

- The value of a limit order includes its *queue position*: being early at the best bid is more valuable than being late.
- Cancellation and resubmission behaviors alter queue dynamics and the distribution of realized waiting times for fills.

Synthetic microstructure data must capture realistic queue lengths, arrival and cancellation intensities, and fill probabilities at different positions in the book.

Order Types and How Orders Become Trades

Orders are instructions submitted to the matching engine. Understanding their behavior is essential for modeling both the execution of strategies and the evolution of the book itself.

Market and Limit Orders

Market orders. A market order is an instruction to buy or sell a specified quantity immediately at the best available prices. It consumes liquidity:

- A buy market order will execute against the best ask, then the next best ask, and so on, until its entire quantity is matched.
- A sell market order does the symmetric operation on the bid side.

Because market orders cross the spread, they pay the spread and any additional cost from walking up (or down) the book.

Limit orders. A limit order is an instruction to buy or sell a specified quantity at a specified price or better:

- A buy limit order at price p will execute immediately against resting asks at prices $\leq p$ and any leftover quantity will rest as a bid at price p.
- A sell limit order at price p will execute immediately against resting bids at prices $\geq p$ and any leftover quantity will rest as an ask at price p.

Limit orders *provide* liquidity when they rest in the book and may earn the spread when they are eventually executed against.

Other Common Order Types

Real venues support richer order types, including:

- **Immediate-or-Cancel (IOC)**: any part of the order that cannot be filled immediately is canceled.
- **Fill-or-Kill (FOK)**: the order must be fully executed immediately or canceled in its entirety.
- **Iceberg orders**: only a portion of the total size is visible in the book; when the visible part is executed, a new slice becomes visible.
- **Pegged orders**: prices dynamically follow a reference (e.g., mid, primary best bid/offer).

From a synthetic perspective, many of these can be abstracted into combinations of simple market and limit behavior plus hidden liquidity. However, they influence:

- The apparent vs. actual depth at each price.
- The timing and size of trades that appear on tape.

A Visual: Book Snapshot and Impact Curve

After defining basic terminology, it is useful to anchor the ideas in a visual representation. The figure below shows, side by side, a sample limit order book snapshot and an empirical market impact curve.

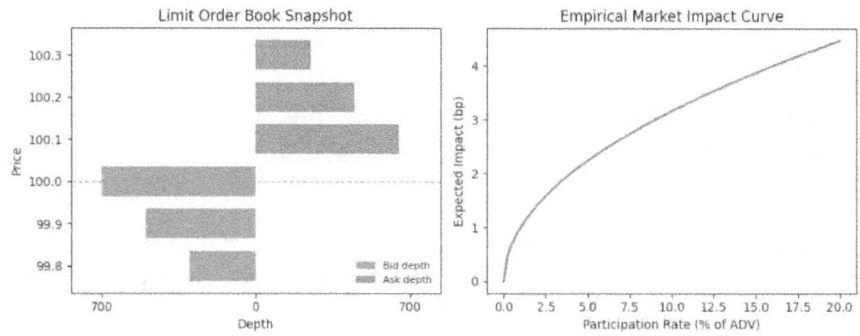

On the left, the bars show how liquidity is distributed at a few price levels; on the right, we see a stylized concave relationship between trade size and expected impact. Synthetic microstructure scenarios should generate order books and impact functions consistent with this qualitative shape, even if the exact numbers change across assets and regimes.

Liquidity: Quoted, Effective, and Realized

Liquidity is the ease with which a position can be traded without significantly moving the price. It is multi-dimensional. For generative models, we need quantitative proxies that can be matched and stressed.

Quoted vs. Effective Spread

The **quoted spread** at time t is simply $a_1(t) - b_1(t)$. However, the actual cost of a trade also depends on how limit orders improve the price, and on whether trades are executed at or inside the spread.

The **effective spread** for an individual trade is defined as

$$\text{eff\_spread}_t = 2 \times side_t \times (trade\_price_t - m_t),$$

where $side_t = +1$ for buyer-initiated trades and -1 for seller-initiated trades, and m_t is the mid-price just before the trade.

Intuitively:

- If a buy trade executes at the ask, the effective spread equals the quoted spread.

- If it executes inside the spread (due to price improvement), effective spread is smaller.

A realistic synthetic tape must reproduce the distribution of effective spreads across assets, times of day, and regimes.

Depth at the Touch and Beyond

Depth at the touch refers to the quantity available at the best bid and best ask. More generally, we can define **cumulative depth profiles**:

- For a given price distance Δp from the mid, sum the available quantity within that band.

Execution algorithms implicitly assume a certain depth profile when they schedule trades. If synthetic depth is too thin, simulated costs will be exaggerated; if too thick, costs will be understated.

Order Book Resiliency

Resiliency measures how quickly the book refills after a shock:

- If a large market order removes most of the best ask, how quickly do new sell limit orders appear?
- Does the spread return to normal levels within seconds, minutes, or longer?

Resilient books cushion impact; fragile books allow small orders to cause large price gaps. Under stress (e.g., during a crisis), resiliency typically weakens. Synthetic models must learn and reproduce these regime changes.

From Order Flow to Price Impact

Market impact is the change in price caused by trading. For a given executed volume Q over some horizon, we can define impact as the expected price change relative to a reference (pre-trade mid or benchmark price).

Temporary and Permanent Impact

It is useful to distinguish:

- **Temporary impact**: The component of price change that reverts after the trade is completed, reflecting short-lived liquidity imbalances.
- **Permanent impact**: The component that persists, usually interpreted as information content (the market infers that your trade reveals new information about value).

Empirically, the average impact as a function of participation rate (fraction of total market volume you trade) is increasing and concave. Small trades move the market less than proportionally; very large trades may saturate as other participants adjust.

Impact as a Function of Participation and Volatility

A common stylized form for the expected impact of a meta-order (sequence of trades) with participation rate ϕ (e.g., $\phi = 10\%$ of total volume over a period) is

$$\mathbb{E}[\Delta p] \propto \sigma\sqrt{\phi},$$

where σ is the volatility over the execution horizon. This captures several intuitive facts:

- At fixed volatility, doubling your participation rate less than doubles your expected impact (concavity).
- In more volatile markets, a given participation rate generally leads to larger impact, because the book is more likely to be thin and rapidly changing.

Synthetic scenarios must therefore model impact jointly with volume and volatility. It is not enough to match price volatility alone; we must ensure that when volume and spread conditions look stressed, impact becomes larger and more uncertain.

Normal vs. Stressed Liquidity Regimes

Under normal conditions:

- Spreads are tight.

- Depth is ample near the top of the book.
- Order book resiliency is high; the book refills quickly.

Under stress:

- Spreads widen significantly.
- Depth at the best prices shrinks; the book *thins out*.
- "Air pockets" appear: price levels with little or no resting liquidity.
- Correlations in order flow rise: many participants try to trade in the same direction simultaneously.

In such environments, even modest-sized orders can cause outsized price jumps as they traverse sparse depth and trigger other participants' stops or margin constraints.

From a synthetic modeling viewpoint, it is important that stressed scenarios be *internally coherent*:

- Widened spreads should coincide with lower depth and higher volatility.
- Impact functions should steepen, meaning given participation rates lead to larger expected impact and greater variance of outcomes.

Microstructure Invariants for Synthetic Markets

To summarize, realistic synthetic microstructure must preserve several classes of invariants:

1. **Order flow statistics**:
    - Arrival rates of market and limit orders as functions of time of day and volatility.
    - Cancellation and modification rates.

- Autocorrelation and clustering in trade signs (buy vs. sell pressure).

2. **Book shape and dynamics**:
   - Distribution of spreads and their dependence on volatility and volume.
   - Depth profiles at and away from the best quotes.
   - Resiliency: how quickly spreads and depth revert after shocks.

3. **Impact-response patterns**:
   - Concave functional form of impact vs. trade size or participation.
   - Relationship between impact, volatility, and background liquidity.
   - Decomposition into temporary and permanent components, including the average reversion profile after executions.

Later, when we design execution algorithms and stress tests, we will use these invariants both as calibration targets and as diagnostic checks. If a synthetic scenario exhibits unrealistically tight spreads given its volatility, or if large trades barely move prices even in thin books, the resulting backtests will be over-optimistic.

Conversely, by deliberately perturbing these microstructure features in controlled ways (e.g., doubling spreads and halving depth), we can construct adversarial synthetic environments that probe the robustness of execution strategies and portfolio allocations under realistic, but historically rare, liquidity crises.

2.3 Transaction Costs and Execution Algorithms

The previous section described how orders interact with the limit order book, how spreads and depth arise, and how order flow generates market impact. We now translate that microstructure into dollars and cents at the portfolio level.

From the perspective of a trading strategy, two portfolios can have identical theoretical returns on mid-prices and yet deliver very different realized P&L once transaction costs are included. Synthetic markets that aim to stress-test strategies must therefore generate not only plausible price paths, but also realistic *execution environments*: spreads, depth, impact, and the behavior of other traders.

This section has three goals:

- Decompose transaction costs into explicit and implicit components.
- Introduce practical execution algorithms, from simple schedules to model-based approaches.
- Present the Almgren–Chriss optimal execution framework and connect its parameters to synthetic microstructure scenarios.

Components of Transaction Costs

Transaction costs are the gap between an *ideal* benchmark value and what you actually realize when you trade. Let V^* be the notional value of an order at some benchmark price (e.g., the pre-trade mid), and let V^{real} be the realized value, including all fees and slippage. The total cost is

$$C_{total} = V^* - V^{real}.$$

We decompose this into explicit and implicit components.

Explicit Costs

Explicit costs are directly observable in fee schedules and tax rules:

- **Commissions**: broker charges per share, contract, or notional traded.
- **Exchange and clearing fees**: charged by venues and central counterparties.

- **Taxes and levies**: e.g., transaction taxes, stamp duties.

In most liquid markets, explicit costs are relatively small compared with implicit ones, but they accumulate over high turnover and can be significant in some jurisdictions (e.g., markets with transaction taxes).

For synthetic markets, explicit costs enter as deterministic or simple stochastic add-ons. They are important for realism, but they do not drive complex dynamics. The real modeling challenge lies in implicit costs.

Implicit Costs

Implicit costs arise from the interaction between your orders and the market microstructure:

- **Bid–ask spread**: If you cross the spread (buy at the ask, sell at the bid), you immediately lose roughly half the spread relative to the mid-price.
- **Slippage**: Execution at a worse price than anticipated due to book dynamics during the order's life.
- **Market impact**: Systematic price movement caused by your trades, as discussed in the previous section.
- **Opportunity cost**: Losses from not executing (or only partially executing) when prices move unfavorably relative to your benchmark.
- **Information leakage**: If your trading reveals information about your intentions, others may front-run you, worsening future execution prices.

These costs are inherently stochastic and depend on the full temporal path of prices, volumes, and other participants' actions. Synthetic microstructure scenarios must reproduce the joint distribution of these quantities.

Implementation Shortfall: A Unifying Measure

In practice, traders often evaluate execution quality using *implementation shortfall.* This concept unifies many cost components and provides a natural objective for both empirical analysis and synthetic stress tests.

Suppose you decide at time t_0 to buy Q shares of an asset. Let:

- P_0: decision price (e.g., mid-price at t_0).
- P_t: price path during the execution horizon.
- P_T: final price used as evaluation benchmark (e.g., close).
- $\tilde{Q}_t$: quantity executed at time t at price $\tilde{P}_t$, with $\sum_t \tilde{Q}_t = Q_{exec} \leq Q$.

The *paper* (ideal) portfolio value if you could instantly buy all Q at P_0 is:

$$V^* = Q \cdot P_T - Q \cdot P_0.$$

The realized portfolio value after actual execution is:

$$V^{real} = Q_{exec} \cdot P_T - \sum_t \tilde{Q}_t \tilde{P}_t.$$

The implementation shortfall (IS) is:

$$\text{IS} = V^* - V^{real} = Q \cdot P_0 - \sum_t \tilde{Q}_t \tilde{P}_t + (Q_{exec} - Q) \cdot P_T.$$

This can be interpreted as:

- The difference between the decision price and the *execution prices*, weighted by executed quantity.
- Plus an *opportunity cost* term for any unexecuted quantity if $P_T > P_0$ (for a buy order).

In synthetic experiments, we can compute IS for each scenario and execution algorithm, then analyze its distribution (mean, volatility, tails). The quality of the underlying synthetic microstructure directly affects these statistics.

Baseline Execution Strategies

We now review some baseline execution strategies that are widely used in practice and form natural reference points for more sophisticated algorithms.

Naïve Strategies: All-at-Once and Uniform Slicing

Two extreme strategies illustrate the basic trade-off:

All-at-once (immediate execution). Submit the entire order Q as an aggressive market order at the start.

- *Pros*: Minimizes timing risk (exposure to future price moves before completion).
- *Cons*: Maximizes market impact and spread cost; the order may walk far up or down the book.

Uniform slicing over time. Split the order evenly over N intervals, trading Q/N units at each step, e.g., once per minute over an hour.

- *Pros*: Reduces instantaneous impact by spreading volume over time.
- *Cons*: Exposes you to price risk: the market may move against you while you are still executing.

Synthetic markets must capture the competing forces at play: impact grows with trading intensity, while price risk grows with execution horizon.

TWAP: Time-Weighted Average Price

A simple and common schedule-based algorithm is **TWAP** (Time-Weighted Average Price). TWAP executes at a constant rate over a predefined time window, effectively implementing the uniform slicing strategy:

$$q_t = \frac{Q}{T_{horizon}} \Delta t,$$

where q_t is the quantity traded in interval Δt.

TWAP implicitly assumes:

- Market liquidity is roughly uniform over the horizon.
- Price volatility and impact per unit traded do not vary strongly with time of day.

In reality, volume and liquidity are highly intraday-dependent (e.g., higher at the open and close). Synthetic intraday scenarios must reproduce these patterns; otherwise, TWAP's performance in backtests will be misestimated.

VWAP: Volume-Weighted Average Price

VWAP (Volume-Weighted Average Price) aims to match the market's volume profile. If V_t is the forecast or observed market volume in interval t, and $\sum_t V_t = V_{total}$, then a VWAP schedule trades

$$q_t = Q \cdot \frac{V_t}{V_{total}}.$$

This strategy concentrates trading when the market is naturally more active:

- *Pros*: Lower impact per unit traded when market volume is high.
- *Cons*: Requires volume forecasts; vulnerable to errors or adversarial conditions (e.g., sudden volume droughts).

For synthetic markets, the joint distribution of prices and volumes—especially intraday seasonalities and their regime shifts—directly influence the relative merits of TWAP vs. VWAP.

Impact-Aware Optimal Execution: The Almgren–Chriss Model

Schedule-based algos are easy to implement but do not explicitly optimize a trade-off between impact cost and execution risk. The Almgren–Chriss framework provides a tractable, model-based approach that does.

Model Setup

Consider the problem of buying $X_0 > 0$ shares of a stock over a fixed time horizon $[0, T]$, divided into N discrete intervals of length $\Delta t = T/N$. Let:

- x_k: shares remaining to buy at the beginning of period k, with $x_0 = X_0$ and $x_N = 0$.
- $v_k = x_{k-1} - x_k$: shares purchased in period k.
- S_k: unaffected (fundamental) price at time k.

Price dynamics are modeled as:

$$S_k = S_{k-1} + \sigma\sqrt{\Delta t}\,\epsilon_k,$$

with ϵ_k i.i.d. with mean zero and variance 1, representing exogenous noise.

The *execution price* for trades in period k is:

$$\tilde{S}_k = S_{k-1} + \eta v_k + \frac{\gamma}{2} v_k,$$

where:

- ηv_k is temporary impact (per-share price concession in that period).
- $\frac{\gamma}{2} v_k$ represents permanent impact (moves the future unaffected price path).

This is a simplified representation; many variants exist, but the key idea is that trading faster (larger v_k) both increases immediate cost and affects future prices.

Objective: Cost–Risk Trade-off

The total cost of executing the order is the difference between what you pay and what you would have paid at the initial price S_0:

$$C = \sum_{k=1}^{N} v_k \tilde{S}_k - X_0 S_0.$$

The expected cost $\mathbb{E}[C]$ increases with the impact parameters η and γ, while the *variance* of cost $\mathrm{Var}(C)$ increases with price volatility σ and with the degree to which execution is spread out over time (later trades are exposed to more noise).

The Almgren–Chriss objective balances these two:

$$\min_{(v_k)} \ \mathbb{E}[C] + \lambda \, \mathrm{Var}(C),$$

where λ is a risk aversion parameter:

- $\lambda = 0$: purely cost-minimizing (tend to trade very slowly to minimize impact).
- Large λ: highly risk-averse (trade faster, accepting higher impact to reduce price risk).

Optimal Trading Trajectory

Under the linear impact and Gaussian noise assumptions, one can derive a closed-form solution for the optimal trajectory $(x_k)_{k=0}^{N}$. It has a characteristic shape:

- For low risk aversion (λ small): the schedule is back-loaded and relatively flat; you trade slowly at first and accelerate slightly near the end.
- For high risk aversion (λ large): the schedule is front-loaded; you trade aggressively at the beginning to quickly reduce exposure.

The key takeaway is that the optimal schedule depends on:

- **Impact parameters** η, γ: determined by liquidity and impact conditions.
- **Volatility** σ: higher volatility increases execution risk, encouraging faster trading.
- **Risk aversion** λ: a preference parameter reflecting the trader's tolerance for execution risk.

Synthetic microstructure scenarios effectively specify η, γ, σ and the distribution of noise ϵ_k. Changing these parameters in synthetic experiments allows us to stress-test the robustness of fixed execution policies and to evaluate whether a given Almgren–Chriss parameterization remains appropriate across regimes.

From Theory to Practice: Adaptive Execution Algorithms

Real-world execution algorithms combine elements of schedule-based and model-based approaches, often with adaptive features:

- **Dynamic participation caps**: target a certain fraction of market volume, but avoid exceeding a maximum participation rate to prevent excessive impact.
- **Liquidity-driven speed**: speed up in high-volume, tight-spread periods; slow down when liquidity evaporates.
- **Impact feedback**: monitor realized impact and adjust aggressiveness if costs are higher than expected.

In many implementations, Almgren–Chriss-style models provide initial schedules and risk/impact estimates, while real-time microstructure signals (spreads, depth, short-term volatility) are used to perturb the baseline schedule.

For synthetic markets, this means:

- The synthetic data must be rich enough to drive meaningful adaptive behavior (e.g., periods of unusually high or low liquidity).

- Evaluation should consider *policy* performance across many synthetic regimes, not just a single historical replay.

Stress-Testing Execution in Synthetic Markets

Bringing the pieces together, we can now articulate how to use synthetic microstructure to stress-test transaction costs and execution algorithms:

- **Define cost metrics**: implementation shortfall, realized spread, impact per unit traded, and tail measures (e.g., 95% worst-case cost).
- **Specify execution policies**: TWAP, VWAP, Almgren–Chriss schedules with different risk aversion, and adaptive variants.
- **Generate synthetic scenarios** that perturb:

- Spreads (e.g., doubling during stress).
- Depth and resiliency (thin and slow-refilling books).
- Volatility and volume (spikes, droughts, structural breaks).
- Impact functions (steeper and more volatile under stress).

- **Simulate executions** under each policy and scenario, computing cost metrics and their distributions.
- **Analyze robustness**: which policies maintain acceptable cost and risk profiles across synthetic regimes?

This process turns generative models into a laboratory for execution design. By explicitly linking microstructure features (spreads, depth, impact) to execution outcomes (implementation shortfall distributions), we bridge the gap between the theoretical returns of asset classes and derivatives, and the realized P&L experienced by actual trading systems.

2.4 Data Engineering and Experiment Tracking

In the preceding sections we treated markets at two levels: economic instruments (assets and derivatives) and microstructure (order books, liquidity, and impact). We now turn to the infrastructure that allows you to *study* such markets systematically, build generative models, and stress-test trading strategies in a way that is reproducible, scalable, and auditable.

In practice, the bottleneck in synthetic market research is rarely the latest neural architecture; it is almost always the quality and organization of data and experiments. Poorly engineered data pipelines or ad hoc experiment tracking make it impossible to trust results, let alone present them to risk committees or regulators.

This section focuses on two pillars:

- **Data engineering**: building lineage-aware, versioned pipelines for market and microstructure data.
- **Experiment tracking**: recording model configurations, random seeds, metrics, and outputs so that synthetic experiments can be reproduced and audited.

Throughout, we assume that many workloads are GPU-accelerated, which puts additional pressure on data formats and throughput.

From Raw Feeds to Research-Ready Datasets

The starting point is raw data from one or more venues and providers. These may include:

- Trade and quote (TAQ) feeds for equities and futures.
- Full-depth order book snapshots or event streams.
- Reference data: instrument identifiers, corporate actions, contract specifications.

- Macroeconomic and alternative data (e.g., news, flows), used as conditioning variables for synthetic scenarios.

Raw feeds are heterogeneous: different time zones, identifier schemes, and data quality. A structured pipeline is needed to transform this chaos into coherent datasets.

Ingestion and Normalization

The first stage ingests data and imposes basic consistency:

- **Timestamp normalization**: convert all times to a canonical time zone (e.g., UTC); record original time zone in metadata.
- **Identifier mapping**: map venue-specific tickers or symbols to a stable internal identifier (e.g., an ISIN plus venue code).
- **Schema harmonization**: standardize field names and types across providers (e.g., price in cents vs. dollars, size in shares vs. lots).

At this step, it is crucial to attach metadata that tracks origin:

- Provider name, feed type, and version.
- Ingestion timestamp and software version.

These metadata form the roots of data lineage: a record of where each observation came from and how it entered the system.

Cleaning and Quality Control

Next, we clean the data and flag issues:

- **Missing data**: identify gaps in time or instruments; decide whether to impute, forward-fill, or drop.
- **Stale quotes**: remove or mark quotes that persist unusually long without trades.
- **Outliers and bad ticks**: detect and filter implausible prices or sizes (e.g., large deviations from prevailing mid, or suspiciously small/large sizes).

- **Corporate actions**: apply split and dividend adjustments so that price and volume histories are economically meaningful.

Robust cleaning often requires both rules (e.g., price bands relative to rolling medians) and statistical methods (e.g., robust z-scores). For synthetic generation, it is particularly important to preserve *true* extreme events (flash crashes, liquidity dry-ups) rather than erroneously flagging them as outliers.

Each cleaning step must be recorded:

- The transformation applied (e.g., "drop trade if price deviates by more than 50% from previous mid").
- The parameters used (e.g., threshold values, window lengths).
- The software version and code commit that implemented the rule.

This information is part of the transformation lineage.

Derived Structures: Bars, Books, and Features

For many modeling tasks we do not work directly with raw events, but with aggregated or derived structures. Common examples include:

Bar data. Time bars (e.g., 1-minute OHLCV), volume bars, or dollar bars. Construction involves grouping trades and quotes into intervals and computing summary statistics.

Order book representations. For example:

- Top-of-book series: best bid/ask, depth at touch, and spread.
- Fixed-level snapshots: prices and depths at the first N levels on each side.
- Event sequences: order submissions, cancellations, and trades with their timestamps.

Features for models. These can include:

- Realized volatility, spread, and volume measures.

- Liquidity indicators (e.g., order book imbalance, depth gradients).
- Cross-asset or factor signals (e.g., market returns, sector indices).

Each derived dataset should be defined by a clear *recipe*:

- Input datasets and their versions.
- Exact aggregation rules.
- Any filtering or winsorization.

This is where treating data as code becomes essential: the recipe should be specified in version-controlled scripts or configurations, so that a future researcher can rebuild exactly the same bars, books, and features.

Data Lineage and Versioning

Lineage and versioning ensure that any experimental result can be traced back to the precise data it used.

Datasets as Versioned Artifacts

One effective pattern is to treat datasets similarly to software releases:

- Assign each dataset a unique identifier and version (e.g., LOB_1min_v0.3.1).
- Store metadata: creation date, source data versions, transformations, and responsible owner.
- Make datasets immutable: instead of mutating in place, create a new version when changes are needed.

This practice avoids the common problem where results become irreproducible because the underlying data were silently updated.

Lineage Graphs

Lineage can be represented as a directed acyclic graph (DAG), where:

- Nodes are datasets (raw, intermediate, or derived).
- Edges represent transformations: a function that maps one or more parent datasets to a child dataset.

Each edge carries:

- The code version (e.g., git commit hash) of the transformation.
- Configuration parameters.
- Runtime environment details (e.g., library versions, hardware).

Querying this graph lets you answer questions such as:

- "Which raw feeds and transformations produced the feature set used for Model X?"
- "If we discover a bug in the corporate actions adjustment code, which downstream datasets and experiments are affected?"

Such traceability is not merely convenient; for many institutions, it is a regulatory requirement.

Storage, Formats, and Performance Considerations

Synthetic market research is often both data- and compute-intensive. Choices about storage and formats directly affect project feasibility.

Partitioning Strategies

Market data naturally lend themselves to multi-dimensional partitioning. Common partition keys include:

- Time (e.g., by day, month, or year).
- Asset or instrument (e.g., ticker, symbol, or internal ID).
- Venue or region.

For example, a typical partitioning scheme might store 1-minute bars by date and asset:

```
s3://market-data/bars_1min/date=2024-01-02/asset=AAPL/...
```

Partitioning should align with anticipated access patterns:

- If you frequently train models across many assets but limited time windows, partitioning by date is beneficial.
- If you often run backtests on specific universes over long histories, partitioning by asset may be more efficient.

Columnar Formats and Compression

Columnar storage formats (e.g., Parquet, ORC) are well-suited to analytical workloads and GPU pipelines:

- They store data column-wise, which improves scan efficiency for wide tables when only a subset of columns is needed.
- They support efficient compression and encoding, reducing storage and I/O.
- They integrate well with distributed processing frameworks and GPU-accelerated libraries.

For microstructure data, trade-offs arise between:

- **Granularity**: storing full event-level logs vs. aggregated bars or snapshots.
- **Storage and I/O**: full order book event streams can be enormous; some applications may only need reduced representations.

When synthetic models require high-frequency detail (e.g., generating realistic order book paths for impact modeling), event-level data are indispensable. In other cases, coarser aggregates suffice.

Experiment Tracking: Making Research Reproducible

Once data pipelines are in place, the next challenge is to track the *experiments* performed on those data: training generative models, running synthetic simulations, and evaluating trading strategies.

What to Track

For each experiment run, at minimum record:

- **Data inputs**:
  - Dataset identifiers and versions.
  - Time periods and instrument universes.
- **Model configuration**:
  - Model architecture (e.g., type of generative model, number of layers, latent dimension).
  - Hyperparameters (learning rate, batch size, regularization coefficients).
  - Random seeds and any stochastic choices (e.g., data shuffling).
- **Training and evaluation settings**:
  - Number of epochs, early stopping criteria.
  - Loss functions and evaluation metrics (e.g., volatility matching, factor correlation preservation).
- **Environment**:
  - Codebase version (e.g., git hash).
  - Library and framework versions.
  - Hardware details (e.g., GPU models, number of devices).
- **Outputs**:
  - Trained model checkpoints.
  - Diagnostic plots (loss curves, calibration metrics).

  - Summary statistics of synthetic vs. historical data.

This information should be stored in a structured form (e.g., a database or dedicated experiment-tracking system), not just in free-form logs.

Runs, Experiments, and Projects

It is helpful to organize work hierarchically:

- A **run** is a single execution of training or backtesting code with a fixed configuration.
- An **experiment** groups runs that vary along controlled dimensions, such as hyperparameter sweeps or different data subsets.
- A **project** aggregates experiments that address a research question, such as "Robustness of execution algos under synthetic liquidity shocks."

Metadata at each level should include descriptive tags (e.g., asset_class=equity, frequency=1min, model=diffusion) to facilitate search and comparison.

Metrics and Artifacts

Experiment tracking should distinguish between:

- **Metrics**: scalar or vector quantities logged during or after a run (e.g., training loss per epoch, divergence between real and synthetic correlation matrices, implementation shortfall distributions).
- **Artifacts**: binary or large objects produced by the run (e.g., model weights, generated scenarios, plots).

For synthetic markets, metrics often include:

- Moment-matching: differences in means, variances, and higher moments of returns.
- Risk metrics: deviations in VaR, ES, drawdown distributions between historical and synthetic data.

- Microstructure metrics: spread distributions, depth profiles, impact curves.
- Strategy metrics: changes in Sharpe ratios, turnover, and drawdown profiles for benchmark strategies under synthetic vs. historical data.

Consistently tracked metrics allow you to compare models and configurations on economically meaningful criteria, not just generic statistical scores.

Integrating GPU Acceleration and Resource Monitoring

Many generative models and large-scale simulations are GPU-bound. Ignoring resource usage can make research slow, brittle, or non-reproducible.

Batching and Data Loaders

To feed GPUs efficiently:

- Use data loaders that prefetch and batch data from storage into GPU memory.
- Align batch sizes with GPU memory limits and model architecture.
- Minimize on-the-fly transformations in the training loop; push as much preprocessing as possible into upstream data pipelines.

This division of labor reinforces the importance of well-defined, precomputed feature datasets and avoids silently changing preprocessing in training code.

Tracking Resource Usage

Experiment logs should include:

- GPU utilization and memory usage over time.

- Wall-clock training duration and throughput (samples per second).
- Any resource-related failures (out-of-memory, timeouts).

These signals help diagnose bottlenecks and make it easier to reproduce experiments on different hardware or in the cloud.

Governance, Auditing, and Risk

Well-structured data pipelines and experiment logs are not just engineering best practices; they are essential for governance and risk management.

Auditability of Synthetic Stress Tests

When synthetic scenarios are used in decision-making—for example, to set risk limits or evaluate new trading strategies—stakeholders will ask:

- Which historical periods and instruments informed these scenarios?
- How were the generative models trained and validated?
- Can we reproduce the results if we rerun the analysis next year or on another system?

A combination of dataset versioning, lineage graphs, and experiment tracking allows you to answer these questions with concrete, verifiable references.

Change Management

Markets evolve: regimes change, microstructure rules are updated, and new instruments appear. Models and pipelines must also evolve. With proper tracking:

- Changes to data cleaning rules or feature definitions can be linked to new dataset versions.

- Model architecture updates can be compared against baselines on the same data.
- Historical synthetic stress tests can be re-run with updated models to see whether conclusions change.

This enables controlled, auditable iteration rather than ad hoc tinkering.

Putting It All Together

By this point in the chapter, we have moved from:

- Economic instruments and risk metrics (what is being traded and how risk is measured).
- Through market microstructure and execution (how orders become trades and incur costs).
- To the data and infrastructure needed to study and simulate these phenomena at scale.

A well-designed, lineage-aware data pipeline provides the raw material and features for generative models. Rigorous experiment tracking ensures that synthetic scenarios and stress tests are reproducible and auditable. Together, they turn synthetic markets from a research curiosity into a practical tool for trading strategy design, execution optimization, and institutional risk management.

Chapter 3

Generative AI Foundations for Financial Time Series

Most generative AI examples focus on images and text-but markets speak a harsher dialect: noisy, heavy-tailed, and reflexive time series driven by event streams and feedback loops. In this chapter, we translate the modern generative toolkit into the language of returns, yield curves, and order books. You'll see how probabilistic modeling and deep learning combine to create synthetic markets, how to measure whether those markets are realistic and useful for strategy stress-testing, and which model families actually respect dependence structures, regimes, and microstructure. By the end, you'll be able to look at any new generative architecture and quickly judge whether it is likely to help-or hurt-your trading research.

3.1 Probabilistic and Neural Foundations

In the previous chapter we argued that synthetic markets are only useful if they preserve the risk-relevant structure of real markets: distributions of returns, dependence across assets and time, and the pathwise features that matter for strategies. In this section we put the mathematical foundation under that idea.

We will treat any generative model—classical or neural—as a *probabilistic object*: a way of defining a joint distribution over financial time series and any latent (unobserved) drivers. This perspective is critical for deciding whether the synthetic data produced by a model is credible enough for backtesting and stress testing.

We proceed in four steps:

1. From random variables to financial time series as joint distributions.
2. Latent-variable models and financial regimes.
3. Likelihoods, loss functions, and what they assume about markets.
4. Neural networks as flexible parameterizations of probabilistic models.

Random Variables and Data-Generating Processes

At the core of synthetic-data generation is the idea that there exists some unknown *data-generating process* (DGP) for market quantities. For concreteness, let

$$R_t \in \mathbb{R}^d$$

denote the vector of (log-)returns on d assets between time $t-1$ and t, and let

$$\mathcal{D} = \{r_{1:T}^{(i)}\}_{i=1}^{N}$$

denote a dataset of N observed return paths, each of length T.

- A *random variable* is a measurable function from an underlying probability space to a value space (e.g., $\mathbb{R}^d$ for returns).
- A *stochastic process* $\{R_t\}_{t\geq 1}$ is a sequence of random variables indexed by time.
- The *joint distribution* of $R_{1:T} = (R_1, \dots, R_T)$ is denoted $p(R_{1:T})$.

Modeling the market means positing a family of distributions

$$\{p_\theta(R_{1:T}) : \theta \in \Theta\}$$

parameterized by θ (volatilities, correlations, neural-network weights), and then using data to select a suitable θ.

Two decompositions are particularly important for time series:

Chain rule and conditional structure.
By the chain rule of probability,

$$p_\theta(R_{1:T}) = \prod_{t=1}^{T} p_\theta(R_t \mid R_{1:t-1}).$$

Any sequential generative model is implicitly specifying these conditionals. For example, an autoregressive neural network implements

$$R_t = f_\theta(R_{1:t-1}, \varepsilon_t),$$

where ε_t is a random innovation (often standard Gaussian), which in turn defines $p_\theta(R_t \mid R_{1:t-1})$.

State-space view.
Alternatively, we can introduce a hidden state S_t summarizing relevant history (e.g., volatility or regime):

$$p_\theta(R_{1:T}, S_{1:T}) = p_\theta(S_1) \prod_{t=1}^{T} p_\theta(R_t \mid S_t)\, p_\theta(S_{t+1} \mid S_t).$$

This is the classical state-space or hidden Markov model (HMM) formulation. Many neural models can be read as powerful, learned state-space models.

The key point is that both classical ARMA–GARCH models and modern sequence models are different parameterizations of the same mathematical object: a joint probability distribution over paths.

Latent Variables and Financial Regimes

Observed market data reflects the interaction of many unobserved forces: risk appetite, liquidity conditions, macro regimes, intraday microstructure, and so on. Rather than attempt to model all such drivers explicitly, we use *latent variables* to stand in for them.

What is a latent variable?

A latent variable Z is a random quantity that is not directly observed but affects the distribution of observed data X. Probabilistically, this means:

$$p_\theta(X) = \int p_\theta(X, Z)\, dZ = \int p_\theta(X \mid Z)\, p_\theta(Z)\, dZ,$$

where $p_\theta(Z)$ is a prior over latents and $p_\theta(X \mid Z)$ is a likelihood (conditional distribution) of data given latents.

For financial time series, we might let:

- Z be a discrete latent regime (calm, stressed, crisis),
- $Z_{1:T}$ be a latent volatility path,
- or Z be a continuous low-dimensional embedding summarizing macro and market conditions.

Latent-variable generative story

A generative model with latents is described by the following conceptual steps:

1. Sample latent variables from a prior:
$$Z \sim p_\theta(Z).$$
2. Given Z, sample the observable path:
$$R_{1:T} \sim p_\theta(R_{1:T} \mid Z).$$

Equivalently, for time-structured latents $Z_{1:T}$,

$$p_\theta(R_{1:T}, Z_{1:T}) = p_\theta(Z_1) \prod_{t=1}^{T} p_\theta(R_t \mid Z_t)\, p_\theta(Z_{t+1} \mid Z_t).$$

This decomposition is useful in practice because:

- It captures *heterogeneity*: different market regimes correspond to different regions of latent space.
- It enables *controlled generation*: by fixing or steering Z, we can generate specifically "crisis-like" or "high-volatility" scenarios.
- It supports *interpretation*: the learned Z can be correlated with known risk factors (VIX, credit spreads) to validate that the model's internal structure matches market intuition.

Likelihoods and Loss Functions

To use data to fit a generative model, we must choose a training objective. In probabilistic modeling, this is usually formulated in terms of the *likelihood* of the observed data under the model.

Maximum likelihood principle

Given observations $\mathcal{D}$ and a model family $\{p_\theta\}$, the maximum likelihood estimate (MLE) is:

$$\hat{\theta}_{MLE} = \arg\max_\theta \log p_\theta(\mathcal{D}) = \arg\max_\theta \sum_{i=1}^{N} \log p_\theta\big(r_{1:T}^{(i)}\big).$$

In practice, we minimize the negative log-likelihood (NLL):

$$\mathcal{L}_{NLL}(\theta) = -\frac{1}{N}\sum_{i=1}^{N} \log p_\theta\big(r_{1:T}^{(i)}\big).$$

When p_θ is tractable and differentiable with respect to θ, we can use gradient-based optimization to minimize this loss. Importantly, *every* loss function used in training a neural generative model implicitly encodes some assumption about p_θ.

MSE as a Gaussian likelihood

Suppose a model predicts a mean return $\mu_{\theta,t}$ and we use mean squared error (MSE) over one-step-ahead returns:

$$\mathcal{L}_{MSE}(\theta) = \frac{1}{NT}\sum_{i=1}^{N}\sum_{t=1}^{T} \big\| r_t^{(i)} - \mu_{\theta,t}^{(i)} \big\|^2.$$

This is equivalent to assuming

$$R_t \mid \text{history} \sim \mathcal{N}(\mu_{\theta,t}, \sigma^2 I)$$

for some fixed variance σ^2: the MSE objective is proportional to the NLL of a Gaussian with constant variance. Thus, minimizing MSE pushes the model toward the *conditional mean* of R_t under a homoskedastic Gaussian assumption. For financial returns, this is usually a poor fit: volatility varies over time and tails are heavy.

Heteroskedastic and heavy-tailed likelihoods

To better match financial data, we often parameterize both conditional mean and volatility via a neural network. A simple example for scalar returns R_t is:

$$R_t \mid R_{1:t-1} \sim \mathcal{N}\big(\mu_\theta(R_{1:t-1}), \sigma_\theta^2(R_{1:t-1})\big),$$

with NLL

$$\mathcal{L}_{Gauss}(\theta) = \frac{1}{NT}\sum_{i,t}\left[\frac{\big(r_t^{(i)} - \mu_{\theta,t}^{(i)}\big)^2}{2\sigma_{\theta,t}^{2(i)}} + \frac{1}{2}\log\sigma_{\theta,t}^{2(i)}\right] + \text{const.}$$

The presence of $\log\sigma_{\theta,t}^2$ penalizes unnecessarily large predicted volatilities, while the squared error term encourages accurate fit. In effect, this is a neural generalization of GARCH: the network outputs a time-varying conditional variance.

To capture heavy tails, one might assume a Student-t distribution:

$$R_t \mid R_{1:t-1} \sim t_\nu\big(\mu_\theta(R_{1:t-1}), \sigma_\theta^2(R_{1:t-1})\big),$$

which assigns higher probability to large deviations than a Gaussian. The corresponding NLL downweights extreme observations less aggressively, leading to models that better respect tail risk.

Bayesian view

In a Bayesian setting, parameters themselves are random with prior $p(\theta)$. We then work with the *posterior*

$$p(\theta \mid \mathcal{D}) \propto p(\mathcal{D} \mid \theta)\, p(\theta).$$

The training objective becomes the negative log-posterior:

$$\mathcal{L}_{Bayes}(\theta) = -\log p(\mathcal{D} \mid \theta) - \log p(\theta),$$

that is, NLL plus a regularization term from the prior. This connects probabilistic modeling directly to regularized neural training: weight decay, for instance, corresponds to a Gaussian prior on parameters.

Neural Networks as Parametric Distributions

Thus far we have described the probabilistic side: $p_\theta(R_{1:T})$, latent variables, and likelihoods. Neural networks enter as extremely flexible parameterizations of conditional distributions and latent mappings.

Basic neural building blocks

A feedforward neural network defines a nonlinear mapping from inputs x to outputs y via layered transformations:

$$h^{(1)} = \phi\big(W^{(1)}x + b^{(1)}\big),$$

$$h^{(2)} = \phi\big(W^{(2)}h^{(1)} + b^{(2)}\big), \ldots,$$

$$y = W^{(L)}h^{(L-1)} + b^{(L)},$$

where ϕ is a nonlinear activation (ReLU, tanh, etc.). When applied to time series, the input x might be the history $R_{1:t-1}$ or some summary thereof.

Core components and their role for financial data:

- **Parameterization.** The weights $\theta = \{W^{(\ell)}, b^{(\ell)}\}$ define a function from history to distribution parameters (means, volatilities, copula parameters, etc.).
- **Nonlinearity.** Activations allow the network to represent nonlinear dependence (e.g., volatility increasing in the magnitude of past returns).
- **Normalization.** Batch or layer normalization stabilize gradients and help with non-stationary scales, but must be used carefully in time series to avoid look-ahead bias.
- **Regularization.** Techniques such as weight decay, dropout, and early stopping control overfitting—crucial when we have limited historical crises but many parameters.

From outputs to distributions

A neural network on its own is just a function approximator. To become a probabilistic model, we interpret its outputs as parameters of a distribution. For example:

- **Gaussian output:**
$$(\mu_{\theta,t}, \log \sigma_{\theta,t}) = f_\theta(R_{1:t-1}),$$
and define
$$R_t \mid R_{1:t-1} \sim \mathcal{N}(\mu_{\theta,t}, \sigma^2_{\theta,t}).$$
- **Mixture output:** For more flexible tails,
$$\{\pi_{k,t}, \mu_{k,t}, \sigma_{k,t}\}_{k=1}^K = f_\theta(R_{1:t-1}),$$
with mixture weights $\pi_{k,t}$ (via softmax). Then
$$p_\theta(R_t \mid R_{1:t-1}) = \sum_{k=1}^{K} \pi_{k,t} \mathcal{N}(R_t; \mu_{k,t}, \sigma^2_{k,t}),$$
yielding multimodal and heavy-tailed conditional distributions.

The loss used to train f_θ is the NLL of the chosen distribution family. Thus, neural networks provide flexible shapes; the probabilistic layer on top specifies how these shapes translate into risk-relevant distributions.

Neural Latent-Variable Models

We now combine latent variables and neural parameterizations. This is the conceptual bridge to the deep generative models used later in the book (VAEs, flows, diffusion), but we keep the discussion at a high level.

Latent factor representation

Suppose each return path $r_{1:T}^{(i)}$ is generated from a low-dimensional latent vector $z^{(i)} \in \mathbb{R}^m$:

$$z^{(i)} \sim p(z),$$
$$R_{1:T}^{(i)} \mid z^{(i)} \sim p_\theta(R_{1:T} \mid z^{(i)}),$$

with $p_\theta(R_{1:T} \mid z)$ parameterized by a neural network. Intuitively, z might encode:

- the broad market regime (bull vs. bear),
- a volatility level,
- cross-sectional factor exposures.

During training, we attempt to find parameters θ and (possibly) an inference mechanism for the latents such that the joint model $p_\theta(R, Z)$ explains the observed data well. Once trained, we can:

- Sample z from its prior and generate synthetic paths $R_{1:T}$.
- Condition on specific z values (or regions) to produce targeted scenarios (e.g., high-volatility, high-correlation regimes).

Training with intractable posteriors

In latent-variable models, the *posterior* $p_\theta(Z \mid R_{1:T})$ often has no closed form. This complicates maximum likelihood, because the marginal likelihood requires integrating out Z:

$$p_\theta(R_{1:T}) = \int p_\theta(R_{1:T}, Z)\, dZ.$$

Approximate inference methods (variational inference, Monte Carlo) are then used. While later sections will formalize this for VAEs and flows, for our purposes here the key point is conceptual:

> A neural latent-variable model is defined not only by its generative story $p_\theta(R, Z)$, but also by how it approximates the unobserved Z given data.

The more accurately we can infer Z, the better we can:

1. Interpret the regimes and states implied by the model.
2. Condition on them to generate realistic, targeted stress scenarios.

Neural Optimization and Non-Stationary Financial Data

Fitting neural generative models involves minimizing a loss (usually an approximation to NLL) with respect to millions of parameters. For financial data, two challenges arise:

1. **Non-stationarity.** The DGP itself evolves: technology, regulation, and macro structure change over time. A model trained on long histories must either adapt to these shifts or focus on regimes relevant to current usage.
2. **Heteroskedasticity and heavy tails.** Returns display volatility clustering and large jumps; naive Gaussian assumptions lead to underestimation of risk and optimistic backtests.

Core mechanics of neural optimization remain the same as in other domains, but their interpretation in finance is specific.

Stochastic gradient descent (SGD)

We typically minimize a loss $\mathcal{L}(\theta)$ using SGD or its variants (Adam, RMSprop). At each iteration:

1. Sample a mini-batch of paths or time windows $\{r_{1:T}^{(i)}\}_{i \in \mathcal{B}}$.
2. Compute the loss (e.g., average NLL) on the batch.
3. Compute gradients $\nabla_\theta \mathcal{L}_\mathcal{B}(\theta)$ via backpropagation.
4. Update parameters:

$$\theta \leftarrow \theta - \eta \, \nabla_\theta \mathcal{L}_\mathcal{B}(\theta),$$

   where η is the learning rate.

From a probabilistic viewpoint, SGD is approximating MLE (or MAP in a Bayesian setting). From a financial viewpoint, the batch choices, learning rate schedule, and regularization affect which regimes are emphasized and how much the model overfits idiosyncrasies of the sample.

Regularization as prior knowledge

Techniques such as:

- weight decay (L2 regularization),
- dropout,
- early stopping,
- spectral normalization on weights,

serve both statistical and financial roles. They reduce variance of the estimator and act as priors about plausible model behavior. For example, penalizing large weights biases the model toward smoother functions of history; in markets, this corresponds to preferring stable dependence structures over wildly fluctuating ones that might merely reflect noise.

Diagram: Linking Latents, Time Series, and Neural Networks

Right after introducing latent-variable models and neural training objectives, it is helpful to visualize how these pieces fit together into a single probabilistic object parameterized by a neural network.

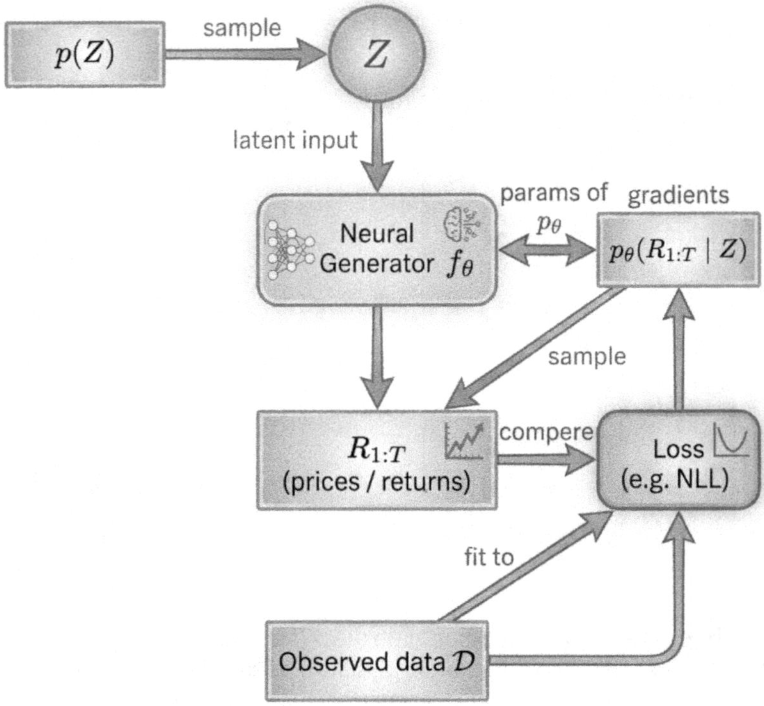

This diagram emphasizes three layers:

1. The **probabilistic layer**: prior $p(Z)$, conditional $p_\theta(R_{1:T} \mid Z)$.

2. The **neural parameterization**: the generator f_θ maps $(Z, \text{history})$ to distribution parameters.

3. The **optimization layer**: a loss (often NLL) compares the model-induced distribution to observed data and updates θ.

Why the Probabilistic View Matters for Synthetic Markets

Interpreting neural generative models as probabilistic constructs is not merely philosophical; it has concrete consequences for stress testing and trading:

- **Coverage.** The support of $p_\theta(R_{1:T})$ tells us which scenarios the model can in principle generate. If certain crisis configurations have near-zero probability under p_θ, they will almost never appear in simulation, no matter how long we sample.
- **Calibrated likelihoods vs. visual plausibility.** A model can produce time series that "look realistic" yet assign implausibly low probability to historical crises. Likelihood-based diagnostics reveal such mismatches.
- **Controlled generation.** Latent variables and conditional structures determine how we can steer simulations toward specific regimes (e.g., high spread, low liquidity) without breaking other stylized facts.
- **Comparability.** Viewing different architectures (RNNs, transformers, VAEs, diffusion models) through the lens of $p_\theta(R, Z)$ and associated losses allows apples-to-apples comparison: how each trades off likelihood fidelity, tail behavior, and control.

In the following sections of the chapter, we will build on this foundation to:

1. Define rigorous evaluation criteria for generative models in finance.
2. Introduce resampling and copula baselines as transparent probabilistic benchmarks.
3. Survey adversarial, latent, and diffusion architectures, always grounding them in their underlying probability models.

Throughout, the guiding principle remains: a generative model is only as useful as the probabilistic structure it encodes and how well that structure matches the risks we care about.

3.2 Evaluation and Controlled Generation

In the previous section we treated every neural generator as a probabilistic model for financial time series, with an explicit or implicit likelihood $p_\theta(R_{1:T})$ and, often, latent variables encoding regimes or volatility states. That probabilistic view is necessary but not sufficient for our purpose in this book.

For trading and risk management, the central questions are:

- *Is the synthetic data good enough for the decisions we want to make?*
- *Can we steer the generator toward scenarios that are relevant but rare in the historical record?*

This section develops a structured way to answer these questions. We will:

- Define a hierarchy of evaluation criteria, from basic distributional checks to pathwise and strategy-level diagnostics.
- Introduce quantitative tools to compare real and synthetic data.
- Show how conditioning and control variables turn a generic generator into a scenario engine for specific regimes and risk factors.
- Emphasize how to verify that controls work *without* destroying other key properties of the data.

A Hierarchy of Evaluation Criteria

Not all discrepancies between real and synthetic data are equally important. A generator that slightly misses kurtosis but nails crisis comovements may be more useful for stress testing than one that perfectly matches first four moments yet never produces liquidity dry-ups.

A practical way to structure evaluation is to move from low-level statistical properties to high-level economic behavior.

Level 1: Basic distributional fidelity

At the most elementary level, we want synthetic data to reproduce familiar stylized facts of asset returns.

Marginal distributions. For each asset or factor:

- Compare empirical histograms of real and synthetic returns.
- Check first four moments (mean, variance, skewness, kurtosis).
- Inspect tail behavior: log-log plots of tail probabilities, Hill tail-index estimates.

A generator that produces nearly Gaussian returns when the real series is heavy-tailed is suspect for risk applications: tail risk will be understated in backtests.

Temporal dependence. Key time-series features include:

- *Autocorrelation of returns* $ACF_R(k)$: usually close to zero at daily or lower frequencies for liquid assets.
- *Autocorrelation of squared/absolute returns* $ACF_{|R|}(k)$: decays slowly, reflecting volatility clustering.
- *Conditional heteroskedasticity*: observation of ARCH/GARCH effects in real vs. synthetic data.

If volatility clustering disappears in synthetic data, any volatility-timing strategy tested on it will be misleadingly stable.

Cross-sectional dependence. For a portfolio of assets or factors, evaluate:

- Correlation matrices and their eigenvalue spectra.
- Rank correlations (Spearman, Kendall) to capture non-linear dependence.
- Tail dependence measures: frequency of simultaneous large losses.

Here we check that the model does not only match average correlations, but also the "correlation goes to 1 in a crisis" behavior relevant to portfolio risk.

Level 2: Pathwise and event-based properties

Trading strategies and risk systems care about entire trajectories, not isolated returns.

Drawdown and recovery profiles. For both real and synthetic P&L or index levels:

- Compute distributions of maximum drawdown over rolling windows.
- Measure average and worst-case time to recovery from large drawdowns.
- Inspect clustering of drawdowns across assets.

A model that produces the right unconditional volatility but only short, shallow drawdowns understates the pain strategies might experience.

Extreme moves and clustering. Examine:

- Frequency of k-sigma moves (e.g., $|R_t| > 4\sigma$).
- Temporal clustering of extremes: do large moves tend to follow large moves?
- Cross-asset co-occurrence: joint probability that multiple assets exceed large thresholds on the same day.

Liquidity and microstructure proxies. When intraday or microstructure data are available:

- Spread distributions and their dynamics.
- Order-book depth and its variation across regimes.
- Volume, trade size distributions, and their autocorrelations.

These features matter for execution strategies and transaction-cost modeling.

Level 3: Task- and strategy-level behavior

Ultimately, synthetic data are a tool for decision support. The final level of evaluation measures whether decisions made on synthetic data behave similarly when applied to real data.

Backtest robustness. One methodology:

- Calibrate a strategy or risk model on a subset of real data.
- Run it on many synthetic paths generated from a model calibrated to the same period.
- Compare the distribution of performance metrics (Sharpe, maximum drawdown, turnover) between:
  - out-of-sample real data, and
  - synthetic data drawn from the model.

If the synthetic backtests are consistently more optimistic than real out-of-sample performance, the generator is over-smoothing or underestimating risk.

Stress testing and scenario analysis. A good generator allows us to pose questions like:

- What happens to this portfolio if a 2008-like liquidity crunch occurs but starts from today's valuations?
- How do execution costs behave if volatility doubles and order-book depth halves?

Here, success is judged not just by distributional similarity but by the plausibility and diversity of generated stress scenarios.

Quantitative Tools for Comparing Real and Synthetic Data

We now list concrete statistical tools that formalize the comparisons just discussed. The goal is not to turn evaluation into an exercise in p-value worship, but to provide a quantitative handle on how and where models deviate from reality.

Two-sample tests and distance measures

Given samples $\{x_i\}$ from the real distribution and $\{y_j\}$ from the generator, two-sample tests ask whether they could be drawn from the same underlying law.

Classical tests.

- Kolmogorov-Smirnov (KS) test for univariate marginals.
- Anderson-Darling test for emphasis on tails.

These tests are easy to apply asset-by-asset and give a coarse sense of fit.

Modern distance measures. For multivariate data and higher-level statistics:

- Maximum Mean Discrepancy (MMD) between feature embeddings of real and synthetic paths.
- Wasserstein distances between empirical distributions of summary statistics (e.g., distributions of 20-day maximum drawdowns).

These metrics create a single number summarizing how close synthetic and real distributions are for the quantity of interest.

Probability integral transform (PIT) diagnostics

If the model outputs conditional distributions $F_{\theta,t}(\cdot)$ for returns, we can perform PIT diagnostics:

$$u_t = F_{\theta,t}(r_t),$$

where r_t is the realized return. Under correct specification, the sequence $\{u_t\}$ should be i.i.d. uniform on $[0, 1]$.

In practice, we:

- Plot histograms of $\{u_t\}$ to detect bias (e.g., too many small values indicate underestimated left tails).

- Compute autocorrelations of $\{u_t\}$ and $\{u_t^2\}$ to detect unmodeled dependence.

PIT diagnostics are powerful because they test the full conditional distribution, not just its first moments.

Feature-based evaluation

Instead of comparing raw series directly, we often compare distributions of engineered features that are particularly relevant for trading.

- Volatility estimates (realized or GARCH-type) over different horizons.
- Rolling correlations and betas.
- Factor returns and factor-mimicking portfolio P&L.
- Microstructure indicators such as order imbalance or price impact measures.

For each feature, we can compute and compare:

- Marginal distributions and tail summaries.
- Autocorrelations and cross-correlations.
- Regime-specific statistics (e.g., conditional on high VIX vs. low VIX).

Visual Comparison of Real and Synthetic Metrics

Before we introduce conditional architectures, it is helpful to have a visual summary of how evaluation metrics differ between real and synthetic data, and how a conditional generator is driven by noise and guidance signals.

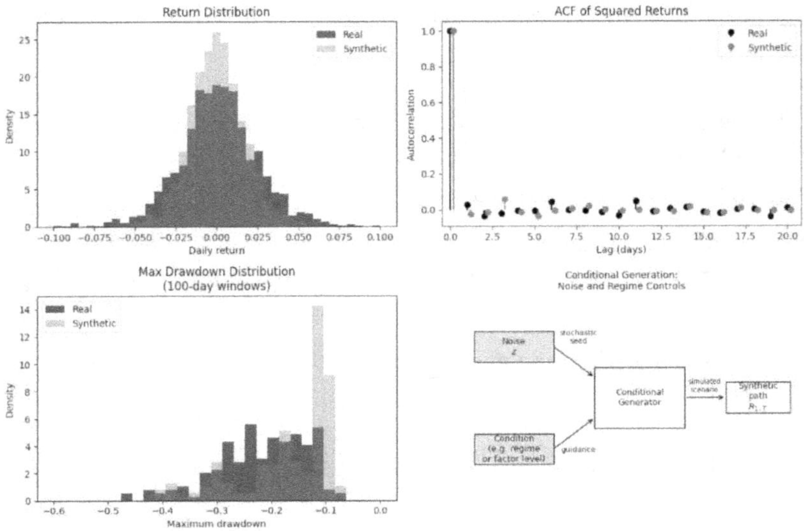

This figure illustrates the core idea: we do not evaluate the generator on one metric alone, but across a suite of distributional and pathwise features, while keeping in mind how noise and conditioning variables drive the synthetic paths.

From Unconditional to Conditional and Controlled Generation

So far we have described evaluation mainly for *unconditional* generators, which aim to match the overall data-generating process. For stress testing, we need more: the ability to generate paths that correspond to specified regimes, factor realizations, or macro conditions.

What do we mean by control?

Formally, a conditional generator models:

$$p_\theta(R_{1:T} \mid C),$$

where C is a control or conditioning variable. Examples include:

- a discrete regime label (calm, stressed, crisis),

- a continuous volatility level or VIX-like index,
- a vector of macro factors (growth, inflation, credit spreads),
- or portfolio-specific conditions (target leverage, liquidity state).

Control means that when we change C, the distribution of generated paths shifts in a predictable, economically meaningful way *along the intended dimension*, while preserving other stylized facts as much as possible.

Architectural patterns for conditioning

There are several standard ways to incorporate C into a neural generator.

Direct concatenation. For sequence models (RNNs, transformers), we can append C to the input at each time step:

$$\text{input}_t = [R_{1:t-1}, C].$$

The network learns how C influences the conditional distribution of returns. This is straightforward but may blur the role of C and history if not carefully regularized.

Conditional embeddings. We map C to an embedding vector $e(C)$ and inject it into the network at multiple layers:

$$h_t^{(\ell+1)} = \phi\big(W^{(\ell)} h_t^{(\ell)} + U^{(\ell)} e(C) + b^{(\ell)}\big).$$

This allows the model to share structure across related conditions (e.g., similar macro states) and can be especially useful when C is high-dimensional or categorical.

Encoder-decoder setups. We can build a model in which:

- An encoder maps past data or desired scenario descriptors into a latent representation.
- A decoder (generator) takes as input both noise and this representation to produce paths.

For example, an encoder could summarize historical crisis episodes into a latent vector that the generator then uses to produce "crisis-like" but not identical scenarios.

Classifier-free and guidance-based methods. In diffusion and other advanced models, we sometimes train both conditional and unconditional versions and then combine their gradients to guide sampling toward or away from certain conditions. The conceptual takeaway is that guidance allows for a smooth knob controlling how strongly C shapes the generated paths, at the cost of higher sampling complexity.

Verifying That Controls Work

Adding conditioning variables is easy; ensuring they behave as intended is not. We need systematic checks that:

- Changes in C move the distribution in the expected direction and magnitude.
- Other properties (e.g., volatility clustering, cross-asset dependence) remain realistic under each condition.

Sensitivity and monotonicity checks

Suppose C is a scalar volatility level. We can:

- Generate many paths at different fixed values of C.
- Estimate realized volatility on each path.
- Plot average realized volatility vs. C.

We expect a roughly monotonic relationship. A non-monotonic or flat relationship suggests the model is ignoring the control or misusing it.

Similarly, if C encodes stress level, we should see:

- higher tail probabilities and drawdowns as the stress level increases,
- increased cross-asset correlations and tail dependence under high stress.

Conditional distribution and feature checks

For each conditioning value c, we can perform the same battery of evaluations as before, but *conditional* on $C = c$:

- Compare real vs. synthetic conditional distributions $p(R_{1:T} \mid C = c)$ when historical analogues exist (e.g., days with VIX in a given range).
- Compare feature distributions (volatility, drawdowns, liquidity measures) conditional on $C = c$.

This is crucial when we use synthetic data to extrapolate from limited historical samples of rare regimes.

Joint behavior across controls and latents

In latent-variable models, we may have both observed controls C and unobserved latents Z. Then

$$p_\theta(R_{1:T} \mid C) = \int p_\theta(R_{1:T} \mid Z, C)\, p_\theta(Z \mid C)\, dZ.$$

For scenario design, we often fix C and sample Z from its (learned) conditional distribution. Evaluation should then:

- Assess diversity across samples of Z at fixed C (coverage of plausible paths).
- Ensure that variation in Z does not break the regime semantics of C (e.g., crisis-labeled C paths should not include many calm, low-volatility periods).

Putting It All Together for Trading and Risk

Suggested evaluation workflow

- **Define the use case.** Is the generator intended for:
  - long-horizon portfolio risk,
  - high-frequency execution stress testing,

  - factor strategy robustness,
  - or regulatory stress scenarios?

  Different use cases emphasize different levels of the evaluation hierarchy.

- **Calibrate the generator.** Fit the probabilistic model $p_\theta(R_{1:T} \mid C)$ to historical data, using appropriate likelihood-based or adversarial objectives.
- **Run unconditional diagnostics.** Before introducing controls, verify that:
  - basic distributional and temporal properties are matched,
  - cross-sectional and tail dependence are realistic,
  - pathwise statistics such as drawdowns are in the right ballpark.
- **Introduce and test controls.** Add conditioning variables C and:
  - visually and quantitatively verify that changing C has the intended effect,
  - re-run evaluation metrics *conditioned* on C.
- **Strategy-level evaluation.** For the targeted use case:
  - run strategies or risk models on synthetic data under different C values,
  - compare to out-of-sample real episodes where available,
  - adjust model or controls if synthetic behavior is inconsistent with historical analogues.

The key trade-off: fidelity vs. controllability

Finally, any practical generator must manage a tension:

- *Fidelity* demands close replication of historical distributions and pathwise properties.

- *Controllability* demands that we can push the model into regions of scenario space that are rare or unseen historically, guided by economically meaningful controls.

Overfitting to the past improves short-horizon fidelity but harms generalization and controllability. Overly strong controls can produce visually extreme but statistically incoherent scenarios. The probabilistic viewpoint from the previous section—treating the generator as $p_\theta(R, Z \mid C)$ with explicit assumptions about likelihoods and latents—provides the language to reason about and manage this trade-off.

In the next section, we will step back from neural architectures and introduce resampling and copula-based baselines. These simpler models will serve as a benchmark for both fidelity and controllability: any complex deep generator we deploy should demonstrably do better than what can be achieved with transparent, low-tech methods.

3.3 Resampling and Copula Baselines

The previous sections treated neural generators as probabilistic models and developed tools to evaluate how well their synthetic series match the real world, both unconditionally and under explicit controls. Before we invest in complex architectures, it is essential to ask a more basic question:

> What can we already achieve with simple, transparent methods that make minimal modeling assumptions?

Resampling and copula-based models provide precisely this baseline. They are not "smart" in the way deep networks are, but they respect dependence in ways that naive i.i.d. bootstraps or Gaussian models do not. Any sophisticated generative AI approach must either demonstrate clear advantages over these baselines or explain why its additional complexity is justified for the task at hand.

We focus on two families:

- **Block bootstrap methods** that generate new time series by reusing actual historical returns in carefully chosen blocks.

- **Copula models** that separate marginal distributions from dependence, allowing us to flexibly model cross-sectional structure.

Why Baselines Matter

From a trading and risk-management perspective, a baseline should be:

- *Transparent*: its mechanics and assumptions are easy to explain to risk committees and regulators.
- *Dependence-aware*: it should capture at least some of the temporal and cross-sectional structure present in markets.
- *Computationally cheap*: it should be feasible to generate many scenarios quickly for Monte Carlo analysis.

Block bootstraps and copulas meet these criteria. They will not solve all problems, but they give us a benchmark: if a deep generative model cannot significantly outperform these methods on the evaluation hierarchy of the previous section, we should think carefully before adopting it in production.

Resampling: From i.i.d. Bootstrap to Block Bootstrap

The i.i.d. bootstrap and its limitations

Consider a univariate return series $\{r_t\}_{t=1}^{T}$. The simplest resampling method is the i.i.d. bootstrap:

- Form the empirical distribution $\hat{F}$ that puts mass $1/T$ on each observed return r_t.
- For each synthetic path $r_{1:T}^*$, draw r_t^* i.i.d. from $\hat{F}$.

This preserves the marginal distribution of single-period returns by construction (up to sampling noise). However, it destroys:

- *Autocorrelation* in returns and volatility.
- *Volatility clustering*: large and small moves no longer cluster in time.
- Any pattern in multi-period aggregates (drawdowns, trend persistence).

For financial time series, these are unacceptable deficiencies. A strategy tested on i.i.d. bootstrapped data will see overly stable volatility and mis-estimate risk.

Fixed block bootstrap

To restore some temporal dependence, we move from single points to blocks of consecutive observations. Let L be a chosen block length. Define overlapping blocks:

$$B_1 = (r_1, \ldots, r_L), \quad B_2 = (r_2, \ldots, r_{L+1}), \quad \ldots, \quad B_{T-L+1} = (r_{T-L+1}, \ldots, r_T).$$

A *fixed block bootstrap* path of length T is generated by:

- Sample integers $k_1, k_2, \ldots, k_M$ i.i.d. from $\{1, \ldots, T-L+1\}$, where $M = \lceil T/L \rceil$.
- Concatenate blocks $B_{k_1}, B_{k_2}, \ldots, B_{k_M}$.
- Truncate the resulting sequence to length T.

Intuitively, each block encodes a short-lived piece of the original dependence structure (including volatility clustering). By stitching blocks together, we preserve local dynamics while allowing new global sequences.

Trade-off in block length.

The choice of L is central:

- **Small** L: better recombination (more diverse paths), but weaker preservation of dependence; may break multi-day patterns that matter for trend or mean-reversion strategies.

- **Large** L: stronger preservation of local dynamics, but synthetic paths become closer to simple replays of history with limited recombination; risk of underestimating uncertainty outside known episodes.

A rough guideline is to choose L larger than the main autocorrelation range in squared returns (to capture volatility clustering), but not so large that M becomes small and recombination rare.

Multivariate block bootstrap

For d-dimensional returns $R_t \in \mathbb{R}^d$, we typically form *vector blocks*:

$$B_j = (R_j, R_{j+1}, \ldots, R_{j+L-1}) \in \mathbb{R}^{L \times d}.$$

We then sample and stitch these matrix-valued blocks.

This preserves:

- Within-block cross-sectional dependence: correlations and tail co-movements across assets over L days.
- Within-block temporal dependence: short-term autocorrelation and volatility clustering.

However, it assumes that:

- The joint dynamics are approximately *stationary* over the sample.
- Dependence beyond L days can be broken without major impact on the features we care about.

These are strong assumptions in the presence of structural breaks (e.g., changes in monetary regimes) or persistent regimes (long bull/bear cycles). Still, for many applications, the multivariate block bootstrap provides a solid baseline that captures much more structure than i.i.d. sampling.

Variants: moving blocks and stationary bootstrap

Several refinements exist to reduce artifacts at block boundaries and better approximate stationarity:

Moving block bootstrap. Uses overlapping blocks as above; the randomness in starting positions already mitigates some boundary effects.

Stationary bootstrap. Instead of fixed-length blocks, this method draws block lengths from a geometric distribution with mean L. This leads to:

- Random block lengths, which better reflect the stochastic variability of regime durations.
- An exact stationary distribution of the resulting resampled series under mild conditions.

The key idea remains the same: preserve dependence within blocks, randomize beyond.

Strengths and weaknesses of block bootstraps

From the perspective of our evaluation hierarchy:

- **Marginal distributions**: exactly preserved (for single-period returns), up to sampling error.
- **Short-horizon dependence**: reasonably preserved when L is well-chosen.
- **Cross-sectional dependence**: preserved within blocks; may be distorted over long horizons due to recombination.
- **Pathwise properties**: drawdowns and volatility bursts similar to historical episodes, but new combinations of episodes may yield paths that have not occurred historically.

Weaknesses include:

- **Limited extrapolation**: the method cannot generate dynamics qualitatively different from those already observed; no new regimes or tail behaviors beyond history.
- **Sensitivity to structural breaks**: mixing blocks from different structural regimes can produce unrealistic hybrids (e.g., pre- and post-crisis volatility in one path).

- **Limited control**: there is no explicit way to condition on macro variables or desired regimes; one can only approximate this by selecting or re-weighting blocks.

Any deep generative model must at least match block bootstrap performance on short-horizon dependence and cross-sectional structure, while providing better long-horizon modeling and more explicit control.

Copula Models: Separating Marginals and Dependence

While block bootstraps focus on time dependence, copula models provide a principled approach to cross-sectional dependence. They are grounded in a simple but powerful idea: we can model marginal distributions and dependence separately.

Sklar's theorem and copulas

For a d-dimensional random vector $R = (R^{(1)}, \dots, R^{(d)})$, with continuous marginal cumulative distribution functions (CDFs) $F_1, \dots, F_d$, Sklar's theorem states that there exists a copula C such that:

$$\mathbb{P}\big(R^{(1)} \leq r_1, \dots, R^{(d)} \leq r_d\big) = C\big(F_1(r_1), \dots, F_d(r_d)\big).$$

In other words, any joint distribution can be written as:

$$F_R(r_1, \dots, r_d) = C(u_1, \dots, u_d), \quad u_j = F_j(r_j) \in (0, 1),$$

where C is a multivariate CDF on $[0, 1]^d$ with uniform marginals.

Conceptually, the steps are:

- Transform each asset's returns to uniform variables $U^{(j)} = F_j(R^{(j)})$.
- Model the joint distribution of $(U^{(1)}, \dots, U^{(d)})$ via a copula C.

This separation is especially attractive in finance because we often have strong prior views about marginals (e.g., heavy tails) but more uncertainty about dependence.

Static copula construction

A basic static copula model for cross-sectional dependence on a given horizon (e.g., daily returns) works as follows.

Step 1: Estimate marginals. For each asset j:

- Fit a parametric distribution (e.g., Student-t) or use the empirical CDF $\hat{F}_j$.
- Transform returns to uniform scores:

$$u_t^{(j)} = \hat{F}_j(r_t^{(j)}).$$

Step 2: Fit a copula to the uniforms. Choose a copula family C_{θ_c} (e.g., Gaussian, t-copula, Archimedean). Estimate its parameters from the empirical uniforms $\{u_t\}$, for instance by:

- Inference functions for margins (IFM): first fit marginals, then copula.
- Maximum likelihood over the joint density implied by marginals and copula.

Step 3: Generate synthetic returns. To draw a new d-dimensional return vector:

- Sample $(U^{(1)}, \dots, U^{(d)}) \sim C_{\theta_c}$.
- Transform back using inverse marginals:

$$R^{(j)} = \hat{F}_j^{-1}\big(U^{(j)}\big).$$

This preserves, by construction:

- each asset's marginal distribution,
- the copula-defined dependence structure (including rank correlations and, for appropriate families, tail dependence).

Gaussian and t-copulas

Two copula families are particularly common:

Gaussian copula. Constructed by:

- Sampling a multivariate normal vector $Z \sim \mathcal{N}(0, \Sigma)$.
- Setting $U^{(j)} = \Phi(Z^{(j)})$, where Φ is the standard normal CDF.

This yields dependence similar to that implied by a multivariate normal distribution but allows non-Gaussian marginals. It captures linear correlations but has no tail dependence: extreme events are not particularly likely to occur simultaneously beyond what correlation implies.

t**-copula.** Constructed by:

- Sampling $T \sim t_\nu(0, \Sigma)$ (a multivariate Student-t with ν degrees of freedom).
- Setting $U^{(j)} = F_{t,\nu}(T^{(j)})$, where $F_{t,\nu}$ is the univariate t-CDF.

The t-copula exhibits tail dependence: large negative realizations in one component increase the probability of large negative realizations in others, even beyond linear correlation. This is more realistic for equity and credit portfolios, where "correlations go to one" in crises.

Dynamic copulas

Static copulas treat dependence as constant over time. In reality, cross-sectional dependence varies with volatility, macro regimes, and other state variables. Dynamic copula models extend the framework by allowing copula parameters θ_c to evolve:

$$\theta_{c,t} = g\big(\theta_{c,t-1}, \text{state variables at } t-1\big),$$

for some update function g (e.g., GARCH-type dynamics for correlations).

For example, a dynamic Gaussian copula may let its correlation matrix follow a DCC (dynamic conditional correlation) process. This allows synthetic simulations to reflect the empirical observation that asset correlations spike in high-volatility regimes.

Strengths and weaknesses of copula models

Relative to the evaluation hierarchy:

- **Marginal distributions**: highly flexible and easily tailored to each asset or factor.
- **Cross-sectional dependence**: can capture non-linear rank dependence and, with appropriate families, tail dependence.
- **Temporal dependence**: basic copulas are static; dynamic versions introduce time variation in dependence but still require additional modeling for serial correlation and volatility clustering.

Main limitations:

- **Complex temporal structure**. Copulas are not a full time-series model; by themselves they do not encode the rich autoregressive and heteroskedastic structure of returns.
- **High dimensions**. Fitting high-dimensional copulas (e.g., hundreds of assets) is challenging; vine copulas and factor copulas help, but complexity grows quickly.
- **Model misspecification**. Choosing the wrong family (e.g., Gaussian copula for assets with strong tail dependence) can give a false sense of security.

Despite these issues, copulas offer a very transparent way to generate cross-sectionally consistent scenarios: we can see exactly how marginals and dependence are constructed, and we can easily adjust each component.

Combining Resampling and Copulas

In practice, we often blend ideas from block bootstrap and copulas to get the best of both worlds: realistic time dependence and realistic cross-sectional dependence.

Two common patterns are:

Copula for cross-section, bootstrap for time.

- Use a dynamic univariate time-series model (or block bootstrap) for each asset's return path.
- At each time step, map model residuals to uniforms and couple them across assets via a copula.

This yields synthetic paths in which each series has realistic temporal dynamics and the cross-section has realistic dependence.

Block bootstrap of copula-transformed data.

- Transform returns to uniform scores via marginal CDFs.
- Perform a multivariate block bootstrap on these scores.
- Transform back to returns using inverse marginals.

Here, the block bootstrap preserves temporal dependence in the copula space, while marginals are controlled separately.

These hybrids highlight a key message of this chapter: dependence modeling is modular. We can separately choose how to handle time dynamics and cross-sectional structure, and then ask how much generative AI really adds on top.

Baselines as Yardsticks for Deep Generative Models

We close by returning to the central theme: deep generative models should be judged against these resampling and copula baselines, not in isolation.

For a given use case (e.g., multi-asset risk or factor strategy stress testing), a deep model should ideally:

- **Match or exceed** block-bootstrap performance on short-horizon dependence and pathwise statistics (volatility clustering, drawdowns).
- **Match or exceed** copula performance on cross-sectional dependence, including tail co-movements.

- **Offer additional benefits**: richer long-horizon dynamics, capacity to extrapolate beyond historical combinations, and explicit, flexible control via conditioning variables as described in the previous section.

If a neural generator fails to do better than a block bootstrap on volatility clustering, or produces cross-sectional dependence no more realistic than a simple t-copula, we should hesitate to deploy it for mission-critical stress testing. Conversely, when a deep model demonstrates clear, quantifiable gains over these baselines on the evaluation metrics that matter for the strategy, we have a compelling case for its use.

In the next section, we will examine the main deep generative families—GANs, VAEs/flows, and diffusion models—through precisely this lens: what probabilistic structure they imply, how they are trained, where they shine relative to resampling and copulas, and where they still fall short.

3.4 Adversarial, Latent, and Diffusion Models

Up to this point we have treated generative models through two complementary lenses. First, we framed them as probabilistic objects—$p_\theta(R_{1:T}, Z)$—with likelihoods, latent variables, and neural parameterizations. Second, we asked how to evaluate them and how to control them for regime-specific stress testing, always comparing to transparent baselines such as block bootstraps and copulas.

We now turn to the three main deep generative families that dominate current research and practice:

- Generative adversarial networks (GANs).
- Latent-variable models with explicit likelihoods: variational autoencoders (VAEs) and normalizing flows.
- Diffusion models based on iterative denoising.

Our goal is not to exhaust every architectural variant, but to understand their core mechanics and, for each family, to answer four questions that matter for trading and risk:

- How is the model trained (what loss, what game)?
- How does it handle likelihoods (explicit, implicit, or approximate)?
- What kind of coverage does it offer over possible market scenarios?
- How does it treat tails and extremes?

Three Families at a Glance

Before diving into details, it is useful to have a visual "map" of the three families and how information flows through them when applied to financial time series.

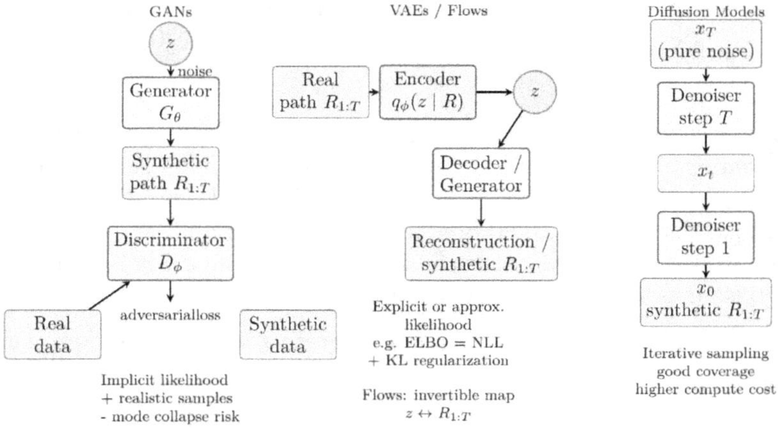

This three-column diagram emphasizes:

- GANs: an adversarial loop between generator and discriminator, no explicit likelihood.

- VAEs/flows: an encoder–latent–decoder chain with explicit or approximated likelihood.
- Diffusion: a multi-step denoising ladder, where sampling is iterative.

We now unpack each family in turn, always relating back to likelihood control, scenario coverage, and tail behavior.

Generative Adversarial Networks for Time Series

Basic GAN mechanics

A standard (unconditional) GAN defines:

- A *generator* G_θ that maps latent noise $z \sim p(z)$ to synthetic paths:
$$\tilde{R}_{1:T} = G_\theta(z).$$
- A *discriminator* (or critic) D_ϕ that receives a path $R_{1:T}$ and outputs a score indicating how "real" it appears.

Training is a two-player minimax game:

$$\min_\theta \max_\phi \mathbb{E}_{R\sim p_{data}}[\log D_\phi(R)] + \mathbb{E}_{z\sim p(z)}[\log(1 - D_\phi(G_\theta(z)))].$$

Variants (Wasserstein GANs, hinge losses) modify the loss but preserve the idea: D_ϕ learns to distinguish real from fake, while G_θ learns to fool D_ϕ.

Crucially, there is *no explicit likelihood* $p_\theta(R_{1:T})$; the model is trained to match the data distribution implicitly via adversarial feedback.

Architectures for financial sequences

For financial time series, G_θ and D_ϕ must process sequences:

- **Recurrent architectures**: LSTMs or GRUs that step through time, suitable for capturing long-range dependencies but may be harder to train in adversarial settings.

- **1D convolutional architectures**: temporal convolutions (e.g., WaveNet-style) can capture local patterns and are often easier to parallelize.
- **Transformers**: self-attention over time allows expressive modeling of long-range interactions, including impacts of distant events on current volatility.

The discriminator is often a mirror of the generator, taking an entire path and summarizing it into a scalar "real vs. fake" judgment.

Strengths: sample realism and flexibility

GANs are designed to produce samples that look realistic under the discriminator's scrutiny. If well trained:

- Generated return paths can exhibit sharp, non-Gaussian features and complex temporal patterns that are hard to capture with simple likelihood models.
- GANs can, in principle, approximate any distribution over paths given enough capacity and data.

From a coverage perspective, adversarial training encourages G_θ to match the data distribution globally, not just in terms of low-order moments. This can be powerful for synthesizing microstructure or intraday data, where exact likelihoods are difficult to specify.

Weaknesses: mode collapse, instability, and likelihood opacity

However, GANs present several challenges that are especially problematic for risk applications:

Mode collapse. The generator may focus on a subset of the true data modes, producing synthetic paths that fail to cover important regions of scenario space. For example, the GAN might learn to generate "typical" volatility regimes but almost never produce severe crisis-like episodes, because the discriminator is satisfied by matching common cases.

Training instability. The minimax game is sensitive to learning rates, network balance, and loss choices. Training may oscillate, diverge, or converge to degenerate solutions. For financial time series, heavy tails and regime shifts exacerbate instability: rare but crucial patterns are difficult for the discriminator to learn and may get ignored.

No explicit likelihood. Without $p_\theta(R_{1:T})$, we cannot:

- compute likelihood-based diagnostics (e.g., PIT tests),
- directly compare likelihoods of different models,
- or incorporate the generator into likelihood-based risk systems.

Evaluation must rely on sample-based metrics (as in the previous section), making it harder to guarantee coverage of extremes.

Implications for tails and stress testing

GANs trained naively often *under-represent tails.* Discriminators see far more normal days than crises; unless we up-weight rare events or design specific loss terms, the generator will optimize for typical behavior.

Mitigation strategies include:

- *Reweighting*: give higher loss weight to misclassification of extreme or crisis periods.
- *Conditioning*: introduce a regime label as input so that the generator explicitly learns crisis vs. calm modes.
- *Wasserstein or energy-distance losses*: which may provide smoother gradients and better sensitivity to distribution support.

Even with such measures, the absence of explicit likelihood makes it difficult to quantify exactly how often the GAN-generated universe visits tail regions compared to history.

Latent-Variable Models: VAEs and Normalizing Flows

Latent-variable models occupy the middle ground between transparent likelihood-based modeling and the flexible but opaque world of GANs.

Variational autoencoders: approximate likelihoods with latent structure

A variational autoencoder (VAE) defines:

- A prior over latent variables $p(z)$ (often standard normal).
- A generative model $p_\theta(R_{1:T} \mid z)$, parameterized by a neural decoder.
- An approximate posterior $q_\phi(z \mid R_{1:T})$, parameterized by an encoder.

The training objective is the evidence lower bound (ELBO):

$$\log p_\theta(R_{1:T}) \geq \mathbb{E}_{q_\phi(z \mid R_{1:T})}[\log p_\theta(R_{1:T} \mid z)] - \mathrm{KL}\big(q_\phi(z \mid R_{1:T}) \,\|\, p(z)\big),$$

which is maximized over (θ, ϕ).

Interpretation:

- The first term encourages accurate reconstruction of the observed path under the generative model (likelihood term).
- The second term regularizes the posterior to stay close to the prior, preventing the model from encoding too much idiosyncratic noise in z.

Architectures for time series.

The encoder and decoder must process sequences:

- *Sequence-to-latent encoder*: RNN, temporal CNN, or transformer that compresses a path $R_{1:T}$ into a latent vector z (mean and variance).
- *Latent-to-sequence decoder*: RNN, temporal CNN, or transformer conditioned on z that outputs the parameters of $p_\theta(R_{1:T} \mid z)$, often factorized autoregressively across time.

The latent z serves as a compact representation of market state or regime. We can inspect z to understand how the model organizes scenarios, or condition on regions of latent space to generate specific types of paths.

Likelihood control and tails.

VAEs provide an *approximate explicit likelihood* via the ELBO: we can compute lower bounds on $\log p_\theta(R_{1:T})$ and use these as diagnostics or for model comparison.

Tail behavior depends on:

- the prior $p(z)$ (usually light-tailed Gaussian),
- and the conditional distribution $p_\theta(R_{1:T} \mid z)$ (which we can choose to be heavy-tailed, e.g., mixtures or t-likelihoods).

If $p_\theta(R_{1:T} \mid z)$ is too Gaussian, the VAE may smooth out extremes; if we use richer likelihoods, we can better capture tail risk.

There is a regularization trade-off: strong KL penalties encourage using fewer latent dimensions and more smoothing; weaker penalties allow more flexibility but can overfit and diminish the usefulness of z for controlled generation.

Normalizing flows: invertible mappings with exact likelihoods

Normalizing flow models represent complex distributions via a sequence of invertible, differentiable transformations:

$$z \sim p(z), \quad R_{1:T} = f_\theta(z), \quad z = f_\theta^{-1}(R_{1:T}).$$

By the change-of-variables formula,

$$p_\theta(R_{1:T}) = p(z) \left| \det \frac{\partial f_\theta^{-1}}{\partial R_{1:T}} \right|.$$

Flows are trained by *maximizing exact likelihood*:

$$\max_\theta \sum_i \log p_\theta\big(r_{1:T}^{(i)}\big).$$

Architecturally, f_θ is built as a composition of simple invertible layers (affine couplings, autoregressive flows, etc.) that handle high-dimensional inputs such as entire return paths or multi-asset panels.

Coverage and tails.

Because flows optimize the full likelihood, they are incentivized to fit the entire support of the data distribution, including tails, provided the base distribution and transformations are expressive enough. We can:

- choose heavy-tailed base distributions $p(z)$ to encourage tail risk,
- or design flow layers that amplify or attenuate extremes as needed.

From a stress-testing perspective, flows offer:

- **Exact likelihoods** for diagnostics and model comparison.
- **Efficient sampling**: one forward pass from z to $R_{1:T}$.
- **Invertibility**: we can map observed paths into latent space and analyze their representation.

Their main challenges are:

- architectural complexity (designing invertible layers for long sequences),
- and potentially large parameter counts, which require careful regularization to avoid overfitting.

Diffusion Models: Iterative Denoising for Time Series

Diffusion models represent a conceptually different approach: rather than directly mapping noise to data, they gradually transform noise into data through a long sequence of denoising steps.

Forward noising process

We define a Markov chain that gradually adds noise to data. For a path $R_{1:T}$ viewed as a vector x_0, the forward process constructs:

$$x_1, x_2, \ldots, x_T,$$

where

$$x_t = \sqrt{\alpha_t}\, x_{t-1} + \sqrt{1-\alpha_t}\, \varepsilon_t, \quad \varepsilon_t \sim \mathcal{N}(0, I),$$

with a schedule $\{\alpha_t\}$ that decreases over time. As t increases, x_t becomes more Gaussian and less dependent on the original data; at the final step x_T is approximately standard normal.

This forward process is fixed and does not involve learnable parameters.

Reverse denoising process

The generative model learns to reverse the noising process: given a noisy sample at step t, predict the less-noisy sample at step $t-1$.

In continuous-time formulations, this is a stochastic differential equation (SDE) with a learned drift; in discrete-time, we parameterize reverse-conditionals:

$$p_\theta(x_{t-1} \mid x_t),$$

often by training a neural network to predict either the noise ε_t or the clean signal x_0 from x_t.

Sampling proceeds as:

- Draw $x_T \sim \mathcal{N}(0, I)$.
- For $t = T, T-1, \ldots, 1$:

$$x_{t-1} \sim p_\theta(x_{t-1} \mid x_t).$$

- Interpret x_0 as a synthetic path $R_{1:T}$.

Likelihoods and training

Certain diffusion formulations admit tractable or approximate likelihoods via variational bounds, but in practice:

- Training uses a surrogate loss (a form of denoising score matching), not direct maximum likelihood.
- Exact likelihood evaluation is often expensive and approximate.

Despite this, diffusion models have strong empirical *coverage* properties: because they model the full noising and denoising dynamics, they can, in principle, represent very complex distributions over paths.

Coverage and tail behavior

Coverage advantages:

- The iterative refinement allows the model to correct coarse-grained errors in early steps with fine-grained adjustments later.
- The score function (gradient of log-density) learned at each noise level helps the model represent multiple modes and complex geometries in data space.

For tails:

- Proper training requires that extreme events be well represented at various noise scales; otherwise, the model may smooth them out.
- In financial applications, we can up-weight or re-sample tail events during training to ensure the score network learns their structure.

From a stress-testing point of view, diffusion models are attractive because:

- They can generate diverse, high-fidelity scenarios, including complex crisis patterns not easily captured by simple likelihood models.
- Conditioning (on regimes, factors, or macro variables) can be integrated via classifier guidance or conditional score networks, providing flexible control over scenarios.

Their main drawbacks:

- **Sampling cost**: generating each path requires many denoising steps; this can be significant when simulating thousands of long time series.

- **Likelihood opacity**: although likelihoods can be approximated, they are not as straightforward as in flows.

Comparing Families: Likelihood, Coverage, and Tails

We can now synthesize the main trade-offs across the three families, focusing on the aspects that matter most for synthetic markets.

Likelihood control

- **GANs**: no explicit likelihood; cannot directly compute $p_\theta(R_{1:T})$. Evaluation relies entirely on sample-based statistics, two-sample tests, and strategy-level backtests.
- **VAEs**: approximate likelihood via ELBO; we can compute lower bounds on $\log p_\theta(R_{1:T})$ and use them for model selection and diagnostics.
- **Flows**: exact, tractable likelihoods; strong support for PIT-based diagnostics and rigorous model comparison.
- **Diffusion**: variational or approximate likelihoods; more opaque than flows but still grounded in a principled probabilistic framework.

For regulatory or risk-management contexts that demand likelihood-based validation, flows and VAEs have a natural advantage over GANs and (to a lesser extent) over diffusion models.

Scenario coverage and diversity

- **GANs**: high-fidelity samples in regions the discriminator has learned well; risk of mode collapse and poor coverage of rare regimes unless training is carefully engineered.
- **VAEs**: coverage is typically broad due to the latent prior, but reconstructions may be somewhat "blurry," especially if the likelihood family is too simple.

- **Flows**: good coverage where data density is high; exact likelihoods discourage ignoring modes but may still struggle in very sparse tail regions if the architecture is not sufficiently expressive.
- **Diffusion**: often the strongest empirical coverage across complex, multi-modal distributions, provided the noise schedule and training are well tuned.

For synthetic markets, coverage is essential: we want the model to generate a rich variety of plausible histories, not simply replays of typical patterns.

Tail behavior and extremes

- **GANs**: tend to under-sample tails unless specifically trained to emphasize them; absence of likelihood makes tail calibration hard.
- **VAEs**: tail behavior can be engineered via the conditional likelihood; risk of oversmoothing if Gaussian assumptions are used.
- **Flows**: tail properties can be directly shaped by the base distribution and flow architecture; likelihood diagnostics help check whether tails are well captured.
- **Diffusion**: capable of representing rich tail structures, but require careful training to ensure extremes are not washed out by noising.

Because stress testing is largely about extremes, this dimension should weigh heavily in model choice and evaluation.

Practical considerations

Other factors affecting model selection:

- **Training stability**: GANs are the most delicate; VAEs and flows are generally more stable; diffusion models are stable but computationally intensive.

- **Sampling speed**: flows and GANs offer fast single-pass sampling; VAEs are similar to flows; diffusion models are slowest due to iterative denoising.
- **Controllability**: all families can be extended to conditional versions, but diffusion and flow models often provide cleaner probabilistic interpretations of conditioning.

Choosing and Using Models in Synthetic Markets

In practice, no single family dominates across all criteria. A sensible workflow for a trading or risk organization might be:

- Start with resampling and copula baselines to set a performance floor.
- Introduce a likelihood-based latent model (VAE or flow) to gain interpretability and likelihood diagnostics, and to learn a compact latent representation of market regimes.
- Experiment with GANs or diffusion models when sample realism and coverage of complex microstructure patterns are paramount, being mindful of training cost and evaluation challenges.
- For each candidate model, apply the evaluation hierarchy from earlier: marginal and temporal statistics, cross-sectional dependence, pathwise properties, and strategy-level behavior under both typical and stressed conditions.

Throughout, the probabilistic perspective from the first section remains the guiding principle: even when likelihoods are implicit or approximate, we should always ask:

> What is the effective $p_\theta(R_{1:T}, Z)$ encoded by this architecture and training procedure, and does it assign reasonable probability mass to the scenarios that truly matter for our strategies?

Only when we can answer that question with some confidence—and when the model clearly exceeds what block bootstraps and copulas can achieve—does it make sense to rely on adversarial, latent, or diffusion models as the engines of our synthetic markets.

3.5 Sequence and Event Models for Order Flow

The earlier sections of this chapter worked mostly at the level of daily or lower-frequency returns and factors. We viewed a market path as a sequence of vectors $R_{1:T}$ and applied generative models (GANs, VAEs/flows, diffusion) to this coarse time grid. For many trading and risk applications, however, this is not enough.

Execution algorithms, market-making strategies, and intraday risk management depend on the microstructure of electronic order books: the precise timing and type of orders, the evolution of bid and ask queues, and the clustering of trades. To build synthetic markets that are credible for these applications, we must model *order flow* itself.

This section introduces two complementary classes of models that, together, form the backbone of high-fidelity order-flow generators:

- **Transformer-based sequence models**, which excel at capturing long-range temporal dependence and context in complex sequences.
- **Hawkes and related point-process models**, which provide probabilistic descriptions of self-exciting event streams.

We begin with the structure and statistics of order-flow data, then describe each model class, and finally show how they can be combined into hybrid generators.

Order-Book and Order-Flow Data Structures

Modern electronic limit-order markets record a rich stream of events. At a minimum, we can distinguish:

- **Limit orders**: instructions to buy/sell a quantity at a specified price or better; they modify the standing bid and ask queues.
- **Market orders**: instructions to buy/sell immediately at the best available prices; they consume liquidity and move the traded price.
- **Cancellations and modifications**: removal or alteration of existing limit orders.

The state of the limit order book (LOB) at time t can be described by:

- Best bid and ask prices (P_t^{bid}, P_t^{ask}) and corresponding queue sizes.
- Deeper levels (second, third best, etc.) and their queues.
- Derived quantities such as mid-price, spread, and imbalance.

There are two common ways to represent this information for modeling:

- **Event streams**: a sequence of time-stamped events

$$\{(t_n, e_n)\}_{n=1}^{N},$$

  where e_n encodes event type (limit/market/cancel, side, level) and attributes (size, price).
- **State snapshots**: a sequence of LOB snapshots at discrete times, e.g., every Δt seconds, each containing a vector of prices and depths plus recent activity statistics.

Order-flow statistics display distinctive features:

- **Clustering of arrivals**: bursts of orders followed by quieter periods.
- **Self-excitation**: one market order tends to trigger further activity (orders and cancellations) shortly after.

- **Feedback loops**: changes in imbalance or spread alter subsequent order-arrival patterns.
- **Regime dependence**: behavior shifts around macro announcements, market opens/closes, and periods of elevated volatility.

Capturing these patterns requires models that can handle both *sequential dependence* (what happens next depends on a long history of events and states) and *event-level timing* (irregular inter-arrival times that exhibit self-exciting dynamics).

Transformer-Based Sequence Models for Order Flow

Transformers were introduced in natural language processing but have since proven powerful for any complex sequence with long-range dependencies. For order flow, they provide a flexible way to model how the next event or next book state depends on a wide context of past events and market conditions.

Encoding order-flow sequences.

To apply transformers, we must convert order-flow data into a sequence of tokens or feature vectors.

Event-level encoding.

Each event (t_n, e_n) is mapped to a vector x_n including:

- Event type (limit/market/cancel) and side (buy/sell), typically one-hot encoded.
- Price level (relative to mid-price) and size (e.g., log-size).
- Time features: inter-arrival time $\Delta t_n = t_n - t_{n-1}$, time-of-day, or log-transformed time-gaps.
- Local state summaries: current spread, imbalance, recent volatility proxies.

The sequence $(x_1, \ldots, x_N)$ feeds into the transformer.

Snapshot-level encoding.

Alternatively, for fixed-interval snapshots, each token x_k can include:

- LOB features: top L price levels and depths.
- Activity features over the last interval: number of trades, total traded volume, number of cancellations, etc.
- External signals: index futures moves, news flags, or volatility indices.

This view focuses more on state evolution than individual event arrivals.

Transformer mechanics in the order-flow context

A standard transformer layer processes the input sequence via self-attention:

$$\text{Attention}(Q, K, V) = \text{softmax}\left(\frac{QK^\top}{\sqrt{d}}\right)V,$$

where queries Q, keys K, and values V are linear projections of the input embeddings. Intuitively, each position in the sequence can attend to any previous position, weighting its importance based on learned similarity.

For order flow, this means:

- The model can learn that certain past events (e.g., a large trade, a sweep of multiple levels, a spike in cancellations) are strong predictors of near-future activity, regardless of how far back they are in clock time.
- Positional encodings (standard or time-aware) provide information about the ordering and timing of events.

In a generative setting, the transformer is typically *causal*: when predicting event n, it only attends to events $1, \ldots, n-1$.

Output parameterization and training objectives

Depending on the representation, the transformer can output:

- **Next-event distribution**: logits over event types and discretized attributes (e.g., price-level bins), plus parameters for a conditional distribution over inter-arrival times.
- **Next-snapshot distribution**: parameters of a multivariate distribution over next LOB state S_{k+1}, given past states $S_{1:k}$.

Typical training losses:

- Cross-entropy for discrete event types and price-level bins.
- Negative log-likelihood for continuous attributes (sizes, inter-arrival times), modeled as Gaussians, log-normals, or mixtures.

Thus, transformers fit naturally into the probabilistic modeling framework of earlier sections: they specify conditional distributions

$$p_\theta(e_n, \Delta t_n \mid \text{history}), \quad \text{or} \quad p_\theta(S_{k+1} \mid S_{1:k}),$$

with θ being the transformer parameters, trained via maximum likelihood (or approximations thereof).

Strengths and limitations for order-flow generation

Strengths:

- Capture complex, long-range dependencies that extend beyond what simple Markov or low-order autoregressive models can handle.
- Naturally incorporate side information (regimes, macro variables) through additional input channels or conditioning tokens, aligning with the controlled-generation ideas from earlier.
- Flexible output parameterizations allow modeling of heavy-tailed and skewed distributions for order sizes and price changes.

Limitations:

- Standard transformers treat sequences as discrete steps, not as realizations of a continuous-time point process; they can struggle with fine-grained modeling of inter-arrival-time distributions and self-exciting intensity structure.
- Without constraints or explicit microstructure priors, they may generate sequences that look plausible statistically but violate subtle no-arbitrage or market-mechanics rules (e.g., negative spread, inconsistent queue evolution).

These limitations motivate complementing transformer-based sequence models with explicit event-level point-process models.

Hawkes and Point-Process Models for Self-Exciting Dynamics

Where transformers excel at learning rich dependence from data, Hawkes processes bring a clean probabilistic model for event arrivals in continuous time, especially for *self-excitation.*

Point processes and conditional intensity

A (univariate) point process on the real line is a random set of event times $\{t_n\}$. Its behavior can be summarized by the *conditional intensity function* $\lambda(t \mid \mathcal{H}_t)$, where $\mathcal{H}_t$ is the history up to time t:

$$\lambda(t \mid \mathcal{H}_t)\, dt \approx \mathbb{P}\{\text{an event occurs in } [t, t+dt) \mid \mathcal{H}_t\}.$$

For marked point processes, each event carries a mark m_n (e.g., side, size, price level), and the model specifies both the intensity of arrivals and the conditional distribution of marks.

Hawkes processes: self-exciting intensities

A Hawkes process is a self-exciting point process where past events increase the current intensity. In its simplest univariate form:

$$\lambda(t) = \mu + \sum_{t_n < t} \phi(t - t_n),$$

where:

- $\mu > 0$ is a baseline intensity.
- $\phi(\cdot) \geq 0$ is an excitation kernel (e.g., exponential $\alpha e^{-\beta(t-t_n)}$).

Interpretation:

- Each event at t_n kicks the intensity up by $\phi(0)$, and this effect decays over time.
- Clusters of events arise naturally as intensity bursts following previous arrivals.

In multivariate Hawkes processes, we have multiple event types or dimensions (e.g., buy/sell, limit/market), indexed by $i = 1, \ldots, d$, with intensities:

$$\lambda_i(t) = \mu_i + \sum_{j=1}^{d} \sum_{t_n^j < t} \phi_{ij}(t - t_n^j),$$

where ϕ_{ij} describes how events of type j excite future events of type i.

This structure is particularly well-suited to order flow:

- A market buy order triggers more buy market orders and sell limit orders.
- Cancellations may be triggered by recent trades or spread changes.
- Buy and sell intensities interact asymmetrically depending on imbalance.

Marked Hawkes processes

In marked versions, each event time t_n comes with a mark m_n (e.g., order size, price level). The intensity may depend on marks of past events, and the conditional distribution of the mark at t_n depends on $\mathcal{H}_{t_n}$. For example:

$$\lambda_i(t) = \mu_i + \sum_{j=1}^{d} \sum_{t_n^j < t} \phi_{ij}(t - t_n^j, m_n^j),$$

coupled with a mark distribution

$$p(m_n^i \mid \mathcal{H}_{t_n}, \text{event type } i).$$

This allows the model to capture, for instance, that large trades are followed by elevated intensity of further large trades or cancellations.

Simulation and likelihood

Hawkes processes have tractable simulation and likelihoods:

- **Simulation**: Ogata's thinning algorithm can be used to simulate event times given $\lambda(t \mid \mathcal{H}_t)$.
- **Likelihood**: For events $\{t_n\}$ on $[0, T]$,

$$\log L = \sum_n \log \lambda(t_n \mid \mathcal{H}_{t_n}) - \int_0^T \lambda(t \mid \mathcal{H}_t)\, dt.$$

This supports maximum likelihood estimation and rigorous diagnostics (e.g., time-rescaling tests).

Strengths and limitations

Strengths:

- Explicit, interpretable model of self-excitation and cross-excitation: ϕ_{ij} directly encodes how events interact.
- Natural handling of irregular event times and bursts of activity.
- Strong theoretical and statistical foundations; likelihood-based inference is possible.

Limitations:

- Parametric kernels (e.g., exponential) may be too rigid for rich microstructure dynamics; nonparametric or neural parameterizations help but increase complexity.

- Hawkes processes focus on event times and counts; modeling full LOB state evolution and rich marks requires additional structure.

These limitations suggest combining Hawkes-type intensities with the representational power of neural networks.

A Unified Picture: Sequence Models and Hawkes Processes

Transformers and Hawkes models address complementary aspects of order flow:

- Transformers: powerful sequence models capturing high-dimensional context, but less grounded in continuous-time point-process theory.
- Hawkes: principled models of self-exciting event timing, but traditionally lower-dimensional and parametric.

A high-fidelity order-flow generator can use both.

Conceptual diagram

After introducing the core ideas of transformer sequence models and Hawkes processes, it is helpful to visualize how raw order-flow events feed into each class of model and how each produces synthetic event streams.

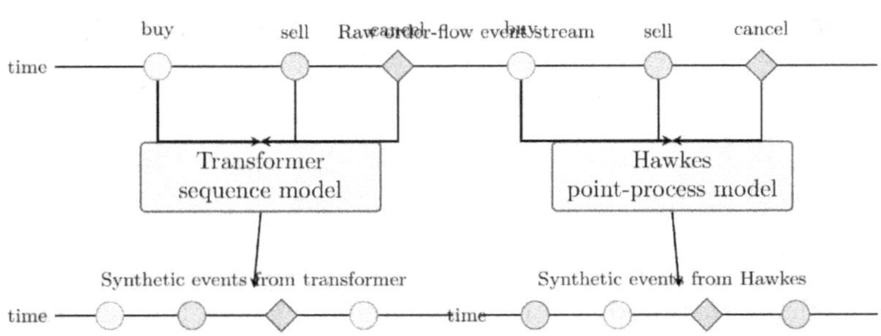

This schematic shows the dual view: both transformer and Hawkes models ingest the same raw event stream for training and each, once fitted, can generate its own synthetic stream with similar statistical properties.

Hybrid Architectures: Deep Sequence Encoders with Point-Process Likelihoods

The most powerful order-flow models combine the strengths of transformers and Hawkes processes.

Neural Hawkes and intensity networks

In *neural Hawkes* models, we let a neural network (often recurrent or transformer-based) parameterize the intensity function. For example:

- A sequence encoder ingests past events and produces a hidden state $h(t)$ summarizing history at time t.
- Intensities are then given by

  $$\lambda_i(t) = f_i(h(t)),$$

  where f_i is a positive-valued function (e.g., softplus of a linear projection).

This blends:

- The continuous-time, likelihood-based structure of point processes.
- The expressive power of neural sequence encoders to capture complex, path-dependent effects.

Training maximizes the point-process log-likelihood with respect to both the encoder and intensity network parameters.

Order-book state plus event streams

Another hybrid pattern mirrors the macro-level generative models in earlier sections:

- A transformer-based sequence model simulates the evolution of the LOB state at coarse granularity (e.g., every Δt).
- Within each interval, a Hawkes process—with parameters conditioned on the current LOB state—generates individual events.

Formally, let S_k be the state at interval k, modeled by a sequence model. Given S_k, we define a Hawkes intensity $\lambda_i^k(t)$ over $t \in [t_k, t_{k+1})$ for event types i, with parameters depending on S_k. The generator thus:

- captures slow-moving regime shifts and context via the sequence model,
- and fast, clustered, self-exciting event arrivals via the Hawkes mechanism.

Controlled generation at the microstructure level

As in previous sections, we can introduce controls C (e.g., volatility regime, target spread or liquidity level) by:

- Feeding C as additional input to the transformer encoder/decoder, so that S_k evolves under the desired regime.
- Conditioning Hawkes intensities $\lambda_i(t)$ on C, thereby modifying event arrival patterns directly.

Evaluation then proceeds along the same hierarchical lines, but with microstructure-specific metrics:

- Distributions and autocorrelations of spreads, depths, and imbalances.
- Clustering statistics of order arrivals and trades.
- Execution-cost distributions for standardized trade profiles under synthetic order flow.

From Microstructure Models to Synthetic Markets

Finally, we emphasize how sequence and event models fit into the broader theme of the book.

- At **daily or lower** frequencies, we use the probabilistic and neural models from earlier sections to generate synthetic return and factor paths for portfolio-level strategies.
- At **intraday** and microstructure levels, transformer-based sequence models and Hawkes processes generate realistic order books and trade streams.

These two layers can be linked:

- High-frequency generators can be conditioned on low-frequency market states (e.g., daily volatility, factor returns) drawn from higher-level generative models.
- Strategy backtests can thus be stress-tested against coherent multi-scale scenarios: from macro regimes down to tick-by-tick order flow.

In this way, sequence and event models for order flow are not standalone curiosities; they are the final piece in constructing synthetic markets that are rich enough to test both portfolio construction and execution under a wide spectrum of plausible and stressed conditions.

Chapter 4

Synthetic Simulation and Stress-Testing Methodologies

Real markets rarely fail in the ways your backtests imagine. In this chapter we fuse stylized facts, regime-aware generators, and execution-level simulators to manufacture synthetic worlds where your strategy can actually break-then show you how to learn from those failures before they occur in live trading.

4.1 Stylized Facts, Constraints, and Regime Modeling

In the previous chapter we motivated synthetic markets as tools for asking "what if" questions about trading strategies: what if volatility doubles, liquidity halves, or correlations flip sign? To ensure that such questions produce meaningful answers, the synthetic worlds we create cannot be arbitrary. They must *look* like financial markets along key statistical dimensions, and they must *behave* like markets in economic terms: no free lunches, realistic frictions, and credible regime structure.

This section provides that foundation. We will:

- Define the empirical *stylized facts* that synthetic data should reproduce.
- Translate basic no-arbitrage and microstructure requirements into explicit constraints on simulators and generative models.
- Introduce *macro* and *micro* regimes as the organizing backbone for scenario design, and show how they condition generative models.

Throughout, keep in mind the guiding principle:

> A synthetic market is useful only insofar as it is *wrong in interesting ways* but *right in the ways that matter.*

We will first specify the ways in which it must be "right."

Stylized Facts as Empirical Targets

Stylized facts are robust empirical regularities that appear across assets, markets, and time periods. They are not exact laws, but they are stable enough that any realistic synthetic market should reproduce them at least approximately.

Let $\{r_t\}$ denote log returns at some time scale (e.g., daily or 5-minute). The key stylized facts we will use as empirical targets are:

Heavy-tailed Returns

Empirically, return distributions have:

- Excess kurtosis: more mass in the tails and center than a Gaussian with the same variance.
- Asymmetry (skewness), often negative for equity indices.

In practice, this means that large moves (e.g., $|r_t| > 4\sigma$) happen far more often than Gaussian models predict. For synthetic data, this implies:

- Marginal return distributions should match tail thickness (e.g., through tail index, Hill estimators, or quantile ratios).
- Backtests that rely on synthetic data should see extreme P&L swings at roughly the right frequency.

Volatility Clustering

While raw returns r_t show little linear autocorrelation, measures of volatility (e.g., $|r_t|$, r_t^2) do. Large moves tend to be followed by large moves, regardless of direction.

Formally, if $v_t = r_t^2$, then

$$\mathrm{Corr}(v_t, v_{t+k}) > 0$$

for lags k over a wide range. In synthetic markets:

- Conditional variance should be time-varying and persistent.
- Drawdown and risk estimates under synthetic paths should reflect episodes of high and low volatility, not constant variance noise.

Leverage Effects

For many equity markets, negative returns tend to be followed by higher volatility—the so-called leverage effect. One intuitive explanation is balance-sheet leverage: a price drop mechanically increases leverage for fixed debt, amplifying risk.

Empirically, this appears as a negative correlation between returns and future volatility:

$$\mathrm{Corr}(r_t, v_{t+1}) < 0.$$

Synthetic data should replicate this asymmetry at the appropriate horizon, especially if strategies are sensitive to volatility changes after losses (e.g., risk-parity, volatility targeting).

Volume–Volatility Relationships

Periods of high volatility typically coincide with high trading volume and turnover. At an abstract level:

- $|r_t|$ and volume Q_t are positively correlated.
- Large price moves are often associated with imbalances in order flow, not just more trades.

In synthetic data, price changes, volume, and order-flow imbalance should be co-generated, not sampled independently, to reproduce these joint patterns.

Serial Dependence in Signs, Not Levels

At many horizons, raw returns $\{r_t\}$ exhibit weak or near-zero autocorrelation, consistent with approximate market efficiency. However, the *signs* of returns and (especially) order-flow directions often show dependence:

- $\text{Corr}(r_t, r_{t+k}) \approx 0$ for modest k.
- $\text{Corr}(\text{sign}(r_t), \text{sign}(r_{t+k}))$ and $\text{Corr}(\text{trade direction}_t, \text{trade direction}_{t+k})$ are often positive for short lags.

This is important for execution-aware backtests: persistent order-flow imbalances impact prices, and simulators that randomize trade signs independently will underestimate implementation shortfall and impact risk.

Why Stylized Facts Matter for Synthetic Markets

If a generative model or simulator ignores these facts, it will systematically understate:

- Tail risk (missing heavy tails),
- Regime risk (missing volatility clustering),
- Execution risk (missing order-flow dependence and volume-volatility links),

- Asymmetric risk (missing leverage effects).

Hence, stylized facts become *empirical constraints* on admissible synthetic data. When calibrating a generator, we will routinely compare empirical metrics from real data and generated data: kurtosis, autocorrelation functions of r_t^2, leverage effect measures, and volume-volatility correlations.

Economic and Microstructure Constraints

Stylized facts are statistical; they say nothing about whether a synthetic market admits obvious arbitrage or implausible microstructure. We therefore impose a second layer: economic and market-microstructure constraints.

No-arbitrage as a Soft Constraint

Fully enforcing no-arbitrage in a highly flexible generative model is typically infeasible. Instead, we impose it as a *soft* constraint: the synthetic market should not admit simple, robust, and unrealistically profitable trading rules after accounting for frictions.

Concretely:

- For a broad class of simple strategies (e.g., linear predictors, moving-average crossovers), the out-of-sample Sharpe ratio computed on synthetic data should not be systematically higher than on real data.
- If a strategy that is marginal in the real world becomes extraordinarily profitable in synthetic worlds, this indicates an unrealistic degree of predictability or an omission of frictions.

This can be operationalized as part of calibration: add penalty terms to the training loss of generative models that reward matching the distribution of achievable Sharpe ratios across a test strategy set.

Realistic Bid-Ask Spreads and Depth

At higher frequency, prices are not single numbers; they are two-sided quotes with finite depth. For execution-aware synthetic markets:

- Bid-ask spreads should follow realistic distributions and dynamics (mean levels, volatility, intraday seasonality).
- Depth at top levels should be finite, with plausible replenishment and depletion.

If spreads are too tight or depth too large, implementation shortfall will be understated. If spreads or depth are too unstable, risk may be overstated. These features can be matched to historical limit-order-book (LOB) data through explicit calibration targets: average spread by time-of-day, depth distributions, and resiliency measures.

Price Impact Consistency

Simulators that treat prices as exogenous to orders (no impact) produce unrealistically generous execution. Conversely, extreme impact functions can over-penalize trading and discourage valid strategies.

We require:

- A monotone relationship between trade size and expected impact, with concave impact functions at the metaorder level (doubling size less than doubles impact).
- Empirical calibration: the synthetic relationship between order-flow imbalance and price change should match historical elasticities at relevant horizons.

This constraint ties trading activity back to returns in synthetic data and prevents "free liquidity" worlds.

Bounds on Predictability under Realistic Costs

Even if the generator is calibrated to weak-statistics like autocorrelations of r_t, it might inadvertently encode strong nonlinear predictability. To keep synthetic markets economically plausible, we can:

- Estimate upper bounds on achievable Sharpe ratios under realistic transaction costs using simple strategy families on real data.
- Constrain the generative model such that similar bounds hold in synthetic data (e.g., by penalizing strategies that achieve unreasonably stable profits).

This effectively adds a layer of "learned no-arbitrage": synthetic markets are tuned so that easy money is not lying on the floor.

From Constraints to Regimes

So far we have listed features that should hold *on average*. Real markets, however, do not live in a single stationary environment. They move through *regimes*: tranquil periods, stressed but functioning markets, and full-blown crises. These regimes differ in:

- Volatility level and clustering behavior,
- Correlation structures,
- Liquidity (spreads, depth, resiliency),
- Macro conditions (inflation, policy stance, growth),
- Microstructure patterns (intraday cycles, event-driven bursts).

Rather than ask our generators to approximate one amorphous "average" market, we will train and use them *conditional on regimes*. This has two benefits:

- It increases realism by allowing different parameterizations in different states.
- It gives us a powerful organizing principle for scenario design: we can explicitly target transitions between regimes that matter to a strategy.

Before formalizing regime models, it is useful to visualize how stylized facts, regimes, and generators fit together.

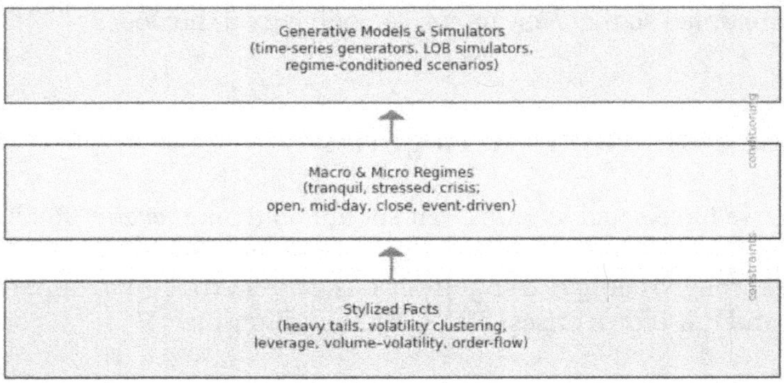

This schematic emphasizes three layers:

- **Stylized facts** at the base: empirical features that must be matched.
- **Regimes** in the middle: macro and micro state variables organizing how those facts manifest over time.
- **Generators and simulators** at the top: models that take regime information as input and produce synthetic paths subject to constraints from the lower layers.

We now formalize the regime layer.

Macro Regimes

Macro regimes describe the slow-moving state of the market and economy. Examples include:

- Volatility states: tranquil, stressed, crisis.
- Monetary environments: tightening, neutral, easing.
- Inflation regimes: low/stable, high/rising, disinflationary.

- Liquidity states: high-liquidity, impaired, frozen.

Let S_t^{macro} denote the macro regime at time t, taking values in a finite set, e.g., $\{1, \ldots, K\}$. In a hidden Markov model (HMM) view:

$$\Pr(S_t^{macro} = j \mid S_{t-1}^{macro} = i) = P_{ij},$$
$$r_t \mid S_t^{macro} = f(\theta_{S_t^{macro}}, \varepsilon_t),$$

where P is a transition matrix and f is some emission model (e.g., Gaussian with regime-specific mean and variance, or a neural generator with regime-specific parameters).

In a generative-AI setting, we typically condition a flexible model on a regime label:

$$r_{1:T} \sim G_\phi(z, S_{1:T}^{macro}),$$

where z is latent noise and S^{macro} is either given (for scenario design) or sampled from an estimated transition model.

Key points:

- Within each macro regime, stylized facts may have different parameters (e.g., tail thickness, volatility clustering strength).
- Regime transitions can be used as stress levers: we can design scenarios where a long tranquil period is followed by a sudden move into crisis, or where the system gets stuck in a stressed regime longer than in history.

Micro Regimes

Micro regimes operate at the intraday and event level. They capture predictable patterns within a trading day and around specific events. Typical examples:

- **Open**: high volatility, wide spreads, fast order-book turnover.
- **Mid-day**: lower volatility, tighter spreads, thinner volume.
- **Close**: rising volume and volatility, imbalances from closing auctions.

- **Event-driven**: around scheduled announcements (earnings, macro data) or unscheduled news.

Let S_t^{micro} denote a micro regime at intraday resolution. At the level of a limit-order-book simulator, S_t^{micro} affects:

- Arrival rates of limit and market orders,
- Typical spread and depth distributions,
- Order-cancellation behavior and order-book resiliency,
- Short-horizon price-impact coefficients.

We can model micro regimes deterministically (e.g., a fixed open/mid/-close pattern by clock time) or stochastically (e.g., event indicators around news). In a generative model for intraday data, we again condition:

$$\text{LOB snapshots, trades} \sim H_\psi(z, S_{1:T}^{macro}, S_{1:T}^{micro}).$$

Regimes as Conditioning Variables for Scenario Design

With macro and micro regimes in place, we can articulate a powerful workflow for synthetic scenario design:

- **Estimate regime processes from history.** Use HMMs, Markov-switching models, or clustering to infer S_t^{macro} and, at higher frequency, S_t^{micro} from observed data. Calibrate transition matrices and regime-specific parameters or embeddings.
- **Train regime-conditioned generators.** Fit generative models (e.g., VAEs, diffusion models, or GANs) that take as input both noise z and regime paths $S_{1:T}$, and learn to generate returns, volatility, volume, or full LOB states conditioned on those regimes.
- **Design regime paths as scenarios.** Instead of sampling $S_{1:T}$ only from the estimated transition model, we also *design* specific regime sequences of interest:

  - Long tranquil → sudden crisis → slow recovery.
  - Rapid alternation between tranquil and stressed liquidity.
  - Extended high-inflation and tight-monetary regimes.

- **Generate synthetic worlds.** For each designed $S_{1:T}$, sample multiple realizations from the generator. Because the generator was trained under constraints that enforce stylized facts and economic plausibility within each regime, the resulting paths remain realistic while exploring new combinations and durations of regimes.

At the micro level, a similar pattern holds:

- Use historical intraday data to map time-of-day and event flags into micro regimes.
- Train execution-level generators or simulators that reproduce, within each micro regime, observed spread, depth, and impact patterns.
- When testing a strategy, construct synthetic trading days with unusual combinations, e.g., "every hour is like the open," or "a macro crisis coincides with repeated event-driven spikes."

This regime-centric design provides a bridge between high-level stress narratives ("a prolonged liquidity drought during a tightening cycle") and low-level data required for backtesting (returns, volumes, LOB states).

Putting It Together: A Constrained, Regime-Driven Synthetic Market

We can now summarize the architecture of a constrained, regime-driven synthetic market that will underpin later chapters:

- **Empirical layer (stylized facts).** Define target statistics (tails, volatility clustering, leverage, volume-volatility, order-flow dependence) and validate that generated data match them within acceptable tolerances.

- **Economic/microstructure layer (constraints).** Impose no-arbitrage as a soft constraint via achievable Sharpe ratios; calibrate realistic spreads, depth, impacts, and predictability bounds under transaction costs.
- **Regime layer (structure).** Model macro and micro regimes, estimate them from history, and use them as conditioning variables in generative models and simulators.
- **Generative layer (models).** Train flexible generators conditioned on regimes and constrained by the empirical and economic layers, capable of producing both price-level and order-book-level synthetic data.
- **Scenario design layer (usage).** Construct scenario families as combinations of regime paths: historical-like, extended, or counterfactual. These become the inputs to stress-testing and adversarial analysis in subsequent sections.

The remainder of the chapter will build on this foundation. Agent-based and order-book simulators will realize the microstructure constraints in detail; stress-testing sections will use regime paths as stress templates; and evaluation frameworks will incorporate these synthetic, regime-conditioned worlds systematically into backtesting.

4.2 Agent-Based and Order-Book Simulation

In the previous section we worked at the level of time series: returns, volatility, volume, and regimes. We imposed stylized facts and economic constraints on synthetic prices so that a strategy's *risk* would be realistic. To understand a strategy's *execution*, however, we must move down a level of detail.

Real-world trading happens in a limit order book (LOB). Quotes are two-sided and finite; orders queue, cancel, and walk the book; and prices respond to order imbalances in state-dependent ways. A synthetic market that only simulates mid-prices and volumes will inevitably understate slippage, impact, and liquidity risk.

This section builds execution-aware simulators grounded in an explicit order book and populated by interacting agents. We will:

- Recap the essentials of limit-order-book structure and how microstructure translates into execution costs.
- Introduce representative agent classes and show how their rules can be tuned to reproduce order-book stylized facts.
- Explain how to calibrate these simulators to historical LOB data while respecting the no-arbitrage and impact constraints introduced earlier.
- Show how to couple learned generative models to the simulator so synthetic regimes and order flows drive agent behavior.
- Outline a reusable architecture in which trading strategies, generators, and agents interact in a unified simulation loop.

Throughout, the goal is not a perfectly faithful reproduction of every microstructural nuance, but a simulator whose errors are understood and whose implications for strategy robustness are informative.

Limit-Order-Book Structure and Execution Outcomes

A modern electronic LOB is a continuous double auction. At any time t:

- The *bid side* consists of limit buy orders, each with a price and quantity, arranged in descending price order.
- The *ask side* consists of limit sell orders, arranged in ascending price order.
- The *best bid* b_t is the highest bid price; the *best ask* a_t is the lowest ask price.
- The *mid-price* is $m_t = (a_t + b_t)/2$ and the *spread* is $s_t = a_t - b_t$.

Order types include:

- Limit orders: specify price and size, rest in the book until matched or cancelled.
- Market orders: demand immediate execution against the best available opposite-side liquidity.
- Cancellations: remove existing resting orders.

Matching is usually price-time priority: orders at better prices execute first; within a price level, earlier orders have priority.

For a trading strategy, realized execution depends on how its submitted orders interact with the existing book and future order flows:

- *Slippage*: difference between the decision price (often mid) and the volume-weighted average execution price (VWAP).
- *Spread cost*: half-spread paid when crossing the spread with marketable orders.
- *Market impact*: adverse price movement caused by a trader's own orders, especially large or persistent flow.

An execution-aware simulator must therefore represent not only the mid-price, but also:

- The state of the book (depth at each price level, on both sides).
- Stochastic arrival of external orders (other agents).
- Matching, queueing, and cancellation dynamics.

Agent Classes and Their Roles

Rather than simulate every real-world participant, we model a few stylized *agent classes* whose interactions reproduce the main microstructural patterns. Common classes include:

- **Market makers:** Continuously post bids and asks around the mid-price, managing inventory and adverse-selection risk. They provide most of the displayed depth.
- **Directional traders:** Agents with a view on future price moves (e.g., based on signals or news). They may trade aggressively (market orders) to quickly express their view, or passively (limit orders) when urgency is lower.
- **Liquidity takers:** Agents with exogenous trading needs (portfolio rebalancing, fund flows). They submit market and marketable limit orders, consuming displayed liquidity.
- **High-frequency market makers / arbitrageurs:** Faster variants of market makers, reacting quickly to microstructure signals or cross-asset price discrepancies. They tighten spreads but can also withdraw rapidly in stress.
- **Noise traders:** Agents whose orders are not informational but add randomness and depth to the book. They help reproduce background volatility and volume.

Each agent class is defined by:

- **State variables:** current inventory, cash, outstanding orders, risk limits, and (possibly) their own belief about future returns.
- **Decision rules:** mapping from current market state and private state to order submissions/cancellations.
- **Parameters:** aggression level, replenishment frequency, spread widths, inventory risk aversion.

By carefully choosing these rules and parameters, we can match microstructural stylized facts analogous to the time-series stylized facts from the previous section:

- Distribution and intraday pattern of spreads.
- Depth profiles (how volume decays away from best bid/ask).

- Resiliency: how quickly the book refills after a large trade.
- Relationship between order-flow imbalance and short-horizon price changes.

From Historical LOB Data to Calibration Targets

To ground the simulator, we calibrate it to historical LOB data at a time resolution Δt (e.g., 100 ms or 1 s) appropriate for the strategies we care about.

Core Calibration Targets

Typical targets include:

- **Spread distribution:** histogram of s_t by time-of-day, asset, and regime (tranquil vs stressed). We want the simulator's equilibrium spreads to match these distributions.
- **Depth distribution:** average and quantile profiles of cumulative depth at each price level relative to the mid (e.g., at ± 1, ± 2, ...ticks).
- **Order arrival processes:** empirical intensities of limit order arrivals, market orders, and cancellations as functions of state (spread, imbalance, volatility) and time-of-day.
- **Impact curves:** average price change over short horizons as a function of signed trade size or order-flow imbalance.
- **Volatility and volume:** joint distribution of short-horizon returns and traded volume, including volatility clustering and volume-volatility correlation.

We can summarize these targets compactly in a table for a given asset:

Target	Description
Spread distribution	Empirical distribution of best bid-ask spread s_t (by regime and time-of-day).
Depth profile	Mean and quantile of cumulative depth at each level from mid.
Order intensities	State-dependent intensities for limit, market, and cancel events.
Impact function	Expected Δm vs signed volume or order-flow imbalance over horizon Δt.
Volatility-volume link	Correlation structure of $\lvert r_t \rvert$, r_t^2, and volume Q_t.

Parameterizing Agent Rules

Once we fix the target statistics, we parameterize each agent class. For example:

- A simple market maker may:

  $$\begin{aligned} a_t &= m_t + \delta_t, \\ b_t &= m_t - \delta_t, \end{aligned}$$

  where δ_t is a spread half-width that depends on recent volatility, inventory, and competition. Parameters control base spread, sensitivity to volatility, and inventory aversion.

- A directional trader with signal $\hat{r}_{t+1}$ might submit a market buy when $\hat{r}_{t+1}$ exceeds a threshold, with size scaling in $\hat{r}_{t+1}$.

- A noise trader might submit random limit orders at prices drawn from a distribution centered on the mid, with simple Poisson arrival times.

Let θ denote the vector of all such parameters across agent classes. The calibration problem then becomes:

$$\theta^* = \arg\min_{\theta} \mathcal{L}_{micro}(\theta),$$

where $\mathcal{L}_{micro}$ measures discrepancies between simulated and real-world microstructural statistics, possibly combined with penalties for violating economic constraints (no-arbitrage, realistic impact).

Economic Constraints at the Microstructure Level

The no-arbitrage and predictability constraints introduced earlier have concrete microstructural counterparts:

- **No free lunch via limit orders:** A strategy that simply posts at the best bid and ask should not realize unbounded Sharpe ratios in the simulator. If market makers earn unrealistically high, low-risk returns, spreads or impact are likely mis-specified.

- **Realistic impact:** For a given metaorder size (e.g., a parent order broken into child trades), the average impact measured in the simulator should align with empirical impact curves. Unrealistically low impact creates too-optimistic capacity estimates.
- **Arbitrage bounds:** Simple cross-venue or cross-asset arbitrage strategies should have profit distributions similar to those in historical data, or at least bounded in a plausible way.

We can encode these as soft penalties in $\mathcal{L}_{micro}$ by simulating a small suite of "test" strategies during calibration and ensuring their performance metrics (Sharpe, turnover, drawdowns) fall into plausible ranges.

Coupling Generative Models to the Order-Book Simulator

The previous section introduced regime-conditioned generative models that produce synthetic paths for prices, volatility, and perhaps coarse order-flow measures. We now explain how such generators interact with the agent-based simulator.

There are two complementary coupling patterns:

Generators as Macro/Meso Drivers

In this pattern, generators provide higher-level signals that influence agent behavior, while the LOB remains the mechanism that translates those signals into executions and prices. The flow is:

- Sample a regime path $S_{1:T}$ (macro and micro) and latent noise z.
- Use a time-series generator G_ϕ to produce:

$$\{(\tilde{r}_t, \tilde{\sigma}_t, \tilde{Q}_t, \widetilde{\text{imbalance}}_t)\}_{t=1}^{T}.$$

- Agents condition their intensities and decision rules on these generated series. For example:

  - Market makers widen spreads when $\tilde{\sigma}_t$ is high.
  - Directional traders' signal $\hat{r}_{t+1}$ is correlated with $\tilde{r}_{t+1}$.
  - Liquidity takers' baseline volume follows $\tilde{Q}_t$.

- The LOB simulation then generates detailed order events and realized mid-price paths m_t which, by construction, are consistent with the higher-level synthetic environment.

Here the generator sets the *weather* (volatility, volume, flow imbalance, regimes) and agents respond within the LOB.

Generators as Order-Flow Proposers

Alternatively, we can ask the generative model to produce detailed order-flow patterns directly, which the simulator executes:

- Train a model H_ψ on historical event sequences (order arrivals, cancellations, trades), possibly with regime conditioning.
- For a given regime path and latent z, sample a synthetic event stream:

$$\{\tilde{e}_t\}_{t=1}^{T}, \quad \tilde{e}_t \in \{\text{limit buy/sell, market buy/sell, cancel}\}$$

  with prices and sizes.

- Feed these events into the LOB engine, which enforces matching and book updates.
- Insert the *strategy* as one additional agent whose orders are injected into this synthetic flow.

In this setup, other agents may be implicit in the generator (their behavior is learned from data), while the strategy under test is explicit. The advantage is that higher-order dependencies in order flow (e.g., clustering, autocorrelation in trade signs) can be learned automatically.

Architecture of an Agent-Based LOB Simulator

To keep these components manageable, it is helpful to think in terms of a modular architecture. Figure illustrates a typical design where agents, generators, the order book, and strategies interact in a simulation loop.

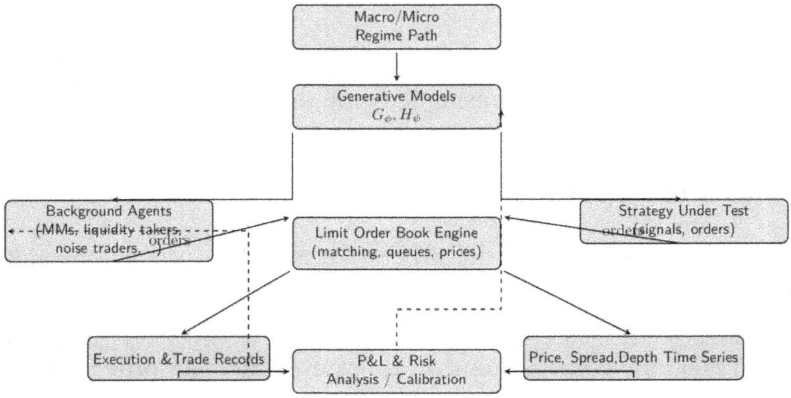

Key aspects of this architecture are:

- **Separation of concerns:** Generative models focus on producing regimes and macro/meso drivers or event proposals; agents focus on decision rules; the LOB engine enforces matching and price formation.
- **Plug-in strategy:** The strategy under test is just another agent with its own state and decision rules. This makes it easy to test many strategies in the same environment.
- **Feedback loop:** P&L and microstructural statistics from the simulator feed back into calibration: parameters of agents and generators are adjusted until target stylized facts and economic constraints are met.

Simulation Loop and Implementation Pattern

At a high level, one iteration of the simulation loop over small time steps Δt looks like:

- Given current time t, read the regime state S_t and any macro/meso drivers from the generator.
- For each background agent:
  - Observe current market state (LOB snapshot, volatility, own inventory).
  - Sample actions (submit/cancel orders) according to its state-dependent decision rule.
- The strategy under test observes its features (which can include synthetic signals from generators) and decides on orders.
- Collect all orders and cancellations for time interval $[t, t+\Delta t)$ and pass them to the LOB engine.
- The LOB engine:
  - Sorts and matches orders according to price-time priority.
  - Updates the book, generates trades, and updates the mid-price.
- Record executed trades, book state, and mark-to-market P&L.
- Advance to $t + \Delta t$ and repeat.

A concrete implementation would manage these components in modular classes (e.g., OrderBook, Agent, Generator, Strategy) with clear interfaces, but the essential logic is as above.

Compatibility with Regime-Based Stress Testing

Finally, note how this microstructure layer naturally connects back to the regime-based framework:

- **Macro regimes** determine long-run volatility, correlation, and liquidity states that feed into agent parameters (e.g., typical spreads, baseline volumes).
- **Micro regimes** correspond to intraday patterns (open, mid-day, close, event-driven intervals) that directly set arrival intensities and spread/depth profiles.
- **Stress scenarios** designed at the regime level (e.g., "extended crisis with repeated event spikes") are translated by the generator into synthetic order-flow environments in which the agent-based LOB simulator operates.

Thus, the agent-based, execution-aware simulator is not an isolated tool: it is the microstructural realization of the synthetic, regime-conditioned markets developed in earlier sections. In subsequent parts of this chapter, we will use this simulator as the engine for historical, hypothetical, reverse, and adversarial stress tests, so that strategy performance under synthetic markets reflects both price-level and execution-level risks.

4.3 Historical, Hypothetical, and Reverse Stress Testing

The previous sections gave us two essential building blocks: (i) synthetic markets that respect stylized facts and economic constraints, and (ii) an execution-aware, agent-based limit-order-book simulator. We can now subject trading strategies to demanding tests that go well beyond vanilla backtests.

Stress testing, in this context, means deliberately exposing a strategy to *hostile yet plausible* environments and asking: *When, how, and why does this strategy lose money, suffer liquidity shortfalls, or breach risk limits?* This section structures stress testing along three complementary axes:

- **Historical stress testing:** replaying real crisis episodes and extreme events.

- **Hypothetical stress testing:** constructing synthetic but plausible shocks and regimes.
- **Reverse stress testing:** starting from a failure criterion and working backward to find scenarios that cause it.

All three can be implemented on top of the synthetic-market and LOB frameworks already developed. They differ mainly in *how scenarios are chosen.*

Historical Stress Testing

Historical stress testing evaluates a strategy by replaying its logic through past periods that were objectively difficult for markets: crashes, liquidity freezes, flash events, and prolonged drawdowns.

Defining Historical Stress Windows

The first step is to identify windows that represent meaningful stress for the strategy's universe and horizon. Examples include:

- Equity index crashes (e.g., sharp multi-day sell-offs).
- Credit dislocations and liquidity crises.
- Sudden volatility spikes or volatility regime shifts.
- Asset-specific events (e.g., earnings surprises, corporate actions gone wrong).

For each episode we fix:

- A start and end date (or intraday time interval).
- The set of instruments and markets to include.
- The data frequency needed to run the strategy (daily, intraday, tick).

These windows then become slices of the historical data feed into our backtest or LOB simulator.

Data Integrity and Execution Assumptions

Historical stress testing is only as reliable as the data and assumptions used. Three issues are particularly important:

Corporate actions and survivorship bias.

Price histories must be adjusted for splits, dividends, and similar actions in a way consistent with how the strategy sees data. The instrument universe must include delisted or bankrupt names where relevant; ignoring them introduces survivorship bias and understates risk.

Look-ahead and information timing.

Signals must be computed using only information available at each point in time. For example, economic releases should enter signals at their announcement time, not retroactively at the period start.

Execution modeling.

We must decide how to translate historical quotes and trades into execution prices for the strategy:

- In a simple mid-price backtest, we may assume fills at mid $\pm$ half-spread plus a parametric impact model.
- In an execution-aware stress test, we use the historical LOB (where available) or our calibrated agent-based LOB simulator, with parameters tuned to match microstructure in the target episode.

The goal is not to perfectly reconstruct every historical fill, but to preserve realistic frictions and price formation mechanisms.

From Individual Episodes to a Stress Suite

A single historical episode can be misleading: a strategy might simply be lucky (or unlucky) in that particular path. We therefore build a *suite* of historical stresses:

- Multiple equity sell-offs of varying speeds and magnitudes.
- Periods of rising vs falling rates, high vs low inflation.
- Crises with and without severe liquidity impairment.

For each episode e in the suite, we compute key performance and risk metrics:

$$\begin{cases} \text{Peak-to-trough drawdown} \\ \text{Maximum intraday loss} \\ \text{Liquidity usage (participation rates, order sizes)} \\ \text{Margin utilization and breaches} \\ \text{Execution quality (slippage vs model)} \end{cases}$$

The collection of these episode-wise metrics forms a historical stress profile of the strategy.

Limitations of Purely Historical Stress Testing

Historical stress testing has two main blind spots:

- **Limited sample of crises.** Markets have not yet experienced all the ways they might break. Historical episodes are few and path-dependent.
- **Structural change.** Market structure, regulations, and participant behavior evolve. A replay of a decades-old crisis may not reflect today's microstructure or liquidity landscape.

To probe beyond these limitations, we introduce hypothetical and reverse stress tests that leverage our synthetic-market machinery.

Hypothetical Stress Testing

Hypothetical stress testing constructs deliberate but plausible *what-if* scenarios. Instead of asking "What would have happened in 2008?", we ask "What if we had a 2008-like volatility spike under today's liquidity regime?"

From Historical Patterns to Stress Templates

We start by extracting stylized patterns from historical crises:

- Volatility trajectories (speed and magnitude of spikes).

- Correlation breakdowns or spikes across assets and factors.
- Liquidity dynamics: spread widening, depth thinning, order-book dry-ups.
- Macro regime transitions (e.g., from tranquil to crisis and back).

These become *stress templates*, which can be applied to different instruments, time periods, or base regimes. For example:

- A template specifying that volatility doubles over a week, then remains elevated for a month.
- A liquidity template where average spreads triple and top-of-book depth halves for several days.
- A correlation template where cross-asset correlations jump from near zero to 0.8.

Using Regimes as a Design Language

The regime framework from earlier sections provides a natural language for defining hypothetical stresses. A macro regime path might be:

$$\text{tranquil} \rightarrow \text{stressed} \rightarrow \text{crisis} \rightarrow \text{stressed} \rightarrow \text{tranquil},$$

with specified durations in each state and transition timings chosen to conflict with typical strategy behavior (e.g., a crisis just after a leverage increase).

Micro regimes add intraday detail: we can design days where "every hour behaves like the open" or where event-driven regimes (e.g., news releases) occur at atypical times.

Conditioning Generative Models on Stress Templates

Once we have a stress template defined in terms of regime paths and macro/micro constraints, we use our generative models to realize full synthetic scenarios:

- **Specify** a regime path $S_{1:T}$ and any additional stress constraints (e.g., a minimum peak drawdown for the reference index).

- **Sample** from a regime-conditioned generator G_ϕ:

$$(\tilde{r}_t, \tilde{\sigma}_t, \tilde{Q}_t, \widetilde{\text{imbalance}}_t)_{t=1}^T \sim G_\phi(\cdot \mid S_{1:T}, z),$$

  for various latent seeds z.

- **Enforce hard constraints** by rejecting or resampling paths that do not satisfy basic stress requirements (e.g., realized index volatility below a certain threshold).

- **Feed** the synthetic price and flow series into the agent-based LOB simulator, ensuring microstructure is consistent with spreads, depth, and volume implied by $(\tilde{\sigma}_t, \tilde{Q}_t, S_{1:T})$.

For example, spreads in the simulator might be a function of the synthetic volatility and liquidity state:

$$s_t^{sim} = f_s(\tilde{\sigma}_t, S_t^{macro}, S_t^{micro}),$$

calibrated so that in non-stress regimes, s_t^{sim} matches historical typical values, and under stressed regimes it matches or slightly extrapolates crisis levels.

Composing and Extending Historical Episodes

Hypothetical stresses let us extend beyond observed episodes by:

- **Lengthening** crises: repeating stress regimes to create multi-year drawdowns not seen historically.

- **Reordering** events: moving a liquidity freeze earlier or later relative to a volatility spike.

- **Transplanting** patterns: applying an equity-like crash template to a new asset class (e.g., crypto) with adjusted microstructure.

Because generators are constrained by stylized facts and economic plausibility, these scenarios are not arbitrary: they respect historical tail properties and regime frequencies while exploring richer combinations than reality has exhibited to date.

Reverse Stress Testing

Historical and hypothetical stress testing both start with a *scenario* and ask, "What happens to the strategy?" Reverse stress testing inverts the question:

> Given a definition of unacceptable performance or risk, what kinds of scenarios would cause the strategy to fail?

This shift is crucial for uncovering *previously unimagined* vulnerabilities.

Defining Failure Criteria

We begin by specifying one or more failure criteria:

- **P&L-based:** peak-to-trough drawdown exceeding a threshold; cumulative loss beyond a risk budget.
- **Liquidity-based:** inability to unwind a position within a required time at acceptable cost; margin calls triggered by illiquidity.
- **Constraint-based:** breach of leverage, concentration, or risk-limit constraints.

Mathematically, let $F(\omega)$ be a function that maps a scenario ω (including regimes, prices, flows, and microstructure) to a scalar measure of stress (e.g., maximum drawdown). A failure event is:

$$F(\omega) \geq \tau,$$

for some threshold τ chosen by risk management.

Scenario Space and Parameterization

The space of possible scenarios Ω is enormous. To make reverse stress testing tractable, we parameterize scenarios via low-dimensional descriptors:

- Parameters of regime paths (durations in each regime, transition times).

- Parameters of shock templates (initial jumps, decay speeds, correlation shifts).
- Latent variables of generative models (z) that control fine-grained variations.

Thus a scenario can be represented as:

$$\omega(\theta, z) = \text{SimulateScenario}\big(S_{1:T}(\theta), z\big),$$

where θ encodes regime and shock parameters, and z is random noise.

Our objective is to find (θ, z) that maximize the stress functional F subject to plausibility constraints.

Optimization and Search Methods

At a high level, reverse stress testing solves:

$$\max_{\theta, z} \quad F(\omega(\theta, z)) - \lambda\, C(\theta, z),$$

where C penalizes implausible scenarios (e.g., those that severely violate stylized facts, deviate excessively from historical regime frequencies, or imply unrealistic microstructure).

Because F is generally non-convex and only observable through simulation, we rely on heuristic or simulation-based optimization methods:

- **Grid or random search** over coarse scenario parameters (e.g., crisis length, volatility level) combined with Monte Carlo draws for z.
- **Evolutionary or genetic algorithms** that iteratively mutate and select scenario parameters based on how stressful they are for the strategy.
- **Gradient-based optimization in latent space** when generators are differentiable: backpropagating through G_ϕ to adjust z or θ so as to increase F.

For example, in a differentiable setting:

- Initialize $(\theta^{(0)}, z^{(0)})$ from a plausible distribution (e.g., based on historical regimes).
- At each iteration k, simulate $\omega^{(k)} = \omega(\theta^{(k)}, z^{(k)})$ and compute $F^{(k)} = F(\omega^{(k)})$.
- Estimate gradients $\nabla_{\theta,z} F^{(k)}$ (possibly via automatic differentiation through the generator and an approximate differentiable P&L proxy).
- Update $(\theta^{(k+1)}, z^{(k+1)})$ in the direction that increases F while respecting plausibility penalties from C.

Even when gradients are unavailable or unreliable, local search methods (e.g., Bayesian optimization in scenario space) can be effective.

Constraining Reverse Stresses to Plausible Worlds

Without constraints, reverse stress testing might find degenerate or absurd scenarios (e.g., simultaneous 20-sigma moves across all assets every day). To avoid this, we impose constraints derived from our earlier stylized facts and regime models:

- Bounds on marginal distributions (e.g., tail indices, volatility ranges).
- Constraints on regime frequencies and transition probabilities (e.g., crises cannot last forever; tranquil regimes cannot disappear entirely).
- Microstructure plausibility: spreads, depth, and impact must remain within calibrated extrapolation ranges.

These constraints are encoded in $C(\theta, z)$ or enforced by construction (e.g., scenario generators that only sample from calibrated models). The result is *extreme-but-plausible* scenarios that meaningfully challenge the strategy.

From Individual Reverse Stresses to a Risk Library

Each reverse stress run typically yields a handful of high-stress scenarios—those that achieve extreme values of F. Rather than discard them after diagnosis, we organize them into a *risk library*:

- Cluster similar scenarios by their regime paths and shock profiles.
- For each cluster, select representative scenarios to serve as regression tests for future strategies.
- Annotate each scenario with the specific vulnerabilities it reveals (e.g., leverage at regime transitions, reliance on tight spreads, exposure to cross-asset correlation spikes).

Over time, the risk library becomes an institutional memory of discovered fragilities, allowing new strategies to be evaluated against previously identified worst cases.

Comparing and Combining the Three Stress Perspectives

Historical, hypothetical, and reverse stress testing are not competitors; they are complementary lenses:

- **Historical** stresses anchor analysis in real events, providing credibility and calibration.
- **Hypothetical** stresses extend reality along plausible dimensions, guided by the regime framework and generative models.
- **Reverse** stresses search for blind spots, uncovering scenarios that violate performance or risk thresholds even if they have not yet occurred.

A robust stress-testing program will:

- Define a diversified suite of historical episodes and replay the strategy under both simple and execution-aware assumptions.
- Design families of hypothetical, regime-based stress templates and realize them using synthetic generators and the LOB simulator.

- Periodically run reverse stress exercises to enrich the library of challenging scenarios and update risk limits or strategy design in response.

In the remainder of the chapter, we will refine the tail-focused and adversarial aspects of scenario generation and then show how all of these stress-testing techniques—historical, hypothetical, and reverse—are integrated into a unified backtesting and evaluation framework.

4.4 Adversarial and Tail-Focused Scenario Generation

The previous section organized stress testing around *how* scenarios are chosen: from history, from handcrafted hypotheticals, or by working backward from a failure condition. In all those cases, the tail behavior of returns and liquidity was implicit: we relied on either historical extremes or stylized templates. We now make the tails explicit and systematic.

This section tackles two closely related problems:

- How to model and sample *extreme* but *statistically plausible* moves in prices and liquidity.
- How to steer generative models and simulators *adversarially* toward scenarios that are especially damaging to a given strategy, while still respecting those statistical and economic constraints.

In other words, we want to manufacture worst-case worlds that are neither arbitrary nightmares nor trivial extrapolations of the past, but lie near the edge of what our tail models and regime structure regard as plausible.

Why Tails Require Special Treatment

Most risk models and even many synthetic generators are calibrated to match central tendencies: means, volatilities, correlations, and perhaps moderate quantiles. Yet the events that define a strategy's survival—margin calls, forced liquidations, career-ending drawdowns—live in the tails.

Two issues make naive Monte Carlo insufficient for tail analysis:

- **Rarity:** If an event has probability 10^{-3} under the data-generating process, a simple Monte Carlo with 10^4 paths will see it only a handful of times, if at all. Estimating how the strategy behaves in those rare cases becomes noisy.
- **Dependence:** Extreme moves are not independent across assets or time. Crises involve clustering of large losses, regime shifts, and correlation spikes. Ignoring this structure yields unconvincing worst cases.

Hence we need tail-focused statistical techniques—especially from extreme value theory (EVT) and dependence modeling—and we must integrate them with our generative models in a way that enables targeted scenario construction.

Extreme Value Theory in a Nutshell

Let $\{r_t\}$ denote (for now) i.i.d. daily returns of some asset, with cumulative distribution F. EVT provides asymptotic approximations for the distribution of *extremes* of such sequences, under broad regularity conditions.

Two standard approaches are particularly useful:

Block Maxima and the Generalized Extreme Value (GEV) Distribution

Partition the series into non-overlapping blocks of length m (e.g., months or years). For each block b, define the maximum return

$$M_b = \max\{r_t : t \in \text{block } b\}.$$

Under mild conditions, as $m \to \infty$, the standardized maxima converge in distribution to a generalized extreme value (GEV) law

$$\Pr\left(\frac{M_b - \mu}{\sigma} \leq x\right) \to G(x; \xi),$$

where G is the GEV distribution with location μ, scale $\sigma > 0$, and shape parameter ξ (the *tail index*). Different signs of ξ correspond to different tail behaviors (Fréchet, Gumbel, Weibull types).

In risk terms, GEV lets us estimate return levels that are exceeded with small probabilities over a block horizon, e.g., "the worst monthly loss that occurs, on average, once every 20 years."

Peaks-Over-Threshold and the Generalized Pareto Distribution (GPD)

Rather than discarding all but the maxima, the peaks-over-threshold approach considers all exceedances above a high threshold u:

$$Y_t = r_t - u \quad \text{conditional on } r_t > u.$$

EVT states that, for large enough u, the conditional excess distribution of Y_t can be approximated by a generalized Pareto distribution (GPD) with shape parameter ξ and scale β:

$$\Pr(Y_t \leq y \mid r_t > u) \approx H(y; \xi, \beta), \quad y \geq 0.$$

This framework is more sample-efficient than block maxima and is widely used to model tail losses. It allows us to estimate quantities like:

- The probability that a loss exceeds a given multiple of the threshold u.
- Quantiles far beyond the range of observed data.

In practice, we:

- Choose a high threshold u (e.g., 95th or 99th percentile of $|r_t|$).

- Fit a GPD to exceedances using maximum likelihood or Bayesian methods.
- Validate the fit using diagnostic plots (e.g., mean excess plots, QQ plots).

Dependence in the Tails

Real market stress is almost never about one asset in isolation. Joint tail events—simultaneous large moves across assets, factors, or time—drive portfolio losses.

To capture joint extremes, we need to go beyond univariate EVT. Two common approaches are:

Copulas with Tail Dependence

A copula C couples marginal distributions $F_1, \dots, F_d$ into a joint distribution:

$$\Pr(R_1 \le r_1, \dots, R_d \le r_d) = C(F_1(r_1), \dots, F_d(r_d)).$$

Certain copulas, such as the t-copula, exhibit *tail dependence*: large moves in one component make large moves in others more likely. Tail dependence is summarized by coefficients like

$$\lambda_U = \lim_{u \to 1^-} \Pr\left(R_2 > F_2^{-1}(u) \mid R_1 > F_1^{-1}(u)\right),$$

and analogously for the lower tail.

By fitting GPDs to marginal tails and a tail-dependent copula to joint exceedances, we can sample multi-asset extreme scenarios that preserve both marginal tail thickness and cross-asset clustering of extremes.

Tail-Focused Factor Models

Alternatively, we can think in terms of factors:

$$r_{i,t} = \beta_i^\top f_t + \varepsilon_{i,t},$$

where f_t are common factors. Tail behavior can be concentrated in the factors (e.g., EVT on factor returns), with residuals treated as lighter-tailed. Under stress, factors jointly experience extremes, driving co-movement.

This is convenient for regime-conditioned generators: macro regimes directly affect the tail properties of f_t.

Tail-Focused Monte Carlo for Scenario Generation

With tail models specified, we can build tail-focused Monte Carlo schemes. The idea is to *oversample* from the tail regions of interest, then, if desired, reweight scenarios to reflect their true probabilities.

A simple two-step construction for a single asset might be:

- With probability p_{tail}, sample returns from a fitted GPD (conditioned on exceeding threshold u), then shift by u and the appropriate sign (loss vs gain). With probability $1 - p_{tail}$, sample from a "body" distribution fitted to non-exceedances.
- Stitch these draws into a time series that also respects volatility clustering and regime behavior, for example by embedding the tail samples within a GARCH-like or regime-switching generator.

For a multi-asset portfolio, we can:

- Sample tail factors from multivariate EVT or from a tail-dependent copula.
- Map them into asset returns using a factor model or joint generator.
- Apply time-series generators conditioned on regimes so that extremes occur in realistic temporal clusters.

This tail-aware sampling provides a baseline supply of extreme-but-plausible scenarios. However, they are not yet adversarial: they are extreme from the *market's* point of view, not necessarily from the *strategy's*.

From Tail Scenarios to Adversarial Ones

We now introduce *adversarial scenario generation*: systematically steering tail-focused generators to find scenarios that are particularly damaging to a chosen strategy, subject to our statistical and economic plausibility constraints.

Defining a Strategy Loss Functional

Let ω denote a full scenario: regime paths, price and return series, volumes, order flows, and microstructure states over a horizon T. Our simulation stack maps ω and a strategy π into P&L and risk metrics. We define a scalar loss functional $L(\pi, \omega)$ that increases with stress:

- L could be peak-to-trough drawdown, maximum margin utilization, or a weighted combination (e.g., drawdown plus penalties for liquidity shortfalls).
- Larger values of L represent more severe stress for the strategy.

Our goal in adversarial scenario generation is then:

$$\max_{\omega \in \Omega_{plausible}} \quad L(\pi, \omega),$$

where $\Omega_{plausible}$ is the set of scenarios deemed statistically and economically plausible given our tail models and regime structure.

Parameterizing Scenarios via Generators

Rather than searching over raw paths ω, we search in a lower-dimensional parameter space controlling our generative models. For example:

- A vector of *regime parameters* θ: durations in each regime, intensity of crisis states, timing of transitions.
- A vector of *tail parameters* ϕ: thresholds, tail indices, or scaling factors applied to tail distributions in certain periods.

- A latent vector z fed to a neural generator G that controls idiosyncratic variation.

A scenario is thus $\omega(\theta, \phi, z) = \text{SimulateScenario}(G, \theta, \phi, z)$, incorporating both the time-series layer and the agent-based LOB layer.

Adversarial generation becomes an optimization over (θ, ϕ, z):

$$\max_{\theta,\phi,z} L\big(\pi, \omega(\theta, \phi, z)\big) - \lambda C(\theta, \phi, z),$$

where C penalizes deviations from tail calibration and stylized facts (more on this below).

Hybrid Strategy: Tail-Heavy Initialization + Adversarial Refinement

An effective and intuitive algorithm combines tail-focused sampling with adversarial refinement:

- **Tail-heavy initialization.** Use EVT-based tail Monte Carlo to generate a pool of scenarios that are already unusually extreme in market terms (e.g., high factor drawdowns, liquidity droughts).
- **Evaluate strategy loss.** Compute $L(\pi, \omega)$ for each scenario using the full simulator.
- **Select candidates.** Identify the most stressful scenarios in this pool (top k by L). These serve as seeds for further adversarial search.
- **Local adversarial refinement.** Around each seed, adjust (θ, ϕ, z) using a local search or gradient-based method to increase L, while monitoring C to ensure plausibility. This may involve:

- Slightly extending crisis regime durations.
- Shifting the timing of shocks to coincide with high-leverage or high-position periods.
- Increasing tail intensity for specific asset clusters to which the strategy is heavily exposed.

- **Plausibility check and filtering.** Discard any refined scenarios that fail statistical diagnostics (tail index, correlation structure) or violate microstructure constraints (e.g., spreads far outside calibrated ranges).

The result is a curated set of *adversarial tail scenarios*: more threatening to the strategy than generic tail events, yet still consistent with our understanding of market behavior.

Constraining Adversarial Search to the Plausible Set

The plausibility constraint $C(\theta, \phi, z)$ is central: without it, adversarial search might produce unreasonably apocalyptic or internally inconsistent markets that shed little light on real-world risk.

Key components of C typically include:

- **Stylized-fact penalties:** Terms measuring discrepancies between generated and target statistics for returns, volatility clustering, leverage effects, and volume-volatility relationships. For example, penalizing deviations in estimated tail index $\hat{\xi}$ from historical estimates.

- **Regime-frequency penalties:** Deviations from empirically estimated regime transition probabilities and stationary frequencies. For instance, scenarios in which the crisis regime dominates 90% of time may be discounted unless explicitly desired.

- **Microstructure constraints:** Penalties for spreads, depths, or impact coefficients leaving calibrated ranges. An example is constraining the average spread multiplier in crisis regimes to be within a factor of what was observed historically plus a modest extrapolation.

- **Pathology filters:** Hard rejections of scenarios that violate basic arbitrage-free or consistency conditions (e.g., negative prices, systematically profitable trivial arbitrages).

In practice, one often uses a two-tier approach: soft penalties during optimization to guide search, followed by hard post-hoc filters for final acceptance.

Algorithmic Patterns for Adversarial Tail Search

Several algorithmic patterns recur in adversarial scenario generation; they can be combined and adapted depending on tools and computational budget.

Black-Box Optimization in Scenario Space

Treat $L(\pi, \omega(\theta, \phi, z))$ as a black box and apply global optimization heuristics:

- Randomized search with importance sampling toward tail-heavy parameter regions.
- Bayesian optimization: model the loss as a Gaussian process over (θ, ϕ) and sequentially query scenarios expected to improve the maximum loss.
- Evolutionary algorithms: maintain a population of scenarios, mutate and recombine parameters biased toward higher L and lower C.

This approach does not require differentiable generators or loss functions and can operate with complex, simulation-based P&L.

Gradient-Based Adversarial Generation in Latent Space

When generative models are differentiable and a surrogate loss $\tilde{L}$ can be differentiated with respect to generator inputs, we can adapt techniques from adversarial machine learning:

- Fix regime and tail parameters (θ, ϕ) consistent with a target stress template.

- Initialize latent vector $z^{(0)}$ from a prior.
- Iteratively update

$$z^{(k+1)} = z^{(k)} + \eta \nabla_z \left[\tilde{L}(\pi, \omega(\theta, \phi, z^{(k)})) - \lambda C(\theta, \phi, z^{(k)}) \right],$$

  where η is a step size.
- Periodically project $z^{(k)}$ back into a region where generated scenarios pass plausibility tests.

The surrogate loss $\tilde{L}$ might approximate P&L using a differentiable model (e.g., a neural approximation to the strategy and execution cost model), while final evaluation still uses the full, possibly non-differentiable simulator.

Stress Testing as a Robustness Game

Conceptually, adversarial scenario generation sets up a two-player game:

- Nature (or an adversary) chooses scenario parameters (θ, ϕ, z) in $\Omega_{plausible}$ to maximize L.
- The strategy designer chooses parameters of π (e.g., leverage, stop-loss rules, position limits) to minimize some risk-adjusted objective, anticipating that Nature will choose adversarial scenarios.

While solving the full min-max game is rarely feasible, iterating between improving π and updating adversarial scenarios yields a practical robustness-improvement loop: each round uncovers new vulnerabilities and prompts design adjustments.

Cataloguing and Reusing Adversarial Tail Scenarios

As with reverse stress testing, the adversarial search process produces a valuable by-product: a growing collection of extreme-but-plausible paths that are especially harmful to certain strategy archetypes.

Rather than keep these scenarios bound to one specific strategy, we can:

- **Abstract and label** them: annotate scenarios with qualitative descriptors (e.g., "prolonged volatility and correlation spike coinciding with liquidity drought in small caps") and quantitative metadata (tail indices, regime durations, peak drawdowns).
- **Cluster and classify** them into scenario families according to their regime and tail characteristics.
- **Build a tail risk library**: a curated set of adversarial scenarios to which all new strategies are automatically subjected, regardless of their original design context.

Over time, this tail risk library becomes an institutional asset, analogous to a unit test suite in software engineering: every new or modified strategy must pass (or at least have explainable behavior under) these challenging synthetic worlds.

Positioning Within the Overall Framework

Adversarial and tail-focused scenario generation completes the palette of stress-testing tools introduced in this chapter:

- Historical and hypothetical stresses anchor our analysis in known patterns and regime-based extrapolations.
- Reverse stresses search for failure modes based on explicit risk criteria.
- Tail-focused adversarial stresses go a step further by combining rigorous tail modeling with optimization over scenario space, actively seeking worst cases compatible with our understanding of market behavior.

In the final section, we will show how to integrate all of these scenario types—historical, hypothetical, reverse, and adversarial tail—into a unified backtesting and evaluation architecture. The goal is to make such synthetic, adversarial testing a routine part of the strategy research lifecycle, not an occasional, heroic exercise.

4.5 Backtesting and Evaluation Integration

Up to this point, we have developed the ingredients of a sophisticated synthetic market:

- Stylized facts and economic constraints that any realistic scenario must satisfy.
- Regime-based generative models that produce synthetic prices, volatility, and order flow.
- Agent-based, limit-order-book simulators that translate orders into executions with realistic liquidity and impact.
- A spectrum of stress-testing methodologies: historical, hypothetical, reverse, and adversarial tail-focused stresses.

This final section explains how to make these tools part of a *routine* research practice rather than ad hoc experiments. The central idea is to embed synthetic scenarios into a robust backtesting and evaluation framework that:

- Respects fundamental principles of time-series backtesting and cross-validation.
- Shares a unified engine architecture for historical and synthetic data.
- Produces evaluation outputs that explicitly account for scenario dependence, fragility, and robustness.

We begin with the architecture, then discuss workflow (cross-validation and walk-forward design), and conclude with evaluation metrics and reporting.

A Unified Backtesting Engine for Historical and Synthetic Worlds

Traditional backtesting engines are often designed around a single data source: historical prices and volumes at a fixed frequency. Synthetic scenarios then get bolted on informally, perhaps via separate scripts or simplified models. This separation leads to inconsistencies: transaction costs, liquidity assumptions, and even strategy logic can differ between historical and synthetic runs.

Instead, we want a *single* engine that can consume either historical or synthetic data streams, apply the same strategy logic, and route orders through the same execution models.

High-Level Architecture

Figure shows a pipeline-style architecture that connects data sources, synthetic generators, stress modules, execution simulators, and reporting components.

The key features are:

- **Two input paths:** one for raw historical data (prices, volumes, order books), and one for synthetic generators and stress modules. Both feed a common *market data stream* interface.
- **Shared core modules:** feature and signal computation, order generation, and execution simulation are *identical* regardless of whether the data are historical or synthetic.
- **Unified P&L and risk attribution:** results from historical and synthetic runs are collected in comparable formats, tagged with scenario identifiers (historical episode, hypothetical template, reverse/adversarial ID).
- **Feedback loops:** calibration and model evaluation use backtest outcomes to refine both data ingestion (e.g., corporate-action handling) and synthetic generators (e.g., matching stylized facts in stressed regimes).

The Unified Market Data Interface

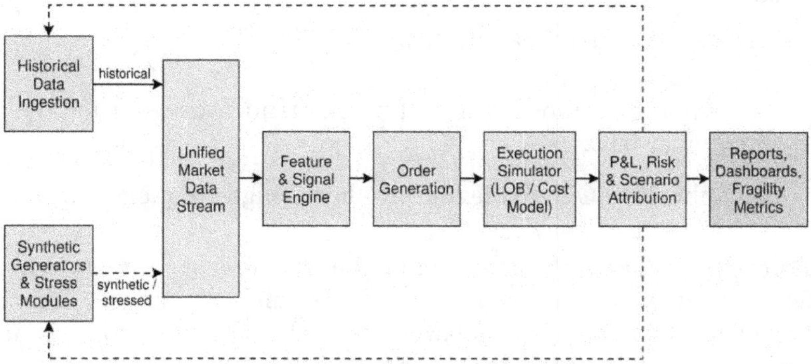

The lynchpin of this design is the *unified market data stream*. Conceptually, it is an iterator over time t that returns an object:

$$\text{MarketState}(t) = \{\text{prices, volumes, LOB snapshot, regime labels, macro features}, .$$

For historical runs, this object wraps real data. For synthetic runs, it wraps outputs from:

- Time-series generators (prices, volatility, volumes).
- Regime and stress modules (macro/micro regime labels, scenario IDs).

- Agent-based LOB simulators (bid/ask, depth, executed trades) if simulation is done "online".

By programming strategies and execution models against this interface, we ensure that swapping historical for synthetic inputs is a configuration choice, not a code rewrite.

Execution Model as a Plug-In

The execution simulator can itself be modular:

- A simple cost model (impact and spread formulas) for daily-frequency backtests.
- A calibrated LOB engine for intraday or high-frequency studies.

The backtesting engine should allow the user to select an execution backend, but the order-generation logic remains unchanged. This is crucial when comparing naive backtests (no book) to execution-aware stress tests (with book) under the same synthetic scenarios.

Time-Series Backtesting Principles with Synthetic Data

Having a unified engine does not exempt us from the usual pitfalls of time-series backtesting; synthetic data add new ways to get into trouble. We therefore revisit core principles and adapt them to a world with generators and scenarios.

Avoiding Look-Ahead and Data Leakage

In a purely historical backtest, we enforce chronological order: signals at time t must be functions only of information available up to t. When synthetic data are involved, we must maintain the same discipline:

- When training generative models, use only the training segment of historical data; do not leak test-period information into the generator.
- When running a backtest over a given period (historical or synthetic), condition signals only on past and current synthetic

states, not on future scenario information (e.g., future regimes or tail parameters).

- If regimes are hidden in reality, strategies should not be allowed to observe the true regime labels from the generator; they must infer them using filters based on observable features.

In implementation, this amounts to ensuring that the MarketState(t) interface does not expose future information, even when the underlying generator has already sampled the full path.

Transaction Costs, Slippage, and Microstructure Consistency

A second principle is making transaction costs and slippage assumptions consistent across historical and synthetic runs:

- Parametric execution-cost models (e.g., a linear or square-root impact formula) should be calibrated on historical data and applied identically to synthetic runs at matching regimes.
- When an agent-based LOB simulator is available and calibrated, it becomes the default execution model for both historical and synthetic intraday scenarios (possibly replaying historical order flows).
- Any simplifying assumptions (e.g., filling at mid-price for illiquid assets) should be explicitly documented and, where possible, stress-tested using more conservative cost models.

These consistencies ensure that performance differences across scenarios are driven by actual market conditions, not by hidden changes in frictions.

Cross-Validation and Walk-Forward with Synthetic Scenarios

In machine learning for time series, we use rolling or expanding-window cross-validation to estimate out-of-sample performance. Synthetic scenarios introduce an additional dimension: we now have both temporal splits and *scenario* splits.

Temporal Cross-Validation on Historical Data

First, we retain standard time-series cross-validation schemes on historical data:

- **Rolling windows:** train on $[t_0, t_1]$, test on $(t_1, t_2]$; then advance the window.
- **Expanding windows:** train on $[t_0, t_1]$, test on $(t_1, t_2]$; then train on $[t_0, t_2]$, test on $(t_2, t_3]$, etc.
- **Purged/embargoed splits:** in cross-sectional models, omit observations around test periods from the training set to avoid leakage via overlapping events or signals.

This yields estimates of performance in actual historical environments and forms the baseline for strategy viability.

Scenario-Conditioned Evaluation

Next, we introduce scenario-conditioned evaluation using synthetic data:

- For a given trained strategy (trained solely on historical data from its training window), we evaluate it across a suite of synthetic scenarios derived from that same training distribution: regime-conditioned, hypothetical, reverse, and adversarial.
- Each synthetic scenario is tagged with meta-information: regime paths, tail parameters, stress type (historical template, hypothetical, reverse, adversarial), and reference to the calibration period.
- We compute not just average performance across all scenarios, but performance broken down by scenario family and meta-features (e.g., crisis duration, maximum volatility).

Conceptually, we extend cross-validation from answering "How does the strategy perform across time?" to "How does it perform across time *and* across kinds of worlds?"

Walk-Forward with Synthetic Augmentation

In a walk-forward research workflow, we might proceed as follows for each step:

- **Train** the strategy $\pi^{(k)}$ on historical data up to time T_k.
- **Calibrate** generators and LOB simulator on the same or slightly extended data window (ensuring no leakage of test-period information).
- **Evaluate** $\pi^{(k)}$ on:
  - Historical test period $(T_k, T_{k+1}]$.
  - A standardized battery of synthetic scenarios calibrated on $[t_0, T_k]$ (stress library).
- **Record** both realized historical performance and synthetic stress performance for $\pi^{(k)}$.
- **Advance** k and repeat.

This process produces a time-series of *pre-launch* evaluations: for each hypothetical launch date T_k, we know how the then-current version of the strategy would have fared not only in subsequent historical data, but also across a consistent set of synthetic stresses.

Evaluation Metrics Tailored to Synthetic Testing

Conventional performance metrics—Sharpe ratio, maximum drawdown, average turnover—remain useful but are insufficient when strategies are tested across a large menu of synthetic scenarios. We need metrics that explicitly summarize *scenario-conditioned* behavior and *fragility*.

Scenario-Conditioned Performance Profiles

Let $\mathcal{S}$ denote the set of scenarios used to evaluate a strategy (historical episodes and synthetic worlds). For each scenario $s \in \mathcal{S}$, we compute a vector of metrics $M(\pi, s)$: e.g., annualized return, volatility, drawdown, maximum loss in a day, liquidity usage.

We can then define:

- **Scenario-wise distributions:** empirical distributions of $M(\pi, s)$ across $s \in \mathcal{S}$, stratified by scenario type, regime characteristics, or tail severity.

- **Response surfaces:** regression or nonparametric mappings from scenario meta-features (e.g., crisis duration, average spread multiplier) to performance metrics, indicating how performance degrades along specific stress dimensions.

This provides a nuanced view: a strategy might be robust to volatility spikes but fragile to extended liquidity droughts, for example.

Fragility and Robustness Scores

To summarize scenario-conditioned behavior succinctly, we can define fragility and robustness scores. For instance:

- **Tail performance quantiles:** the 5th or 1st percentile of scenario P&L or Sharpe across $\mathcal{S}$.
- **Stress coverage:** proportion of scenarios in which key risk limits are respected (e.g., maximum drawdown below a threshold, no margin breach).
- **Fragility index:** a weighted count of constraint violations across adversarial and reverse stress scenarios, potentially scaled by their tail probability under the calibrated model.
- **Robustness premium:** difference between average performance in benign scenarios and performance in stressed scenarios, perhaps normalized by the severity of stress.

These scores are not replacements for detailed scenario analysis, but they provide actionable summaries for governance and portfolio construction.

Realized vs Stressed Risk Comparisons

For live or paper-traded strategies, we can compare:

- **Realized risk and performance:** empirical metrics from live deployment or out-of-sample historical periods.
- **Ex ante stressed metrics:** synthetic stress results computed at launch or at the last major strategy revision.

Discrepancies between realized and stressed outcomes can indicate:

- Underestimation of certain risk channels (e.g., under-modeled liquidity risk).
- Overly conservative stress assumptions (good news, but important to recognize).
- Model drift: changes in market structure making earlier calibrations obsolete.

Maintaining this "realized vs stressed" ledger closes the loop between synthetic testing and actual performance.

Embedding Synthetic Testing in the Research Lifecycle

Finally, to make synthetic markets and stress-testing methodologies effective, they must be embedded into the routine lifecycle of strategy research and deployment:

- **At idea stage:** quick synthetic experiments to identify obvious vulnerabilities before investing heavily in model development.
- **At pre-launch:** full historical cross-validation plus a standardized synthetic stress battery, with explicit go/no-go thresholds based on fragility metrics.
- **Post-launch monitoring:** periodic re-evaluation of the live strategy against updated synthetic scenarios, especially when regime shifts are suspected.
- **Model governance:** documentation of synthetic testing results as part of risk committee materials, alongside traditional backtests and risk reports.

The unified architecture described in this section makes these tasks operationally feasible: switching between historical replay, hypothetical stresses, reverse, and adversarial scenarios becomes a matter of configuration, not bespoke coding.

In sum, integrating synthetic scenarios into backtesting and evaluation is not just about adding more tests; it is about elevating the role of *possible worlds* in our understanding of strategy risk. By grounding these worlds in stylized facts, economic constraints, regimes, and execution-aware microstructure, and by embedding them into disciplined backtesting workflows, we turn generative AI from a curiosity into a core instrument of robust trading research.

Chapter 5

Risk, Portfolio Construction, and Decision Integration

Stress-testing only matters if it changes how you size trades, guard against ruin, and react when markets misbehave. In this chapter, we turn synthetic scenarios into hard numbers-VaR, drawdowns, and tail losses-then push those numbers through portfolio construction and decision rules. The goal is simple but demanding: every position in the book should be justifiable not only under the base case, but under the worlds your generative models say are plausible, painful, and still survivable.

5.1 Risk Measures under Synthetic Scenarios

In earlier chapters we built generative models that produce synthetic prices and P&L paths conditioned on market regimes and strategy states. We now turn these raw paths into the risk quantities that drive limits, capital allocation, and governance. The core idea is simple but powerful:

> Instead of estimating risk only from the single historical path observed in reality, we estimate it from a large ensemble of plausible paths drawn from a generative model that has been calibrated—and then conservatively stressed—using historical data.

This section develops that idea for three workhorse metrics:

- Value-at-Risk (VaR): a quantile of the loss distribution.
- Conditional Value-at-Risk (CVaR, or Expected Shortfall): an average of tail losses beyond VaR.
- Drawdown metrics: path-dependent notions of peak-to-trough loss and time-under-water.

We begin with definitions, then explain how to compute these quantities on synthetic paths, how to compare them to their historical counterparts, and how to manage estimation error, regime sensitivity, and back-testing of risk forecasts.

From Historical to Synthetic Risk Distributions

Classically, risk is estimated from historical returns or P&L:

- We collect a time series of daily (or intraday) P&L $\{L_t\}_{t=1}^{T}$, where L_t denotes loss (so positive values are bad).
- We treat the empirical distribution of $\{L_t\}$ as a proxy for the true loss distribution under current conditions.
- VaR and CVaR are computed from this empirical distribution, and drawdowns from its cumulative sum.

This "single-path" view has two limitations that synthetic scenarios aim to address:

- **Data scarcity in the tails.** Even with decades of data, we have only a handful of large losses, making high-quantile risk estimates unstable.
- **Regime mixing.** The historical record blends calm and crisis regimes with some realized frequency that may not match the regime mix relevant to the next year.

A generative synthetic engine augments this with many simulated years:

- We generate N independent scenarios, each a path of length T days:

$$\{L_t^{(i)}\}_{t=1}^T, \quad i = 1, \dots, N.$$

- Each scenario is a full P&L trajectory consistent with learned dynamics, regime switches, cross-asset co-movements, and any explicit stress overlays.
- We then compute risk metrics across this enlarged sample, exploiting the fact that we now have $N \times T$ loss observations and N full paths.

Intuitively, the historical path tells us "what actually happened once," while the synthetic ensemble asks "what else could plausibly have happened, given what we know, plus a conservative stress layer?"

VaR on Synthetic Paths

Definition

Fix a horizon h (e.g., one day, 10 days) and a confidence level $\alpha \in (0, 1)$ (e.g., $\alpha = 0.99$). Let L_h be the random loss over horizon h. The (loss-based) Value-at-Risk at level α is the α-quantile of L_h:

$$\text{VaR}_\alpha(h) = \inf \{\ell : \mathbb{P}(L_h \leq \ell) \geq \alpha\}.$$

With this sign convention, a higher VaR means a worse (larger) loss.

Under historical estimation, we typically form horizon losses from returns (e.g., sum or compound h daily returns) and take the empirical α-quantile.

Scenario-based estimation

Under synthetic scenarios, we have many realizations of L_h:

- For each scenario i and starting date t, construct the h-day horizon loss:
$$L_{t,h}^{(i)} = L_{t+1}^{(i)} + \cdots + L_{t+h}^{(i)}.$$
- Aggregate all horizon losses into a sample
$$\{L_{t,h}^{(i)} : i = 1, \ldots, N,\ t = 0, \ldots, T - h\}.$$
- Sort these losses in ascending order to obtain an empirical distribution.
- The synthetic VaR estimate is the empirical α-quantile of this enlarged sample.

Formally, let $\{\tilde{L}_j\}_{j=1}^{M}$ denote the stacked horizon losses, where $M = N(T - h + 1)$, and let $\tilde{L}_{(1)} \leq \cdots \leq \tilde{L}_{(M)}$ be their order statistics. Then:

$$\widehat{\mathrm{VaR}}_\alpha^{\mathrm{syn}}(h) = \tilde{L}_{(\lceil \alpha M \rceil)}.$$

Compared to purely historical VaR, two things change: the sample size is larger, and the data points are drawn from a model-implied distribution rather than reality alone. The larger M reduces sampling noise, but model misspecification becomes a central concern.

CVaR on Synthetic Paths

Definition

Conditional Value-at-Risk (CVaR), also called Expected Shortfall, looks beyond the quantile to the average of the worst losses. At level α:

$$\mathrm{CVaR}_\alpha(h) = \mathbb{E}\left[L_h \mid L_h \geq \mathrm{VaR}_\alpha(h)\right].$$

CVaR is more sensitive to the shape of the tail than VaR. It answers: "Given that we are in the worst $(1-\alpha)\%$ of outcomes, what is our average loss?"

Scenario-based estimation

Using the stacked sample $\{\tilde{L}_j\}_{j=1}^M$ and $\widehat{\mathrm{VaR}}_\alpha^{\mathrm{syn}}(h)$:

$$\widehat{\mathrm{CVaR}}_\alpha^{\mathrm{syn}}(h) = \frac{1}{M_\alpha}\sum_{j=1}^{M} \tilde{L}_j \mathbf{1}\{\tilde{L}_j \geq \widehat{\mathrm{VaR}}_\alpha^{\mathrm{syn}}(h)\},$$

where $M_\alpha = \sum_{j=1}^{M} \mathbf{1}\{\tilde{L}_j \geq \widehat{\mathrm{VaR}}_\alpha^{\mathrm{syn}}(h)\}$ is the number of tail observations.

The advantage of synthetic scenarios is particularly clear here: historical CVaR at, say, 99.5% is based on very few data points, whereas the synthetic ensemble can generate thousands of extreme events across many paths and dates. This makes tail averages more stable—if and only if the generative model is correctly calibrated and appropriately stressed.

Visual Comparison: Historical vs. Synthetic Risk

To assess whether synthetic risk measures make sense, it is helpful to compare the empirical loss distribution from history with the synthetic loss distribution. We want to see how VaR and CVaR computed from each line up.

The following figure overlays two loss distributions (historical vs. synthetic) and annotates their respective VaR and CVaR levels.

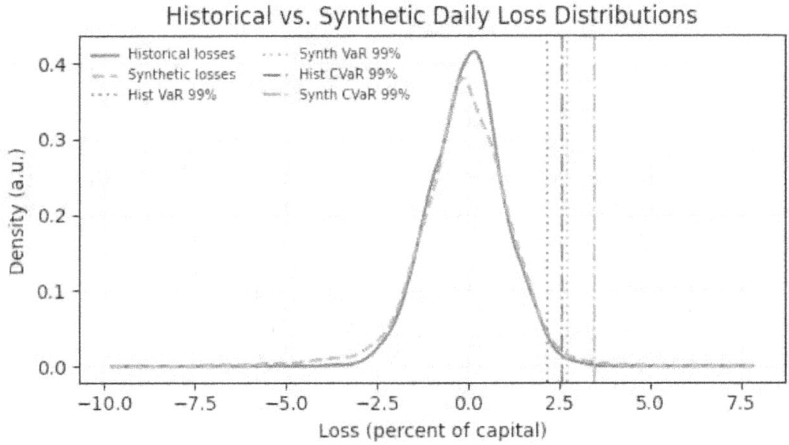

In practice, such a figure helps answer questions like: Does the synthetic distribution reproduce the bulk of historical losses while deliberately thickening the left tail to reflect stress? Are synthetic VaR and CVaR appropriately conservative relative to history?

Drawdown and Time-Under-Water

VaR and CVaR look at losses over a fixed horizon. Drawdown metrics instead care about the shape of the entire P&L path.

Definitions

Let P_t be the cumulative P&L of the portfolio, starting at $P_0 = 0$, over a horizon T (e.g., T trading days). The running peak process is:

$$P_t^{\max} = \max_{0 \le s \le t} P_s.$$

The drawdown at time t is then:

$$D_t = P_t^{\max} - P_t.$$

Key summary measures include:

- **Maximum drawdown** over $[0, T]$:

$$\mathrm{MDD} = \max_{0 \le t \le T} D_t.$$

- **Time-under-water** for a given peak: the duration from a peak until the P&L recovers to that peak.
- **Average time-under-water**: the average length of all such underwater episodes.

These measures are naturally path-based. They are difficult to infer from cross-sectional shocks alone but become straightforward once we have full synthetic paths.

Scenario-based estimation

Given synthetic P&L paths $\{P_t^{(i)}\}_{t=0}^{T}$ for $i = 1, \ldots, N$:

- For each path, compute running peaks $P_t^{\max,(i)}$ and drawdowns $D_t^{(i)}$.
- Extract maximum drawdown on each path:

$$\mathrm{MDD}^{(i)} = \max_t D_t^{(i)}.$$

- Optionally, compute time-under-water statistics per path by marking, for each new peak, the number of days until $P_t^{(i)}$ returns to that peak.
- Summarize across scenarios, for example:
  - Distribution of maximum drawdown: quantiles, mean, worst case.
  - Distribution of longest time-under-water.

Historical analysis gives only one maximum drawdown and one pattern of time-under-water. Synthetic scenarios provide a distribution of such experiences: "In 95% of plausible futures, maximum drawdown does not exceed 20%; in 5%, it is worse, sometimes reaching 35%." This is far richer input for risk appetite discussions and capital planning.

Sampling Error and Tail Instability

Synthetic scenarios are not a magic cure for estimation noise. They simply move the problem: instead of being limited by the realized sample size T, we are limited by the fidelity of the generator and the number of high-quality synthetic paths N we produce.

Two types of uncertainty matter:

- **Finite-scenario error.** Even under a perfect model, VaR and CVaR estimated from M samples exhibit sampling variability. The smaller $(1 - \alpha)$ is, the fewer tail observations we see, and the noisier the estimate.
- **Model error.** If the generator underestimates or overestimates tail thickness, dependence in crises, or regime persistence, the synthetic tail distribution will be biased, regardless of N.

In practice, we:

- Use a large number of scenarios and dates to increase M.
- Report confidence bands on $\widehat{\mathrm{VaR}}_{\alpha}^{\mathrm{syn}}$ and $\widehat{\mathrm{CVaR}}_{\alpha}^{\mathrm{syn}}$ obtained via bootstrap over scenarios or via repeated sub-sampling of synthetic paths.
- Monitor the sensitivity of tail measures to changes in model assumptions and regime conditioning.

Importance Weighting and Tail Reweighting

Generative models are typically calibrated to reproduce the observational data distribution, perhaps with some regularization. Risk management, however, often wants the distribution of *adverse but plausible* outcomes, which may be more conservative than the historical mix.

Two practical techniques bridge this gap:

Importance weighting

Suppose each synthetic scenario i is generated with an internal probability (or weight) w_i implied by the model. Risk management may wish to reweight scenarios to emphasize stressed regimes (e.g., higher volatility, tighter liquidity). Given a new set of weights $\tilde{w}_i$, with $\sum_i \tilde{w}_i = 1$, we can compute weighted empirical distributions:

$$\widehat{\mathrm{VaR}}_\alpha^{\mathrm{w}} = \inf\left\{ \ell : \sum_{j:\tilde{L}_j \leq \ell} \tilde{w}_j \geq \alpha \right\},$$

where $\tilde{L}_j$ are horizon losses and $\tilde{w}_j$ are the corresponding (normalized) weights. CVaR is then computed as a weighted tail mean. This allows us to shift attention toward regimes and scenarios that are more relevant to risk appetite, even if they are relatively rare in the generator's baseline output.

Tail reweighting and stress overlays

An even more direct approach is to:

- Explicitly insert extreme stress scenarios into the synthetic set (e.g., historical crises rescaled to current portfolio, or hypothetical disorderly moves).
- Assign them non-trivial weights (e.g., a minimum floor probability or scenario count) so that VaR and CVaR necessarily reflect their presence.

This produces a hybrid distribution: it preserves the learned structure from the generative model, but overlays exogenous stress scenarios that ensure the left tail is at least as conservative as required by risk policy or regulation.

Regime Sensitivity

Generative models often represent regimes (e.g., low-volatility bull, high-volatility bear, crisis) either explicitly (e.g., hidden Markov states) or implicitly via conditioning variables (e.g., volatility index level, cross-sectional dispersion).

Risk estimates should recognize that:

- Forecasts for the next month should condition on the regime we are in today.
- Enterprise-level stress testing may instead look at worst-case risk across multiple regimes.

Two complementary uses of synthetic scenarios follow:

Conditioned risk

We generate synthetic scenarios *conditional* on the current estimated regime. For example, if the model believes we are currently in a "late-cycle, high valuation, rising rates" regime, we restrict scenarios to those initialized from or constrained to that state. VaR, CVaR, and drawdown estimated from these paths answer: "If the current regime persists and evolves according to its historical dynamics, what are our risks?"

Regime-mix and worst-case risk

Alternatively, we can:

- Generate scenarios under each regime separately (e.g., calm, stressed, crisis).
- Compute risk metrics within each regime.
- Combine them by a policy rule:
  - A probability-weighted average based on regime transition probabilities.
  - A conservative worst-case or high-quantile across regimes:

$$\mathrm{VaR}_\alpha^{\mathrm{worst}} = \max_{r \in \mathcal{R}} \mathrm{VaR}_\alpha^{(r)}.$$

This gives a clear risk narrative: "In the current calm regime, 99% 10-day VaR is 8%, but if the crisis regime is entered, it jumps to 20%; our capital and leverage policies are set based on a blend of these." Synthetic scenarios make it easy to generate such regime-specific distributions.

Back-Testing Synthetic VaR and CVaR

Any risk measure that is going to influence capital, leverage, or trading limits must eventually face reality. Synthetic VaR and CVaR forecasts are no exception. We back-test them in two intertwined dimensions:

Coverage tests for VaR

At each day t, the scenario engine produces a forecast distribution for h-day loss $L_{t,t+h}$, and we compute a VaR forecast $\widehat{\text{VaR}}^{\text{syn}}_{\alpha,t}$. After h days, we observe the realized loss $L^{\text{real}}_{t,t+h}$ and record whether a breach occurred:

$$I_t = \mathbf{1}\left\{ L^{\text{real}}_{t,t+h} > \widehat{\text{VaR}}^{\text{syn}}_{\alpha,t} \right\}.$$

Over many such forecast–realization pairs, the empirical average

$$\hat{p} = \frac{1}{K} \sum_{t=1}^{K} I_t$$

should be close to $(1 - \alpha)$ if the VaR level is calibrated correctly. Standard back-testing uses binomial tests and runs tests to assess whether breaches occur with the right frequency and without clustering.

For synthetic VaR, the key questions are:

- Is synthetic VaR systematically *lower* than historical VaR (underestimation of risk) or *higher* (overly conservative)?
- Do breaches cluster in particular regimes, indicating that the generator underestimates risk specifically during those conditions?

Tail loss diagnostics for CVaR

CVaR back-testing is less standardized but can use tail loss statistics:

- Compare realized average loss on VaR breach days to the forecasted CVaR.
- Examine whether the realized tail distribution shape is consistent with the synthetic tail shape.

Graphical tools are extremely helpful: for example, plotting realized losses against forecast VaR and CVaR bands, or QQ-plots comparing realized tail losses to the synthetic distribution. Where significant discrepancies are persistent, the scenario engine or its stress overlays must be revisited.

Turning Synthetic Paths into Risk Reports

Finally, synthetic risk measures must be consumable by portfolio managers, risk committees, and regulators. A few practical guidelines:

- **Report both historical and synthetic metrics.** Side-by-side VaR, CVaR, and drawdown figures, as in Figure, make the contribution of the synthetic engine transparent.
- **Separate model-based and stress-based contributions.** Distinguish between risk implied by the fitted generative model and incremental risk imposed by explicit stress overlays or tail reweighting.
- **Highlight regime-conditioned results.** Provide risk numbers by regime (current, stressed, crisis) so that decision-makers can see how sensitive risk is to a regime shift.
- **Summarize path-dependent metrics.** Show distributions of maximum drawdown and time-under-water, not just single historical figures. These are often the most intuitive to PMs and investors.

In the next section, we will feed these synthetic risk measures into portfolio construction and position sizing frameworks, replacing static mean–variance inputs by scenario-conditioned risk/return distributions that reflect both learned structure and conservative tail overlays.

5.2 Portfolio Construction and Position Sizing

In the previous section we learned how to turn synthetic P&L paths into risk measures such as VaR, CVaR, and drawdown distributions. Those quantities are only useful if they drive concrete portfolio choices: which strategies to hold, in what size, and under which constraints.

This section shows how to embed synthetic scenarios directly into portfolio construction. Instead of feeding an optimizer with a static vector of expected returns and a covariance matrix estimated from one historical sample, we work with a large panel of scenario outcomes and derive allocations that reflect the full shape of the synthetic P&L distribution.

We proceed in four steps:

- Define a scenario-based representation of portfolio returns.
- Construct mean–variance, risk-parity, and Kelly-style objectives from that representation.
- Introduce real-world constraints: leverage, capacity, turnover, and drawdown limits.
- Discuss practical issues of numerical stability and sensitivity.

From Synthetic Scenarios to Optimization Inputs

Assume we have N synthetic scenarios, each with T time steps, for d tradable strategies or assets. Let $R_t^{(i)} \in \mathbb{R}^d$ be the vector of strategy returns (or P&L as a fraction of capital) at time t in scenario i.

A portfolio with weights $w \in \mathbb{R}^d$ (interpreted as fractions of capital, possibly allowing shorting) has scenario and time-specific return:

$$r_t^{(i)}(w) = w^\top R_t^{(i)}.$$

We can think of all these outcomes as a rectangular data set:

$$\{r_t^{(i)}(w) : i = 1, \dots, N, \quad t = 1, \dots, T\}.$$

From this object we derive:

- Scenario-based expected return:

$$\hat{\mu}(w) = \frac{1}{NT} \sum_{i=1}^{N} \sum_{t=1}^{T} r_t^{(i)}(w).$$

- Scenario-based risk metrics:
  - Variance or volatility of $r_t^{(i)}(w)$.
  - VaR and CVaR at horizons built from $r_t^{(i)}(w)$.
  - Pathwise drawdown statistics computed from cumulative sums of $r_t^{(i)}(w)$ within each scenario.

Crucially, all of these are functions of w but are evaluated through the same scenario engine. This allows us to design an optimization problem that operates not on parametric estimates (μ, Σ) alone, but on the implicit distribution of outcomes revealed by the synthetic scenarios.

High-Level Flow: From Scenarios to Weights

Before diving into the mathematics of each optimization style, it is helpful to visualize the overall process. The following block diagram summarizes the flow from synthetic scenarios to portfolio weights under different objectives.

This picture emphasizes three key messages:

- *All* risk and return quantities are computed from the same synthetic scenario set.
- Different objective functions (mean–variance, risk-parity, Kelly) are just different ways of scoring those scenario-based outcomes.
- Constraints are first-class citizens: they are integrated alongside the objective into a single optimization problem.

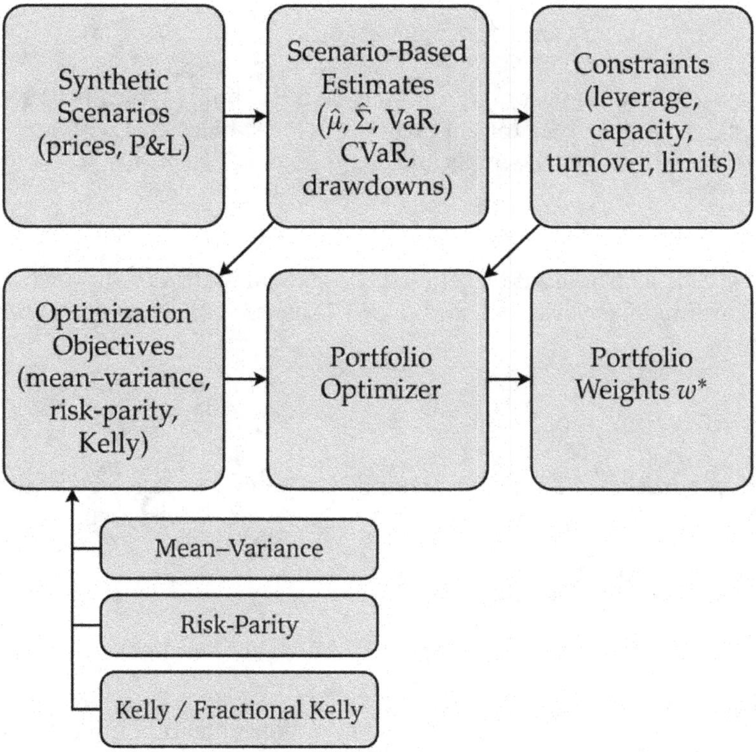

Scenario-Based Mean–Variance Optimization

Estimating mean and covariance from scenarios

The traditional mean–variance approach takes as input an expected return vector $\mu \in \mathbb{R}^d$ and a covariance matrix $\Sigma \in \mathbb{R}^{d \times d}$. Under synthetic scenarios we estimate these directly:

$$\hat{\mu} = \frac{1}{NT} \sum_{i=1}^{N} \sum_{t=1}^{T} R_t^{(i)},$$

$$\hat{\Sigma} = \frac{1}{NT-1} \sum_{i=1}^{N} \sum_{t=1}^{T} \left(R_t^{(i)} - \hat{\mu}\right) \left(R_t^{(i)} - \hat{\mu}\right)^\top .$$

Because NT can be very large, $\hat{\Sigma}$ may be noisy but is typically less singular than a purely historical estimate. Nevertheless, as with any covariance estimation, we apply shrinkage or regularization:

$$\hat{\Sigma}_\lambda = (1-\lambda)\hat{\Sigma} + \lambda D,$$

where D is a structured target (e.g., a diagonal matrix of variances, or a factor model covariance), and $\lambda \in [0,1]$ controls the shrinkage intensity.

Optimization problem

A simple risk-averse investor maximizes a penalized expected return:

$$\max_{w} \quad w^\top \hat{\mu} - \frac{\gamma}{2} w^\top \hat{\Sigma} w,$$

subject to constraints such as:

$$\begin{aligned}
&\mathbf{1}^\top w = 1 && \text{(fully invested or budget constraint)},\\
&\|w\|_1 \le L_{max} && \text{(leverage limit)},\\
&Aw \le b && \text{(exposure, sector, or concentration limits)},\\
&w \in \mathcal{W} && \text{(box constraints, long-only, etc.)},
\end{aligned}$$

where $\gamma > 0$ is a risk aversion parameter.

Even though the objective is written in standard quadratic form, its inputs are scenario-based. This means that, for example, a generative model that produces fatter tails or stronger crisis correlations will widen $\hat{\Sigma}$ and push the optimizer toward more conservative weights than a naïve Gaussian fit to history.

Risk-Parity and Risk-Budgeting with Scenario-Based Risk

Mean–variance optimization focuses on total variance at the portfolio level. Many practitioners instead want *risk-parity*: each strategy or asset should contribute a similar amount of risk to the total.

Risk contributions under synthetic variance

Let portfolio volatility under scenario-based covariance be:

$$\sigma(w) = \sqrt{w^\top \hat{\Sigma} w}.$$

The (marginal) contribution of asset k to portfolio variance is

$$RC_k^{var}(w) = w_k \left(\hat{\Sigma} w\right)_k .$$

Risk-parity aims for:

$$RC_1^{var}(w) \approx RC_2^{var}(w) \approx \cdots \approx RC_d^{var}(w),$$

or more generally for pre-specified risk budgets b_k:

$$RC_k^{var}(w) \approx b_k, \quad k = 1, \ldots, d, \quad \text{with} \quad \sum_k b_k = \sigma^2(w).$$

When risk is defined not by variance but by CVaR or drawdown, we adjust the notion of risk contribution accordingly.

CVaR-based risk-parity

Using the synthetic paths, we can define portfolio horizon losses $L_{t,h}^{(i)}(w)$ and compute CVaR at level α:

$$\widehat{CVaR}_\alpha(w) = \frac{1}{M_\alpha} \sum_{j=1}^{M} L_j(w) \mathbf{1}\{L_j(w) \geq \widehat{VaR}_\alpha(w)\},$$

where $L_j(w)$ indexes all scenario–date horizon losses as before.

Risk contributions under CVaR can be defined via gradients:

$$RC_k^{CVaR}(w) = w_k \frac{\partial \widehat{CVaR}_\alpha(w)}{\partial w_k},$$

which can be approximated numerically using the synthetic sample:

$$\frac{\partial \widehat{CVaR}_\alpha(w)}{\partial w_k} \approx \frac{1}{M_\alpha} \sum_{j \in \text{tail}} R_{j,k},$$

where $R_{j,k}$ is the return of asset k in tail observation j. Intuitively, we are asking: in the worst $(1-\alpha)\%$ of outcomes, how much does asset k move, and in which direction?

A CVaR-based risk-parity portfolio then solves:

$$\min_w \sum_{k=1}^{d} \left(RC_k^{CVaR}(w) - b_k \right)^2,$$

subject to the same constraints as before. The optimization is typically non-convex, but in practice can be tackled with iterative methods that alternate between estimating gradients from scenarios and updating weights.

Drawdown-sensitive allocations

Drawdown risk is inherently path-dependent. Using the synthetic paths, we can compute for each w:

- The distribution of maximum drawdown across scenarios.
- The expected maximum drawdown, or a high quantile thereof.

We can then:

- Add a penalty to the objective:

  $$\max_w \hat{\mu}(w) - \lambda_1 \sigma(w) - \lambda_2 \widehat{MDD}_q(w),$$

  where $\widehat{MDD}_q(w)$ is, say, the q-quantile of maximum drawdown across scenarios.

- Or impose a hard constraint:

$$\widehat{MDD}_q(w) \leq D_{max},$$

meaning that in at least $(1-q)\%$ of synthetic futures, maximum drawdown does not exceed D_{max}.

Here again, the synthetic scenario engine provides all required path-wise information; the optimization layer merely decides how to trade off expected return and different notions of risk.

Kelly-Style and Fractional Kelly Sizing from Synthetic P&L

Kelly sizing aims to maximize the long-run growth rate of capital, assuming repeated bets with known probabilities. In a multi-asset, scenario-based setting, the logic is similar but we work with a distribution of portfolio returns obtained from the synthetic paths.

Growth-optimal criterion

Let $r_t^{(i)}(w)$ be the portfolio return over some rebalancing period (e.g., daily) in scenario i. The Kelly criterion maximizes the expected log growth:

$$\max_{w} \quad G(w) = \frac{1}{NT} \sum_{i=1}^{N} \sum_{t=1}^{T} \log\left(1 + r_t^{(i)}(w)\right),$$

subject to admissibility constraints ensuring $1+r_t^{(i)}(w) > 0$ for all paths (no bankruptcy in any scenario). In practice, we often enforce:

$$1 + r_t^{(i)}(w) \geq \epsilon > 0 \quad \forall i, t,$$

for a small ϵ, to keep the log well-defined and avoid extreme leverage.

This optimization naturally accounts for:

- Mean returns: higher typical $r_t^{(i)}(w)$ increases $G(w)$.

- Volatility: high variance depresses $G(w)$ because $\mathbb{E}[\log(1+R)] < \log(1+\mathbb{E}[R])$ when there is uncertainty.
- Tail risk: very negative outcomes dramatically reduce $G(w)$, since the log of small numbers is large and negative.

All of these effects are mediated by the synthetic distribution of $r_t^{(i)}(w)$.

Fractional Kelly and ruin constraints

Pure Kelly portfolios are often too aggressive for institutional investors. Scenario-based stress testing makes this evident: in many synthetic paths, leverage implied by Kelly sizing may lead to large drawdowns or even breach risk limits.

A practical compromise is *fractional Kelly*:

$$w_{frac} = \phi\, w_{Kelly}, \quad 0 < \phi < 1,$$

where w_{Kelly} is the solution to the growth-optimal problem and ϕ is a scaling factor chosen to satisfy additional risk constraints. Using synthetic paths, we can choose ϕ to ensure:

- Probability of maximum drawdown exceeding D_{max} is below a threshold.
- Probability of a capital loss beyond some level (e.g., -50%) over a planning horizon is below a target.
- Regulatory capital ratios remain within bounds across most scenarios.

Instead of setting ϕ arbitrarily, we can embed it in a constrained optimization:

$$\max_{w} \quad G(w) \quad \text{subject to} \quad \mathbb{P}^{syn}\left(MDD(w) > D_{max}\right) \leq \delta, \quad \|w\|_1 \leq L_{max}, \quad \ldots$$

where probabilities and drawdowns are computed from the synthetic ensemble. This yields a *growth-aware but tail-conscious* allocation.

Incorporating Real-World Constraints

So far we have treated constraints somewhat abstractly. In practice, constraints are where synthetic scenario-based construction earns much of its value, because they can be expressed in terms of outcome distributions rather than static heuristics.

Leverage and capacity

Leverage constraints control $\|w\|_1$ or gross exposure, possibly by bucket:

$$\sum_k |w_k| \leq L_{max}, \quad \sum_{k \in \mathcal{B}_j} |w_k| \leq L_{max}^{(j)}.$$

Synthetic scenarios help calibrate L_{max}: we can search over plausible leverage levels and examine how VaR, CVaR, and drawdown distributions behave, choosing thresholds that keep risk within appetite.

Capacity constraints reflect liquidity and market impact. A simple version bounds dollar exposure:

$$|w_k| \leq c_k,$$

where c_k is chosen based on estimated capacity of strategy k. More sophisticated versions model trading costs and impact as functions of turnover (below) and average daily volume, which can be simulated directly with the scenario engine if it includes volume dynamics.

Turnover and transaction costs

Turnover constraints link current weights w^{old} to proposed weights w:

$$\sum_k |w_k - w_k^{old}| \leq \tau_{max},$$

limiting how much the portfolio can change at each rebalancing. Transaction costs can be included in the objective by subtracting a cost term:

$$\hat{\mu}_{net}(w) = \hat{\mu}(w) - \text{Cost}(w, w^{old}),$$

where Cost$(\cdot)$ may be linear (commissions) plus non-linear (impact) in $\Delta w = w - w^{old}$. If the scenario engine simulates spreads and liquidity, we can even let costs depend on market state and evaluate them across synthetic futures.

Drawdown and risk limits

Institutional portfolios are subject to multiple layers of risk limits:

- **VaR/CVaR limits**: e.g., 99% 1-day VaR must not exceed a fraction of capital.
- **Drawdown limits**: projected maximum drawdown over a horizon must remain below a threshold for most scenarios.
- **Stress-test limits**: losses under specified stress scenarios must not exceed certain levels.

Because the previous chapter has already detailed how to compute these quantities from synthetic paths, we can integrate them directly into the optimization:

$$\begin{aligned}
\widehat{VaR}_{0.99}(w) &\leq VaR_{max}, \\
\widehat{MDD}_{0.95}(w) &\leq D_{max}, \\
L_s^{stress}(w) &\geq -L_{max,s}^{stress}, \quad \forall s \in \mathcal{S},
\end{aligned}$$

where $L_s^{stress}(w)$ is the loss of portfolio w under stress scenario s (which may be part of the synthetic set or an overlay).

Stability, Numerics, and Sensitivity

Scenario-based optimization offers a rich and realistic description of risk, but also raises practical challenges.

Numerical considerations

- **High dimensionality.** With large d and complex constraints, the optimization problem may be high-dimensional and non-convex (particularly for CVaR- and drawdown-based objectives). Practitioners often resort to:

  - Convex approximations (e.g., linearized CVaR formulations).
  - Factor models that reduce dimensionality of $\hat{\Sigma}$.
  - Sequential optimization: first find a mean–variance or variance-parity solution, then locally adjust for CVaR/drawdown.

- **Non-smooth objectives.** VaR and drawdown are non-smooth; CVaR is smoother but still piecewise-defined. Gradient-based optimizers must handle kinks and may need subgradient methods or smoothing techniques.

Sensitivity to scenario set

Portfolio weights can be overly sensitive to small changes in the scenario set (e.g., adding or removing a few extreme paths). To diagnose this:

- **Resample scenarios.** Randomly resample the synthetic dataset (or perturb model parameters) and recompute optimal weights. Large variability indicates fragile allocations.
- **Regularize the solution.** Penalize large changes from a reference portfolio or from the previous allocation:

$$\max_{w} \text{Objective}(w) - \eta \|w - w^{ref}\|_2^2,$$

  which encourages stability over time.
- **Limit concentration.** Impose tighter box constraints on weights to avoid extreme positions driven by small features of the scenario set.

Communicating results

Finally, the outputs of scenario-based portfolio construction must be explainable to portfolio managers and risk committees. The narrative should tie together:

- *Inputs:* Key properties of the synthetic scenario distribution, especially tail behavior and regime conditioning.
- *Objective:* Whether the portfolio is tuned for mean–variance efficiency, balanced risk contributions, or long-run growth.
- *Constraints:* Which limits are binding (leverage, drawdown, regulatory capital) and how they shape the final weights.
- *Outcomes:* Distribution of returns, VaR, CVaR, and drawdown for the chosen w, compared with alternatives (e.g., historical-only optimization).

In the next section we will move from static portfolio construction to *scenario-based decision frameworks*: playbooks and governance processes that specify how allocations should evolve as synthetic diagnostics change over time.

5.3 Scenario-Based Decision Frameworks

Up to this point, we have treated synthetic scenarios as inputs to *measurement* (VaR, CVaR, drawdowns) and *optimization* (portfolio construction and sizing). In a live trading organization, however, these numbers are only the middle of the story. The end of the story is *action*: changing position sizes, adding hedges, deleveraging, or seeking explicit governance sign-off.

This section develops a practical bridge from synthetic diagnostics to concrete actions. We will:

- Define the notion of a *scenario-based playbook*: a pre-agreed mapping from risk indicators to actions.
- Introduce *decision surfaces*: continuous mappings from a small set of synthetic risk indicators to recommended portfolio adjustments.

- Describe how these mechanisms operate across the trade lifecycle: pre-trade checks, intra-day and overnight monitoring, and periodic governance reviews.
- Discuss documentation, communication, and auditability, so that synthetic decisions stand up to internal and external scrutiny.

Throughout, we maintain a tight focus on how insights from the synthetic risk engine are translated into resizing, hedging, deleveraging, and approvals—not just more elaborate reports.

From Diagnostics to Playbooks

Synthetic scenarios produce a rich set of diagnostics:

- Forward-looking VaR and CVaR at various horizons, under different regimes.
- Distributions of maximum drawdown and time-under-water for given portfolios.
- Losses under explicit stress overlays (e.g., disorderly rate shocks, liquidity freezes).
- Scenario-conditioned distributions of leverage, margin utilization, and capital ratios.

If these diagnostics merely appear in long PDFs, they have limited impact on behavior. A *scenario-based playbook* instead specifies, in advance:

> Given particular ranges or patterns in these diagnostics, which concrete actions must portfolio managers and risk managers take?

A playbook transforms fuzzy language (*"if risk looks high, we will reduce positions"*) into a set of operational rules (*"if 95%-quantile projected 6-month drawdown exceeds 25%, reduce gross exposure by at least 30% within 3 trading days"*).

Core ingredients of a playbook

A well-designed playbook has four ingredients:

- **Indicators:** functions of synthetic scenarios that summarize risk. Examples:
  - $D_{0.95}^{(6m)}$: 95th percentile of 6-month maximum drawdown from synthetic paths.
  - $\text{CVaR}_{0.99}^{crisis}$: 99% CVaR under crisis-conditioned scenarios.
  - $L_{rates+equity}^{stress}$: loss under a combined rates/equity stress scenario.
  - p_{breach}: synthetic probability that regulatory capital falls below a threshold.
- **Thresholds (or bands):** numerical levels for indicators that define regimes: *normal, stressed, crisis.*
- **Actions:** specific, verifiable steps triggered when an indicator crosses a threshold:
  - Resizing (reduce gross or net exposure by a specified fraction).
  - Hedging (enter predefined hedge instruments or overlays).
  - Deleveraging (tighten financing, unwind derivatives, reduce margin usage).
  - Governance (require risk-committee review or CIO sign-off before additional risk is added).
- **Timeframes and responsibilities:** clear statements of *who* must act, and *by when*. For example: "PM and desk risk manager jointly responsible for executing de-risking steps within 48 hours."

By grounding indicators in synthetic scenarios, the playbook reflects not only what has happened historically but a wide range of plausible futures, including stressed regimes that may not have occurred in the observed sample.

Decision Surfaces: Mapping Indicators to Actions

While playbooks are often described as threshold rules, it is helpful to think of them more systematically as *decision surfaces*. A decision surface is a function that maps a small number of risk indicators into recommended portfolio actions.

A simple two-indicator example

Consider two synthetic indicators:

- x_1: current portfolio leverage (gross or net), measured as $\|w\|_1$.
- x_2: crisis-conditioned 99% 10-day CVaR as a fraction of capital, $\text{CVaR}_{0.99}^{crisis}$.

We can view (x_1, x_2) as coordinates in a two-dimensional risk space. A decision surface partitions this space into regions associated with different actions:

- Region A (*green*): low leverage and low crisis CVaR → allow new risk, no restrictions.
- Region B (*amber*): moderate leverage and/or elevated crisis CVaR → new risk allowed only after PM justification; hedging encouraged.
- Region C (*red*): high leverage and high crisis CVaR → mandatory deleveraging and hedge activation; no new net risk without committee approval.

Formally, if $a \in \mathcal{A}$ denotes an action (e.g., "reduce gross exposure by 30%"), the decision surface is a mapping

$$\delta : \mathbb{R}^2 \to \mathcal{A}, \quad \delta(x_1, x_2) = a.$$

In implementation, δ is usually defined by inequalities, such as:

$$\begin{aligned} x_1 \le L_{low}, \quad x_2 \le C_{low} \qquad & \Rightarrow \text{Region A}, \\ x_1 \le L_{high}, \quad x_2 \le C_{high} \qquad & \Rightarrow \text{Region B}, \\ x_1 > L_{high}, \quad x_2 > C_{high} \qquad & \Rightarrow \text{Region C}. \end{aligned}$$

The important point is that x_2 (crisis CVaR) comes directly from synthetic scenarios, conditional on crisis regimes and overlay stress. The organization is not guessing what might happen in a crisis; it has a modeled distribution, plus a conservative overlay, and builds the decision surface on top of it.

More complex surfaces

In more sophisticated settings, decision surfaces can involve:

- Multiple indicators (e.g., measures of liquidity, basis risk, or margin consumption).
- Smooth transitions, where actions ramp up gradually rather than jumping at a single threshold.
- Asymmetric rules: e.g., stricter conditions for adding risk than for maintaining risk.

For example, a continuous resizing function might specify that gross exposure should scale with a factor $f(x_2)$ that declines as crisis CVaR increases:

$$w_{allowed} = f(x_2) \cdot w_{baseline}, \quad f'(x_2) < 0.$$

Here the synthetic risk engine computes x_2 daily, and the decision framework translates this into permissible risk budgets for the portfolio.

Pre-Trade: Gating New Positions

Before a new trade is executed, we can query the scenario engine to assess its *marginal* effect on synthetic risk. This leads naturally to pre-trade decision checks.

Marginal risk contribution under scenarios

Suppose the current portfolio has weights w, and we propose a trade that changes weights to $w' = w + \Delta w$. Using the synthetic scenarios:

- Compute key risk metrics for w: e.g., $\mathrm{CVaR}_{0.99}(w)$, $\widehat{\mathrm{MDD}}_{0.95}(w)$, and select stress losses.

- Compute the same metrics for w'.
- Define marginal changes:

$$\Delta \text{CVaR}_{0.99} = \text{CVaR}_{0.99}(w') - \text{CVaR}_{0.99}(w),$$

$$\Delta \widehat{\text{MDD}}_{0.95} = \widehat{\text{MDD}}_{0.95}(w') - \widehat{\text{MDD}}_{0.95}(w).$$

These marginal changes are direct functions of the synthetic P&L paths, because both VaR/CVaR and drawdown are computed on simulated outcomes of w and w'.

Pre-trade gating rules

A pre-trade playbook might specify rules such as:

- *Soft gate:* If $\Delta \text{CVaR}_{0.99} > \theta_1$ or $\Delta \widehat{\text{MDD}}_{0.95} > \theta_2$, the trade must be explicitly justified in a comment field and flagged to risk management.
- *Hard gate:* If $\text{CVaR}_{0.99}(w')$ exceeds a global VaR limit, or if the probability of breaching drawdown limits across synthetic paths exceeds a given level, the trade cannot be executed without risk-committee approval.
- *Hedge requirement:* If adding the trade moves the portfolio into a higher-risk regime on the decision surface (e.g., from amber to red), the playbook can require simultaneous execution of an approved hedge package.

The crucial feature is that all these rules depend on *modeled* future distributions, not just on historical measures or simple deltas. For example, two trades with the same immediate delta exposure to the market can have very different effects on synthetic crisis CVaR if one is known to perform poorly in crisis scenarios generated by the model.

Intra-Day and Overnight Monitoring

After trades are in place, the portfolio evolves with the market. Scenario-based decision frameworks guide how we monitor risk in real time and across days.

Tracking within the "scenario envelope"

The synthetic scenario set implicitly defines an envelope of plausible paths. At each monitoring point (e.g., end-of-day, or intra-day snapshots), we can:

- Update the current state variables that condition the scenario engine (e.g., volatility, spreads, macro indicators).
- Regenerate (or reuse) conditional synthetic paths from the new state.
- Compute updated risk indicators (VaR, CVaR, drawdown, stress losses).
- Compare the actual realized P&L trajectory so far to the distribution implied by the synthetic ensemble.

If realized P&L is consistently worse than, say, the 5th percentile of synthetic outcomes, something is off: either the model is mis-specified, or the portfolio is behaving atypically (e.g., due to slippage, unmodeled costs, or structural breaks).

Monitoring playbook triggers

Monitoring playbooks can define thresholds for:

- **Indicator levels.** For example, if crisis-conditioned 1-month VaR rises above a threshold for two consecutive days, initiate a hedging program.
- **Indicator changes.** For example, if 95%-quantile maximum drawdown over 6 months worsens by more than 5 percentage points in a week, cap gross exposure growth until a risk review is completed.
- **Scenario envelope breaches.** If realized path falls outside a given quantile band of synthetic paths (too good or too bad), require model validation or portfolio review.

Actions may be graduated. For instance:

- *Watch level:* increased monitoring, daily commentary by PMs explaining performance relative to synthetic envelope.
- *Action level:* automatic or mandated resizing of positions; hedges must be added or increased.
- *Escalation level:* portfolio temporarily barred from adding new risk; formal meeting with risk committee scheduled.

Even though the computations behind these triggers rely on high-dimensional generative models, the actions themselves are stated in simple operational language.

Periodic Governance and Model Review

Beyond daily trading, scenario-based decision frameworks must interact with the slower, governance-focused rhythm of the firm: monthly risk committee meetings, quarterly model validations, annual capital planning.

Using synthetic diagnostics in governance

At governance horizons (monthly, quarterly), synthetic diagnostics support decisions such as:

- Setting or revising risk appetite statements (e.g., acceptable ranges of synthetic drawdown and CVaR across businesses).
- Allocating risk budgets across strategies, desks, and asset classes, based on their synthetic tail profiles and regime sensitivities.
- Approving or adjusting capital allocation and leverage levels, reflecting modeled worst-case outcomes.

For example, a risk committee might review a table whose rows are business units and whose columns include:

- Synthetic 99% 10-day VaR under current regime.
- Synthetic 95%-quantile 1-year maximum drawdown under a blended regime mix.

- Losses under specified cross-asset stress scenarios.

The committee can then ask: Do these synthetic outcomes align with board-level risk appetite? If not, they can mandate structural changes: reduce leverage in some units, increase hedging in others, or revise trading mandates.

Challenging and updating the scenario engine

Governance is also the right venue to question the scenario engine itself:

- Are back-testing results (from the previous chapter) acceptable? Are VaR coverage ratios in line with expectations over the past year?
- Have there been persistent model failures in particular regimes or asset classes?
- Should new stress overlays be added, given emerging risks not present in the calibration period (e.g., geopolitical shocks, regime changes in monetary policy)?

Decisions here are meta-actions: instead of resizing the portfolio directly, the committee adjusts *how* synthetic scenarios are generated or weighted, which in turn will affect all downstream diagnostics and playbooks.

Linking Resizing, Hedging, and Deleveraging Rules to Synthetic Metrics

To make scenario-based actions concrete, it is helpful to see how resizing, hedging, and deleveraging rules can be parameterized directly by synthetic risk metrics.

Resizing as a function of projected drawdown

Suppose $D_q^{(H)}(w)$ denotes the q-quantile of maximum drawdown over horizon H (e.g., $H = 6$ months, $q = 0.95$) computed from synthetic paths for current portfolio w. A simple resizing rule could be:

$$f(D_q^{(H)}(w)) = \begin{cases} 1.0, & D_q^{(H)}(w) \leq D_1, \\ \dfrac{D_2 - D_q^{(H)}(w)}{D_2 - D_1}, & D_1 < D_q^{(H)}(w) < D_2, \\ 0.5, & D_q^{(H)}(w) \geq D_2, \end{cases}$$

and the allowed gross exposure becomes

$$\|w\|_1^{allowed} = f(D_q^{(H)}(w)) \cdot \|w\|_1^{baseline}.$$

Here D_1 and D_2 are calibrated drawdown levels where risk appetite begins to tighten and where it hits a hard floor, respectively. As synthetic drawdown projections worsen, allowed size shrinks in a predictable, pre-agreed manner.

Hedging triggered by scenario losses

Similarly, consider a set of explicit stress scenarios (e.g., parallel rate shocks, volatility spikes) that are included in the synthetic ensemble. Let $L_s^{stress}(w)$ be the loss under stress s. A hedging playbook might specify:

- If any $L_s^{stress}(w)$ exceeds a limit $L_{max,s}$, enter a standard hedge package h_s sized so that $L_s^{stress}(w + h_s)$ falls below $L_{max,s}$.
- The exact choice of h_s (e.g., index options, futures overlays, CDS) is determined by pre-agreed menus, but sizing depends on synthetic sensitivity of stress losses to hedge notional.

Because the synthetic engine can simulate the combined behavior of the portfolio and hedge instruments under stressed conditions, the effectiveness of h_s is likewise scenario-based, not just based on static risk weights.

Deleveraging based on tail probabilities

Finally, deleveraging rules can be tied to synthetic probabilities of ruin-like events. Let

$$p_{ruin}(w) = \mathbb{P}^{syn}(\text{capital drawdown} \leq -R),$$

where R is a ruin threshold (e.g., $R = 50\%$) computed over some horizon. A deleveraging playbook may require:

- $p_{ruin}(w)$ must stay below π_1 under the baseline regime and below $\pi_2 < \pi_1$ under crisis-conditioned scenarios.
- If $p_{ruin}(w)$ exceeds these thresholds, reduce leverage until the probability falls below them, as re-evaluated by the scenario engine.

This embeds a probabilistic notion of survival, derived from synthetic paths, directly into leverage decisions.

Documentation, Communication, and Auditability

A scenario-based decision framework will only be trusted if it is transparent and reproducible.

Documenting assumptions and mappings

Each playbook and decision surface should be accompanied by clear documentation:

- Definitions of all indicators used, including horizon, confidence level, and conditioning regime.
- Description of how indicators are computed from the underlying generative model (e.g., number of scenarios, stress overlays).
- Explicit formulas or tables translating indicators into actions (thresholds, fractions, timeframes).

This documentation ensures that, for example, when risk appetite or regulatory guidance changes, the firm can review and adjust the mapping consciously rather than tinkering informally with model parameters.

Logging decisions for post-mortem learning

Finally, decisions taken under the framework should be logged alongside the synthetic indicators that motivated them. For instance:

- On the date of a deleveraging action, record the values of key synthetic indicators and the triggered rules.

- When a hedge package is activated, log the stress losses before and after, as implied by the scenario engine.
- During governance reviews, link committee decisions explicitly to synthetic diagnostics presented at the time.

Over time, this creates a rich dataset for post-mortem analysis: did the playbook lead to sensible actions given what actually unfolded? Were thresholds too tight or too lax? Did certain indicators prove more informative than others?

In summary, scenario-based decision frameworks complete the chain from generative models to real-world trading behavior. Synthetic scenarios feed into risk measurement; those measurements feed into portfolio optimization; and finally, through playbooks and decision surfaces, optimization outputs and risk diagnostics feed into concrete actions. The result is a trading organization in which generative AI is not just an analytical curiosity, but a central component of disciplined, transparent, and adaptive risk-taking.

Chapter 6

Validation, Governance, and MLOps

Building a synthetic market is the easy part; proving that it's trustworthy, well-governed, and resilient under live trading conditions is where the real work begins. In this chapter we turn fragile prototypes into institutional-grade systems-linking model risk, privacy, evaluation, and MLOps into a single, auditable pipeline that risk managers and regulators can actually sign off on.

6.1 Model Risk Management and Robustness

In the earlier chapters we treated synthetic markets primarily as quantitative objects: stochastic processes that can be fit to data, sampled, and plugged into trading and risk engines. To deploy these systems inside an institution, however, you must confront a second, equally important view: synthetic markets as *models subject to governance*. Risk committees, regulators, and auditors will not ask whether the scenarios are clever; they will ask whether the models are *controlled*.

This section builds a concrete model risk management (MRM) framework tailored to generative synthetic markets. We will:

- define what "the model" is in this context—far beyond a single neural network;
- construct a model inventory that captures ownership, purpose, and lineage;
- design a validation plan that blends statistical fit with economic and trading realism;
- introduce the concept of a *stress envelope*: a clearly delimited region in which the model is formally trusted;
- specify the documentation and sign-off workflow that makes these engines acceptable to model risk and governance functions.

Throughout, the guiding principle is simple: a synthetic-market engine is safe to use only when its capabilities, limitations, and operational boundaries are explicit, tested, and monitored.

What Is "the Model" in a Synthetic Market?

Traditional MRM often pictures a model as a self-contained formula (e.g., Black–Scholes) or a calibrated risk engine (e.g., a VaR system). Synthetic markets, by contrast, are *systems of systems*. Treating only the core generator as "the model" is a category error and a common source of governance gaps.

For our purposes, a synthetic-market model comprises at least the following components:

1. **Data layer**:
   - historical prices, order books, and transaction records;
   - feature engineering logic (e.g., realized volatility windows, order-flow imbalances);
   - data filters (outlier handling, corporate-action adjustments, holiday calendars).

2. **Generative engine**:
   - the architecture (e.g., GAN, diffusion model, autoregressive transformer);
   - hyperparameters, training losses, and optimization routines;
   - conditioning interfaces (prompts or control variables for regime, asset, liquidity).
3. **Scenario post-processing**:
   - transformation of raw samples into price paths, order events, or factor shocks;
   - application of market microstructure rules (tick sizes, matching rules, circuit breakers);
   - aggregation into scenario sets used by downstream tools (risk, PnL, liquidity).
4. **Trading and risk logic**:
   - mapping from synthetic paths to orders, fills, and PnL (your backtest engine);
   - slippage, fees, and execution models layered on top of synthetic prices;
   - portfolio aggregation, risk measures, and reporting.
5. **Operational and governance wrapper**:
   - interfaces (APIs, batch jobs, notebooks) through which users request scenarios;
   - access controls, logging, and audit trails;
   - documented usage restrictions and approval records.

For MRM, the "model" is the *entire chain* from raw data to decision-making outputs. Any change in this chain—a new data vendor, a tweak to the loss function, a different backtest fill algorithm—can change the risk profile of the outputs and must therefore appear in the model inventory and validation scope.

A Layered Model Risk Stack

It is helpful to visualize the MRM structure as a set of layers, from data at the bottom up to governance at the top. Figure presents a compact representation of this stack, which we will refer back to in the remainder of the section.

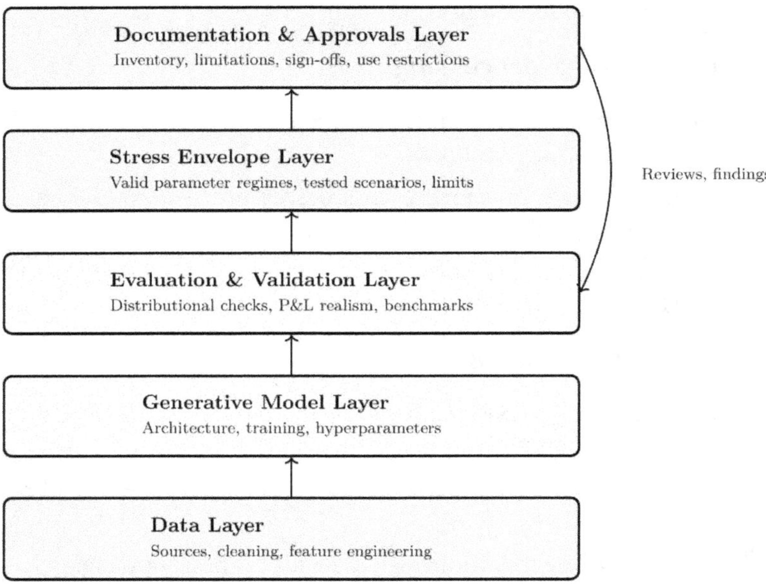

The rest of this section walks through these layers with an emphasis on practical controls that satisfy institutional model risk standards.

Model Inventory and Lineage

A *model inventory* is the central catalogue of models in use across the firm. For synthetic markets, a robust inventory entry should answer the following questions:

1. Identity and ownership. Each model instance must have:

- a unique identifier (e.g., SM-GEN-EQ-001);
- a clear owner (typically a head of quantitative research or trading desk lead);
- a designated MRM contact and a technical maintainer.

2. Purpose and scope. This includes:

- *Intended use*: e.g., "scenario generation for equity stat-arb back-testing" or "stress design for FX liquidity risk";
- *Outputs in scope*: price paths, order-flow streams, factor shocks, or order-book snapshots;
- *Users*: desks or functions allowed to consume the outputs.

3. Dependencies and interfaces. Document:

- *Upstream*: data vendors, reference data sets, model libraries;
- *Downstream*: backtest engines, risk systems, reporting dash-boards;
- how users invoke the model (batch jobs, APIs, notebooks) and expected input formats.

4. Versioning and change history. Every materially different configuration should be treated as a separate version, with:

- a semantic version number (e.g., 2.1.0: major–minor–patch);
- a concise change log (e.g., "v2.1.0: updated to 2015–2024 data, added volatility conditioning");
- links to code repositories, parameter files, and validation reports for that specific version.

A simple but effective practice is to maintain a tabular inventory (using tabularx for layout in internal documentation) that lists one row per model version and references more detailed documentation.

The inventory is not a mere formality. In most institutions, only models present in the official inventory can be used for certain classes of decisions (e.g., capital allocation, limit setting). For synthetic markets this means: if a generator is not in the inventory with an approved status, its outputs should be treated as exploratory research only.

Designing a Validation Plan

Once a model is inventoried, you must define how it will be validated. Synthetic markets require both *statistical* and *economic* tests. A model that passes one but fails the other is not fit for purpose.

A helpful mental model is to distinguish between three families of tests:

1. **Distributional alignment tests**:
    - Are the univariate and multivariate distributions of synthetic data plausibly aligned with historical data?
    - Are temporal dependencies (autocorrelation, volatility clustering) respected?
    - Are cross-asset and cross-venue relationships reproduced?
2. **Tail and stress behavior tests**:
    - Does the model generate realistic extremes, both in magnitude and frequency?
    - Can it reproduce stylized crises, at least qualitatively?
    - Does it avoid pathological artifacts such as negative prices or infinite liquidity?
3. **Trading and P&L realism tests**:
    - When strategies are run on synthetic data, is the resulting P&L distribution consistent with what we see in live or historical trading?
    - Do liquidity and market-impact assumptions remain plausible?
    - Are risk measures (drawdowns, VaR, expected shortfall) in line with empirical experience?

We elaborate on each category.

Distributional Alignment

Let X^{real} denote a vector of empirical market features (returns, spreads, volumes, etc.) and X^{syn} the corresponding vector computed from synthetic data. At minimum, you should compare:

- **Means and variances**: $\mathbb{E}[X^{real}]$ vs. $\mathbb{E}[X^{syn}]$, $\text{Var}(X^{real})$ vs. $\text{Var}(X^{syn})$;
- **Higher moments**: skewness, kurtosis, especially for returns and volumes;
- **Empirical distributions**: via quantile–quantile plots, Kolmogorov–Smirnov statistics, or Wasserstein distances between empirical CDFs;
- **Dependence**: autocorrelation functions, cross-correlation matrices, and simple copula summaries.

These tests are not about perfect equality—by design, synthetic markets may explore regimes outside the historical record. Rather, they check that *within the intended regime*, the generator does not systematically distort basic properties in ways that would mislead strategies (e.g., suppressing volatility clustering, flattening cross-asset correlations).

Tail and Stress Behavior

In finance, most risk comes from the tails. A synthetic market that matches the center of the distribution but fails in the tails is dangerous.

- **Extreme quantiles**: compare empirical quantiles (e.g., 1% and 99%) of key risk factors between real and synthetic data.
- **Block maxima/minima**: review distributions of maximum drawdowns or intraday extremes over fixed windows.
- **Scenario replay**: define a set of historical stress days (e.g., 2008-09-15, 2020-03-16) and inspect whether synthetic scenarios conditioned on similar volatility or macro states produce comparably severe moves.

- **Pathology checks**: scan synthetic paths for impossible or highly implausible events, such as sustained arbitrage loops or unrealistically persistent one-way order flow with no liquidity response.

These tests help define the boundary of the *stress envelope* introduced later: where the model has been demonstrated to behave reasonably under stress, and where it has not.

Trading and P&L Realism

Ultimately, synthetic markets are tools for trading design and risk management. Your validation must therefore look through to strategy outcomes.

Suppose S is a strategy, M the synthetic-market model, and $P(S, M)$ a mapping that runs backtests and returns P&L and risk metrics. For each candidate strategy:

- run $P(S, M)$ on synthetic scenarios;
- run the same logic $P(S, real)$ on historical data;
- compare the distributions of returns, Sharpe ratios, drawdowns, turnover, and liquidity consumption.

You are not aiming for equality of P&L paths; you are checking for obvious distortions. Red flags include:

- synthetic backtests that consistently show much higher Sharpe ratios or much smaller drawdowns than historical tests, without a clear explanation;
- liquidity-sensitive strategies that suddenly appear insensitive to volume and spreads under synthetic data;
- strategies that profit from artifacts of the generator (e.g., predictable oscillations) rather than recognizable market structure.

These tests are especially powerful when applied across a portfolio of strategies: *does the synthetic market reshape the relative attractiveness of strategies in ways that contradict live experience?*

Defining the Stress Envelope

The central conceptual tool for robust model risk management in synthetic markets is the *stress envelope*. Informally, the stress envelope is the region in which:

- the model has been trained;
- the model has been *validated*;
- the institution *accepts* its outputs as a reasonable basis for decision-making.

Outside this envelope, synthetic scenarios may still be useful for exploration, but they must carry a clear "out-of-scope" label and cannot be used for critical decisions without additional justification.

Dimensions of the Stress Envelope

The envelope typically spans several dimensions, for example:

- **Time and data coverage**: e.g., "Equity cash markets, US and Europe, 2010–2024 trading days."
- **Assets and venues**: list of ticker universes, asset classes, and trading venues included in training and testing.
- **Market regimes**: regimes defined by volatility quantiles, liquidity levels, or macro states for which explicit tests have been run.
- **Model parameters and prompts**: allowable ranges for conditioning inputs (e.g., volatility multipliers between 0.5 and 2.0, not 10.0).
- **Use cases**: which applications are approved (e.g., relative ranking of strategies, execution stress tests) and which are not (e.g., regulatory capital calculation).

Formally, you can think of the envelope as a set

$$\mathcal{E} \subseteq \mathcal{D} \times \Theta \times \mathcal{U},$$

where $\mathcal{D}$ is the space of data regimes, Θ the space of model configurations and prompts, and $\mathcal{U}$ the space of uses. Validation work provides evidence that for $(d, \theta, u) \in \mathcal{E}$, the model behavior is acceptable.

Operationalizing the Envelope

In practice, the stress envelope should be *enforced* by systems, not just documented:

- **Input validation**: APIs or user interfaces should constrain parameters to the approved ranges or flag them as experimental.
- **Metadata tagging**: each scenario set produced by the generator should be tagged with its configuration and a flag indicating "in-envelope" or "out-of-envelope" status.
- **Usage controls**: downstream systems (e.g., limit-setting tools) should reject or heavily warn on out-of-envelope scenarios.

This is where the MRM and MLOps perspectives meet: envelope boundaries are defined by validation and governance, and then enforced in production by automated checks and logs.

Sensitivity and Robustness Analysis

Defining a stress envelope also requires understanding how sensitive the model is to:

- **Data revisions**: re-run training and validation on updated data sets (e.g., adding one more year) and compare key metrics.
- **Hyperparameters**: perturb key hyperparameters (learning rates, regularization strengths, network sizes) within reasonable bounds and observe changes in validation statistics and P&L outcomes.

- **Scenario amplification:** e.g., scaling volatility or correlation to design more extreme scenarios—check whether the model extrapolates gracefully or breaks down (e.g., producing unstable paths).

Sensitivity analysis informs where the boundaries of $\mathcal{E}$ should lie: you want to stay in regions where the model's behavior is stable under small perturbations and where failures are at least predictable.

Adversarial Probing and Failure Modes

Generative models are prone to subtle failure modes. Beyond classical statistical tests, it is prudent to perform *adversarial probing*: deliberately attempting to elicit problematic behavior.

Examples include:

- **Prompt abuse** (for promptable generators): try conditioning on extreme or contradictory prompts (e.g., "zero volatility and record trading volume"), and examine whether outputs become inconsistent or pathological.
- **Exploit detection**: search for strategies that achieve suspiciously high Sharpe ratios in synthetic data but not in historical data. Often, these exploit correlations or patterns that are artifacts of the generator.
- **Mode collapse and diversity checks**: assess whether the model produces a narrow band of scenarios, missing important variations, by analyzing the dispersion of key metrics across many draws.

Each discovered failure mode should be:

- documented in the model limitations;
- associated with mitigation steps (e.g., restrict certain prompts, update architecture, or downweight certain use cases);
- used to refine the stress envelope (exclude problematic regions).

Documentation and Governance Pack

To be accepted by an institutional model committee, your synthetic-market engine needs a documentation pack that is both technically informative and accessible to non-specialist stakeholders. At minimum, this should include:

1. **Model development document.** A technical note that covers:
   - high-level objectives and intended use cases;
   - model design choices (data, architecture, loss functions, training setup);
   - key assumptions and simplifications (e.g., how you treat transaction costs or market microstructure).
2. **Validation report.** A structured report that summarises:
   - the battery of tests performed (distributional, tail, P&L realism, adversarial);
   - quantitative results (tables and charts, with commentary);
   - sensitivity analyses and robustness findings;
   - conclusions and recommendations for use, including caveats.
3. **Limitations and use restrictions.** A concise, explicit list of:
   - known weaknesses and failure modes;
   - regimes and use cases that are out of scope;
   - conditions under which the model must be revalidated (e.g., data changes, architecture updates, new asset classes).
4. **Stress envelope definition.** A dedicated section that:
   - defines the envelope dimensions and boundaries (in tables and diagrams);

- describes how envelope compliance is checked in production;
- explains how users are expected to interpret in-envelope vs. out-of-envelope results.

5. Approval and sign-off workflow. Finally, the pack should record:

- review steps (model owner, independent validator, risk committee);
- approval dates and conditions (e.g., pilot phase, restricted to certain desks);
- version-specific status (e.g., v1.0 approved, v1.1 under review).

The goal is that a knowledgeable but non-technical reader can understand what the model does, where it works, where it does not, and who is accountable for its use.

Bringing It Together: Robustness as a Governance Property

In purely mathematical terms, robustness often means stability under perturbations. In institutional practice, robustness is equally a *governance property*: a robust synthetic-market system is one for which:

- the full system—from data to decisions—is clearly defined as a model object;
- every version is captured in a living inventory with lineage and ownership;
- validation tests are systematic, reproducible, and tied to economically meaningful questions;
- the stress envelope is explicit, enforced, and refined in light of new evidence;
- limitations are acknowledged, documented, and reflected in usage restrictions;

- approvals, monitoring, and revalidation are embedded into day-to-day MLOps.

The next sections of the chapter will build on this foundation, turning these governance concepts into concrete operational machinery: evaluation harnesses, deployment pipelines, and drift monitoring that keep synthetic markets aligned with both the statistical reality of data and the institutional realities of risk management.

6.2 Data Privacy and Ethical Synthetic Data

The previous section treated synthetic markets as models that must be inventoried, validated, and governed. We now add a second, equally important lens: *ethical and privacy-aware* use of data in building those models.

In trading, the raw material for synthetic markets is often highly sensitive: client order flow, dealer quotes, and internal execution strategies. Synthetic data is sometimes marketed as a magic bullet—"just generate fake data and privacy is solved"—but reality is more subtle. Synthetic data can reduce privacy risk, yet it can also *amplify* that risk if the generator overfits or memorizes individuals.

This section explains how to balance privacy and utility when using synthetic data for trading research. We will:

- map out the main privacy risks in trading datasets;
- distinguish anonymization, pseudonymization, and synthetic generation—and clarify what each does *not* guarantee;
- introduce quantitative disclosure-risk tests, especially membership- and attribute-inference attacks against generators;
- discuss defenses, including differentially private training and structural constraints;

- propose governance patterns and ethical guidelines for the responsible use of synthetic data in trading.

The goal is to ensure that your synthetic markets are not only statistically and economically sound, but also compliant with legal obligations and aligned with the firm's ethical standards.

Privacy Risks in Trading Data

Market and order-flow datasets contain several layers of sensitive information. To reason clearly about disclosure risk, it helps to categorize the types of identifiers and linkages that can appear.

Direct Identifiers

These are fields that uniquely and explicitly identify a participant or account, such as:

- client or account identifiers;
- internal trader or desk IDs;
- legal entity identifiers or booking codes.

Direct identifiers are usually easy to spot and are often removed as a first step. However, removing them is *not* sufficient for strong privacy because many participants are still re-identifiable through their trading patterns.

Quasi-Identifiers and Behavioral Signatures

A quasi-identifier is any combination of fields that may not uniquely identify someone on its own, but becomes identifying when combined. In trading, typical examples include:

- characteristic trade sizes (e.g., a client always trades in multiples of 17,500 shares);
- venue and time-of-day patterns (e.g., a systematic 9:32–9:38 opening routine);

- product preferences (e.g., always trading short-dated single-stock options in a narrow sector band);
- liquidity usage patterns (e.g., consistently posting at the same depth or using specific dark pools).

Such patterns can act as a "behavioral fingerprint." Even after stripping direct identifiers, it may be possible to relink an anonymized dataset to external information, or to infer proprietary strategies from these patterns.

Linkage and Inference Risks

Beyond direct re-identification, two broad classes of inference risk matter in quantitative trading:

- **Counterparty privacy risk:** An external analyst could infer sensitive information about a particular client or trader from the data (e.g., that a hedge fund is systematically long a sector, or that a client is in distress).
- **Strategy confidentiality risk:** An external analyst or even an internal user in another desk could reconstruct your execution algorithms, alpha signals, or routing strategies from synthetic or anonymized order flow.

These risks exist whether you share the data outside the firm or simply within a large internal community. Synthetic data does not automatically neutralize them; instead, it shifts the question to: *how well does the generator hide or blur individual patterns while preserving the statistics your models need?*

Anonymization, Pseudonymization, and Synthetic Generation

To understand what synthetic data can and cannot do, we must distinguish three basic approaches.

Anonymization

Anonymization aims to transform data so that individuals are no longer identifiable, even when the data is released publicly and can be linked with external information. Typical techniques include:

- removing direct identifiers;
- aggregating data (e.g., daily volumes instead of individual trades);
- coarsening values (e.g., binning order sizes);
- adding limited noise.

True anonymization is very difficult with high-dimensional trading data, because many seemingly innocuous combinations of features can be unique. For example, the pattern "trades AAPL each Monday at 10:01 on venue X for roughly 50,000 shares" might uniquely describe a single participant.

Pseudonymization

Pseudonymization replaces direct identifiers with consistent but meaningless tokens; for example, mapping each client ID to a random hash.

This preserves linkages within the dataset (you can still track a given pseudonymous client over time), which is valuable for modeling behavior, but it does *not* prevent re-identification if an attacker has auxiliary knowledge about that client's trading pattern. Pseudonymization is mainly a data-management tool; by itself, it is not a strong privacy guarantee.

Synthetic Generation

Synthetic data is generated by a model trained on real data, with the hope that:

- the overall statistical structure (distributions, dependencies, regimes) is preserved;
- individual records and their precise trajectories are not copied or reconstructable.

If the generator does not memorize the training data and produces sufficiently diverse samples, then synthetic data can significantly reduce disclosure risk, because there is no one-to-one mapping between synthetic records and real clients.

However, this is a *hope*, not a certainty. Overparameterized generative models can memorize rare or influential training examples, especially in small or skewed datasets, and can leak them through their outputs. That is why we need explicit, quantitative privacy tests.

Balancing Privacy and Utility

There is an inherent trade-off between privacy protection and utility. Intuitively, the more aggressively you distort or obscure individual behavior, the harder it becomes to fit high-fidelity models or to stress-test execution strategies.

For example:

- Coarsening order sizes protects against re-identifying clients with distinctive size patterns, but may make it impossible to accurately simulate limit-order book depth or market impact.
- Enforcing strict k-anonymity constraints on combinations of quasi-identifiers can remove rare but important regimes, such as crisis liquidity events that occurred only a few times.
- Highly noisy or strongly differentially private training may blur tail dependencies that matter for stress testing.

The core principle is to manage this trade-off *explicitly and quantitatively*. Instead of assuming that "more privacy is always better," you should:

- define concrete privacy threat models (what are we afraid of?);
- measure disclosure risk against those threats for a given generator;
- measure utility using the same metrics and strategies you care about for synthetic markets (distributional alignment, P&L realism, etc.);

- search for configurations (model architecture, noise levels, constraints) that deliver acceptable risk at acceptable utility.

The next subsections address the first two steps in more detail.

Threat Models: Membership and Attribute Inference

In recent years, two families of attacks have become standard in privacy evaluations of machine learning models: *membership inference* and *attribute inference*. Both can be adapted to synthetic-market generators.

Membership Inference Attacks

A membership inference attack aims to answer the question:

> Given a record x and black-box access to a trained generator G, can an attacker determine whether x was part of the training dataset?

If the answer can be determined with accuracy significantly above random guessing, the model is leaking information about the training set.

In a trading context, x might represent:

- a specific sequence of orders from a client over a day;
- a characteristic execution trajectory (child orders, venues, timing);
- a trajectory of quotes from a market maker.

A simple membership test could proceed as follows:

- For each candidate record x, condition the generator (if applicable) on the same context (e.g., date, asset, volatility regime) and sample many synthetic records.

- Compute a similarity score between x and each synthetic sample, using a distance function over sequences (e.g., dynamic time warping, event-based metrics).
- Aggregate these similarities into a statistic $s(x; G)$, such as the minimum or average distance to generated samples.
- Compare the distribution of $s(x; G)$ for records that were in training vs. held-out records. If the in-training records consistently appear "closer" to the generator, then membership is inferable.

The *membership advantage* can be measured as the difference between the attacker's accuracy and random guessing (50% in a balanced test). A well-behaved synthetic generator should have membership advantage close to zero under plausible attacks.

Attribute Inference Attacks

Attribute inference focuses not on "was x in training?" but on "what can I infer about some sensitive attribute a given access to G and partial information about x?"

For example:

- given partial order-flow history for a client, can an attacker infer whether that client belongs to a certain segment (e.g., HFT vs. long-only);
- given a position snapshot, can the attacker infer whether the client has a concentrated risk in a particular sector;
- given pre-trade attributes of an order, can the attacker infer whether it is part of a large parent order.

To test for this risk, you can:

- Train a *shadow model* that tries to infer a from synthetic samples generated by G.
- Evaluate that model on real data. If its performance is close to what would be achievable with full access to the real training data, then G leaks substantial information about a.

Both membership and attribute inference tests can be automated as part of the validation harness for your synthetic-market models (see later chapter sections), and their results can be included in the model's documentation and approval pack.

Defenses and Design Choices

Once you can measure disclosure risk, you can meaningfully evaluate mitigation strategies. We highlight three broad classes of defenses and discuss their implications for trading research.

Differentially Private Training

Differential privacy (DP) provides a mathematically rigorous framework for limiting the influence of any single training record on the learned model. In its standard form, a learning algorithm is (ε, δ)-differentially private if, for any two training datasets that differ in one record, the distribution of outputs (e.g., learned parameters or generated samples) changes only slightly, controlled by (ε, δ).

In practice, DP training for generative models usually involves:

- clipping per-sample gradients to limit sensitivity;
- adding calibrated noise to gradients during optimization.

Pros.

- Provides a strong, general guarantee against both membership and many attribute inference attacks.
- Delivers a tunable privacy budget (ε, δ) that can be aligned with legal or policy requirements.

Cons.

- Introduces additional noise into the model, which can degrade fidelity, especially in tails and rare regimes.
- Requires careful hyperparameter tuning and sufficient data volume; small, thin, or highly skewed datasets may suffer substantial utility loss.

For synthetic markets, DP is most attractive when used on large, relatively homogeneous datasets (e.g., high-frequency quotes for liquid futures) where noise averages out, and less attractive for niche, data-scarce products where each record carries a lot of information.

k-Anonymity-Inspired Constraints and Coarsening

Another family of defenses comes from the k-anonymity tradition: ensuring that no individual record is uniquely identifiable within the dataset, even after transformations.

For synthetic data, you can implement analogous ideas by:

- enforcing that certain combinations of quasi-identifiers (e.g., trade size bucket, venue, time-of-day bin) are sufficiently common in the training set;
- excluding rare patterns below some frequency threshold from the training dataset, or deliberately coarsening them;
- adjusting the generator or post-processing to smooth out extremely distinctive behavior.

Pros.

- Conceptually simple; easier to explain to non-technical stakeholders than DP.
- Directly targets linkage risks associated with rare behavior.

Cons.

- Rare events often matter most for trading risk. Excluding or heavily coarsening them can undermine stress-testing utility.
- Lacks a universal, formal guarantee; k-anonymity-like conditions can be broken under richer attack models.

In practice, you might apply these techniques only to the most sensitive quasi-identifiers (e.g., client segments) while leaving market-wide quantities (prices, volumes, spreads) more granular.

Post-Processing Filters and Access Controls

Even if the generator itself is trained without explicit privacy constraints, you can reduce disclosure risk by controlling *how* synthetic data is released and used:

- **Scenario aggregation:** Provide only aggregated statistics or scenario-based stress tests (e.g., factor shocks) rather than raw, tick-level synthetic order flow.
- **Sampling limits:** Restrict the number and granularity of synthetic samples that any one user can obtain for a given configuration, reducing the ability to probe the model.
- **Template-based outputs:** Offer high-level synthetic scenarios through templated interfaces (e.g., "generate 1,000 crisis-like equity paths") rather than low-level API access to arbitrary sampling.

These measures resemble rate limiting and abstraction in software security: they limit the attack surface without fundamentally changing the underlying model.

Governance Patterns for Responsible Use

Technical defenses are necessary but not sufficient. An institution needs *governance* around who can create, access, and act on synthetic data. This governance should be explicit, documented, and integrated with the broader model risk framework.

Data Access Tiers

A practical approach is to define tiers of data access, each with different privacy guarantees and allowed uses. For example:

- **Tier 0: Raw sensitive data.** Full order- and client-level records, accessible only to a small, vetted group (e.g., core quant research, data engineering), under strict audit and with clear legal basis.

- **Tier 1: Protected analytical data.** Pseudonymized and partially aggregated data used for core model development and calibration. Internal access only, under non-disclosure obligations.
- **Tier 2: Synthetic research data.** Outputs of vetted synthetic generators, with documented privacy tests and limitations. Suitable for wider internal research use (e.g., across desks) and some vendor collaborations under contract.
- **Tier 3: Public or near-public data.** Aggregated or fully anonymized statistics or scenarios with negligible disclosure risk, possibly shareable outside the firm (e.g., in academic collaborations).

Synthetic data used for trading research will typically live in Tier 2. The generator that produces it should itself be a governed model, with MRM sign-off, and subject to periodic revalidation on both utility and privacy metrics.

Purpose Limitation and Consent

Regulatory and ethical norms increasingly emphasize *purpose limitation*: using data only for the purposes for which it was collected or reasonably expected.

For synthetic trading data, this may imply:

- restricting certain client flows (e.g., from sensitive mandates) from being used even for synthetic generation, unless explicit consent and contractual terms allow it;
- using different generators or configurations for internal strategy development vs. external sharing with vendors or academic partners;
- documenting in the model development notes which sources of data feed which synthetic engines, and under what legal basis.

Consent and contractual terms are legal topics beyond the scope of this book, but as a model developer you should be aware that not all data you can technically access is appropriate to use for synthetic models.

Retention, Deletion, and Audit Trails

Good governance also addresses *time*. Key questions include:

- How long will raw training data be retained? Are there policies for automatic deletion or archiving?
- If a client exercises a right to erasure (where applicable), do you have a process to:
  - remove their records from raw datasets;
  - assess whether any deployed synthetic generators must be retrained to honor the request?
- Are accesses to synthetic datasets logged, including who generated which scenarios under which configuration?

Incorporating synthetic generators into the broader data-retention and audit framework ensures that privacy commitments made at the contractual or regulatory level are operationally enforceable.

Ethical Guidelines for Synthetic Data in Trading

Beyond compliance and technical defenses lies a broader ethical question: *what is the right way to use synthetic data in trading research?* A few guiding principles are particularly relevant:

- **Respect client intent.** If clients provided data to execute trades, not to train speculative AI models, be cautious about using their flows for ambitious synthetic engines, even if contracts allow it. At minimum, ensure that such use genuinely benefits clients (e.g., better execution quality) and not only proprietary trading.
- **Do not disguise risk as safety.** Synthetic data can create an illusion of safety: "it's fake, so we can share it widely." Avoid using synthetic labels as a shortcut to bypass internal controls. If a synthetic generator has not passed rigorous privacy tests and governance, treat its outputs as potentially sensitive.

- **Avoid unfair profiling.** Synthetic data can be used to build profiles of counterparty behavior that go beyond legitimate trading and risk-management needs. Consider whether such uses are aligned with your firm's code of conduct and with market fairness principles.
- **Be transparent internally.** Traders and quants relying on synthetic data should understand its origin, limitations, and privacy safeguards. Transparency builds trust and encourages responsible use.

These principles will not answer every hard case, but they set a tone: synthetic data is a powerful tool that must be wielded with care, not a loophole to escape ethical scrutiny.

Synthetic markets promise a way to explore rich trading scenarios without exposing raw, sensitive data. Realizing that promise requires more than technical ingenuity. It requires:

- a clear understanding of privacy risks in trading datasets, including quasi-identifiers and behavioral fingerprints;
- a realistic view of what anonymization, pseudonymization, and synthetic generation can and cannot guarantee;
- quantitative disclosure-risk tests, especially membership- and attribute-inference attacks, as part of the validation harness;
- carefully chosen defenses—differentially private training, structural constraints, post-processing, and access controls—tuned to the privacy–utility trade-off relevant for your use cases;
- governance patterns (access tiers, purpose limitation, retention policies, audit trails) that make synthetic data a first-class citizen in the firm's risk and compliance framework;
- explicit ethical guidelines to keep the use of synthetic data aligned with client expectations and market integrity.

In the next section we will connect these privacy and governance concepts to the operational machinery of MLOps: how evaluation harnesses, deployment pipelines, and drift monitoring can continuously enforce both model validity and privacy constraints as synthetic-market systems evolve over time.

6.3 Evaluation Harness, Deployment, and Drift Monitoring

The previous sections established what a synthetic-market model *is* as an object of governance, and how to use it responsibly from a privacy and ethics standpoint. We now turn to the operational question: *how do you keep such a model reliable once it is in continuous use by quants and traders?*

In practice, this means building an MLOps pipeline around the synthetic-market engine. The pipeline must:

- provide a reproducible *evaluation harness*—a suite of tests that can be run on demand or on schedule;
- support robust *deployment* patterns (batch and online) that integrate with trading and risk systems;
- monitor the system for *drift*—in data, in model behavior, and in governance status—and trigger incident response when necessary.

An End-to-End MLOps View

Before diving into details, it is helpful to visualize the full lifecycle of a synthetic-market model in production, from raw data to monitored service. Figure provides a high-level pipeline view.

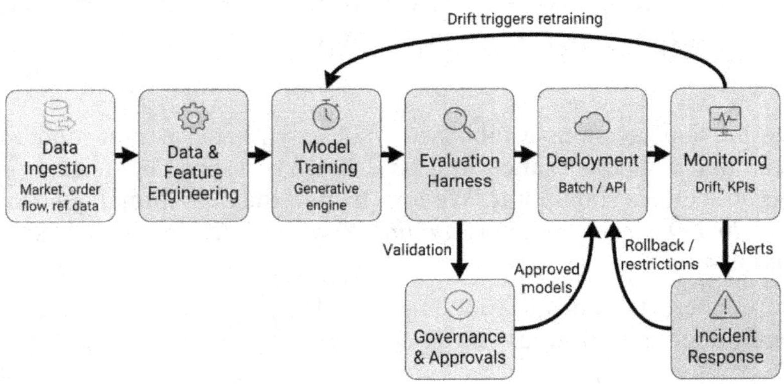

This diagram highlights three messages:

- Evaluation is not a one-off event before go-live; it is embedded in the lifecycle.
- Deployment is not the end; continuous monitoring feeds back to retraining and governance.
- Governance (approvals, usage restrictions) and incident response are first-class components of the pipeline.

We now develop each part in more detail, starting with the evaluation harness.

The Evaluation Harness: Tests as Code

In the model risk section, we described *what* to test: distributional alignment, tail behavior, P&L realism, and privacy leakage. An evaluation harness is the *implementation* of those ideas as a reproducible suite of tests.

Principles of a Good Evaluation Harness

A production-ready harness should satisfy four properties:

- **Comprehensive.** It covers the key dimensions of validity for synthetic markets:
  - statistical goodness-of-fit to historical data;
  - economic and trading realism (P&L, liquidity, execution);
  - privacy and disclosure risk (where data is sensitive);
  - computational performance and capacity usage.
- **Automated.** Tests can be run with minimal manual intervention, triggered by version changes (code, hyperparameters, data) or on a schedule.
- **Versioned.** Each test run is tied to specific versions of:
  - the data snapshot used for training and evaluation;
  - the model artefacts (weights, hyperparameters, prompts);
  - the test configuration itself (metrics, thresholds).
- **Explainable.** Outputs are not just pass/fail flags; they include plots, tables, and narrative summaries that can be understood by reviewers.

Structuring the Test Suite

A practical way to organize the harness is to define a layered structure analogous to unit, integration, and system tests in software engineering:

- **Unit-like tests:** quick checks on individual components:

- data sanity checks (missing values, extreme outliers);
- basic statistics of synthetic vs. real returns or volumes;
- validation of constraints (e.g., no negative prices).

- **Integration-like tests:** end-to-end checks of the synthetic market interacting with simplified trading logic:
  - run benchmark strategies on both historical and synthetic data;
  - compare distributions of returns, turnover, and liquidity usage;
  - evaluate path-dependent risk metrics (drawdowns, VaR, ES).

- **System-level tests:** full-scale experiments:
  - large scenario sets covering multiple regimes and assets;
  - stress scenarios combining synthetic generation with risk engines;
  - privacy and drift stress tests run on representative workloads.

In an institutional setting, these tests are usually encoded as:

- parameterized notebooks for exploratory runs and documentation;
- CI/CD jobs (e.g., `pytest`-style test suites) for regressions;
- orchestrated pipelines (e.g., in Airflow, Prefect, or similar tools) for scheduled full validations.

The key is that the harness itself is treated as a maintained codebase: version-controlled, reviewed, and improved over time.

Metrics and Thresholds

Each test must produce measurable outputs and, for many, *decision thresholds*. For example:

- The Kolmogorov–Smirnov distance between real and synthetic one-day returns must be below a threshold d_{max} for major assets.
- For a benchmark execution strategy, the ratio of synthetic to historical estimated impact must lie within a band, say $[0.7, 1.3]$.
- Membership-inference attack accuracy must not exceed a specified bound (e.g., 55%) under a defined threat model.
- Scenario generation must complete within a wall-clock time budget for given asset universes and horizons.

Some thresholds may be *soft*: exceeding them triggers human review rather than automatic rejection. Others are *hard*: violations block deployment until resolved.

A useful design pattern is to define a small number of summary badges for each model version:

- VALIDATION_STATUS ∈ {PASS, WARN, FAIL};
- PRIVACY_STATUS ∈ {OK, REVIEW, BLOCKED};
- PERF_STATUS ∈ {OK, SLOW}.

These badges feed into governance dashboards and deployment gates.

Deployment Patterns for Synthetic Markets

Once a model version passes evaluation and receives governance approval, it must be deployed so that users can generate and consume scenarios. Synthetic-market systems typically support at least two deployment patterns: *batch* and *on-demand*.

Batch Scenario Generation

In batch mode, the system runs scheduled jobs that generate large sets of synthetic scenarios, which are then stored for later use. Typical use cases include:

- overnight generation of next-day stress scenarios for risk reports;

- periodic creation of scenario libraries for backtesting strategies;
- regulatory stress-test preparation.

Key design choices:

- **Scheduling.** Jobs may run daily, weekly, or around major events (earnings seasons, macro releases). Schedules should align with trading and risk calendars.
- **Configuration.** Each batch run should be driven by a configuration file or database entry specifying:
  - model version and hyperparameters;
  - data cut and conditioning (e.g., regime labels);
  - scenario count, horizon, and assets.
- **Output format.** Scenarios should be stored in a standardized format (e.g., Parquet files with metadata) and registered in a scenario catalogue with tags (regime, asset class, generation date, envelope status).

Batch jobs are usually orchestrated by a workflow manager. Failures (e.g., due to data issues or performance bottlenecks) must be logged and alerted, and partial results handled carefully to avoid silent use of incomplete scenario sets.

On-Demand APIs

On-demand or interactive usage is common when traders and quants want to explore "what-if" questions, such as:

> "What happens to my strategy if volatility doubles in this sector for the next two weeks?"

Here the model is exposed via APIs or services that accept requests with parameters (model version, conditioning prompts, assets, horizon) and return generated paths or aggregated scenario statistics.

Important operational considerations:

- **Latency and throughput.** Response times must be compatible with interactive workflows (seconds to minutes, not hours) for intended use cases.

- **Resource management.** Large generative models can be computationally heavy. You may need:
  - separate clusters or priority queues for production vs. experimental requests;
  - autoscaling policies to handle load spikes;
  - limits on scenario counts per request.

- **Access control and envelopes.** APIs should:
  - enforce allowed parameter ranges based on the stress envelope;
  - tag outputs as in- or out-of-envelope;
  - restrict certain advanced options (e.g., extreme volatility multipliers) to expert users.

For both batch and on-demand modes, every call should be logged with user identity, configuration, and output metadata. These logs are essential for audits, incident response, and governance drift monitoring.

Hybrid Flows with Risk and Pricing Engines

In many institutions, synthetic generation is not an endpoint but a stage in a larger pipeline that includes:

- risk engines (VaR, stress testing, capital allocation);
- pricing engines (derivatives pricing under alternative paths);
- backtesting and optimization suites.

A typical hybrid pipeline might be:

- Generate synthetic factor or price paths under specified stress conditions.

- Feed these paths into the existing risk engine to compute portfolio losses and capital metrics.
- Aggregate results and surface them in dashboards or reports.

From an MLOps perspective, you must ensure that:

- the interfaces between synthetic generators and downstream engines are standardized and versioned;
- downstream systems are envelope-aware and can log which scenarios and model versions were used;
- failures at any stage trigger appropriate alerts and, where necessary, fall back to previous model versions or conservative assumptions.

Monitoring and Drift: Data, Concept, and Governance

Deploying a synthetic-market model is not the end of the story. Live markets evolve; users change how they interact with the system; new regulations and governance norms emerge. Monitoring must track not only standard ML notions of *data* and *concept* drift, but also *governance drift*.

Data Drift

Data drift occurs when the distribution of incoming data (e.g., fresh market prices, order flow) deviates from the training data used for the model.

To monitor data drift, you can:

- maintain rolling windows of recent real data and compare summary statistics to the training snapshot:
  - mean and volatility of returns;
  - spreads, depth, and realized impact for standard trade sizes;
  - order-type and venue mix.

- use distance measures (e.g., population stability index, Wasserstein distance) between feature distributions in recent data and training data;
- track the frequency of "novel" events, such as:
  - new venues becoming dominant;
  - significant changes in tick-size regimes or auction patterns.

Thresholds for these metrics can trigger:

- alerts for human review;
- recommendations for retraining or re-weighting recent data in the generator;
- temporary tightening of the stress envelope (e.g., marking certain asset regimes as out-of-envelope until retraining).

Concept Drift and Model Performance

Concept drift refers to changes in the underlying relationships the model tries to capture. For synthetic markets, signs of concept drift include:

- systematic divergence between synthetic and real market behavior, even within the nominal envelope;
- degradation of trading P&L realism when strategies are re-evaluated with mixed real and synthetic data;
- emergence of new patterns in live data that are absent or underrepresented in synthetic outputs (e.g., new microstructure norms or regulatory changes).

Operationally, you can monitor concept drift by:

- rerunning a subset of evaluation harness tests on a regular schedule (e.g., weekly) using:
  - the same model version;

  - updated real data slices from the recent past.
- comparing key evaluation metrics over time (time series of fit statistics, P&L realism measures);
- tracking the frequency of user-reported anomalies (e.g., traders flagging unrealistic synthetic scenarios).

When drift is detected, playbooks should specify:

- under what conditions retraining is triggered;
- whether retraining is done incrementally (update with new data) or via full rebuild with revised architectures or conditioning variables;
- how retrained versions pass back through the evaluation harness and governance approval before replacing the production model.

Governance Drift

Governance drift arises when there is a gap between the *intended*, approved use of the model and the *actual* usage observed in practice. Examples:

- users invoking the model with parameters outside the validated stress envelope, perhaps via undocumented API endpoints;
- synthetic scenarios originally intended for internal backtesting being reused for external vendor engagement without fresh privacy review;
- desk-level tools building dependencies on experimental model versions that have not been through full validation.

To monitor governance drift, you should:

- log all calls to the synthetic generator with:
  - user identity or application;
  - model version and configuration;

    - envelope status (in/out-of-scope);
    - intended use tag (research, risk, production trading decision support).
- periodically analyze logs to compute governance KPIs, such as:
    - fraction of calls outside the envelope;
    - number of distinct users or systems calling experimental models;
    - frequency of overrides to validation or privacy warnings.
- surface these KPIs on dashboards for model owners, risk managers, and compliance.

Governance drift metrics close the loop between MRM policy and day-to-day behavior: if usage patterns diverge from what the risk committee approved, you have objective evidence and a basis for corrective action.

Incident Response and Rollback Strategies

No matter how careful the design, incidents will occur: a bug in the generator, a previously unseen market regime, a misconfigured access control. The MLOps pipeline must therefore include clear, tested incident-response procedures.

What Counts as an Incident?

Examples of incidents include:

- generation of obviously invalid scenarios (e.g., negative prices, liquidity far above any historical precedent) that were not caught by pre-deployment tests;
- discovery of severe privacy leakage (e.g., a membership-inference attack with very high accuracy);
- evidence that synthetic-based risk analyses severely underestimated losses in a live event;

- regulatory or internal-audit findings that challenge the approved use of the model.

Institutions should define severity levels (e.g., critical, major, minor) with associated response requirements and timelines.

Core Elements of an Incident Runbook

An effective incident runbook for synthetic markets typically includes:

- **Detection.** How incidents are reported:
  - automated alerts from drift and validation monitors;
  - user reports via dedicated channels (e.g., a "model-issue" ticket type);
  - external triggers (regulatory or audit findings).
- **Immediate containment.** Short-term steps to prevent further impact, which may include:
  - disabling certain API endpoints or configurations;
  - reverting to a previous, known-good model version;
  - marking all recent synthetic scenario outputs as "under review" in downstream systems.
- **Analysis.** Root-cause analysis by a small team comprising:
  - model developers;
  - model risk and governance representatives;
  - where relevant, data privacy or legal experts.
- **Remediation.** Actions to fix or mitigate the issue:
  - model changes, retraining, or reparameterization;
  - tightening of the stress envelope or use restrictions;
  - updates to the evaluation harness to catch similar issues earlier.
- **Communication and documentation.** Clear records of:
  - what happened, how it was detected, and how it was fixed;

- which trades or decisions may have been affected;
- any notifications to regulators or clients, where required.

These steps are not unique to synthetic markets, but the presence of powerful generative components and tight coupling to trading decisions makes speed and transparency particularly important.

Bringing It All Together

A synthetic-market engine that is validated and ethically designed but poorly operated is still a model risk. Conversely, robust MLOps can amplify the benefits of a well-designed engine by:

- making validation repeatable and scalable through an evaluation harness;
- enabling safe, flexible deployment modes that match research and production needs;
- continuously monitoring for data, concept, and governance drift;
- providing clear incident-response mechanisms and rollback paths.

The common thread across the chapter is that model quality, privacy, governance, and operations are not separate concerns. For synthetic markets to be credible tools for stress-testing trading strategies, they must live inside an integrated framework where:

- risk committees can see evidence that models remain fit for purpose;
- developers can iterate quickly without compromising control;
- traders and quants can trust that the scenarios they use are traceable, appropriately stressed, and compliant with internal and external expectations.

With this operational backbone in place, synthetic markets become not just a clever modeling trick, but a disciplined infrastructure for exploring the space of possible futures in a controlled, auditable, and resilient way.

Chapter 7

Case Studies and Applications

In this chapter we leave theory behind and sit on the trading desk. We will replay real strategies inside synthetic markets-first an intraday equities strategy battling vanishing liquidity, then an options portfolio caught in a volatility shock-and watch what breaks, what survives, and what has to change. The goal is not to show off models, but to show how generative AI can surface risks your backtests never saw, and turn those insights into concrete adjustments to signals, sizing, execution, and governance.

7.1 Equities LOB Strategy under Liquidity Stress

In previous chapters we have treated the synthetic market as a general concept: a controllable environment that lets us ask "what if" questions about trading strategies under regimes that may be rare or absent in historical data. We now make this concrete with a case study: an intraday equity strategy executed inside a synthetic limit order book (LOB), subjected to adversarial liquidity conditions.

The goal of this section is twofold:

- To show, step by step, how to deploy a realistic intraday equity alpha into a generative LOB simulator.
- To illustrate how adversarial order-flow scenarios translate into actionable changes in execution rules and risk limits.

Throughout, we will keep the financial intuition explicit. We will move gradually from the trading idea, to the simulator, to the stress scenarios, and finally to what changes in the production strategy once we have seen the synthetic stresses.

From Intraday Alpha to Executable Strategy

Consider a mid- to large-cap equity universe with continuous trading on a primary exchange and several off-exchange venues. Our research team has developed a short-horizon intraday alpha that predicts the next 1–5 minutes of returns for each stock. The signal is built from three broad feature families:

- **Event features:** order-book imbalance just before and after auctions, opening/closing rotations, and scheduled news events.
- **Microstructure features:** short-term order flow imbalance, recent cancellations vs. trades, spread changes, and quote volatility.
- **Short-horizon technicals:** moving averages of midprice, realized volatility, and simple reversal/momentum indicators at 30-second to 5-minute scales.

The model outputs a predicted excess return $\hat{r}_{i,t}$ for stock i over the next horizon. On top of this, we apply a simple portfolio construction rule:

- Rank stocks by $\hat{r}_{i,t}$ within a universe (e.g. the S&P 500).
- Allocate gross exposure up to a fixed notional budget, with a symmetric long/short book.

- Impose single-name and sector concentration caps.
- Enforce an inventory constraint: intraday net position per stock is bounded to a multiple of its expected daily dollar volume.

In a traditional backtest, one might simply execute all desired trades at mid plus some simple slippage model. In a synthetic LOB market, we resist this temptation. Execution is not a side detail; it is where much of the strategy's risk lives.

Execution Logic: From Signals to Child Orders

The execution layer operates a standard "parent–child" order framework:

- A *parent order* is the target position change derived from the alpha signal and portfolio constraints.
- This parent is translated into a schedule of *child orders* that are actually sent to the LOB, spread over time and venues.

We specify the baseline execution policy as follows:

- **Participation caps:** We limit our trading rate to at most ρ percent of the observed market volume in each stock over rolling windows (e.g. 5–15 minutes).
- **Passive vs. aggressive mix:** When the signal is strong and liquidity appears abundant, we use a higher fraction of passive limit orders at the best bid/ask or slightly within the spread. When we are behind schedule or liquidity is thin, we allow more aggressive marketable orders.
- **Child order slicing:** Parent orders are sliced into child orders with fixed maximum size, constrained by current depth-at-touch (volume available at the best bid or ask).

In code terms (omitting implementation detail), the mapping from target position $\Delta q_{i,t}$ to child orders $\{o_{i,t,k}\}$ resembles:

$$
\begin{aligned}
\text{schedule\_horizon} &\leftarrow \min(T_{max}, T_{signal}) \\
\text{child\_size} &\leftarrow \min(\text{max\_clip}, f(\text{depth\_at\_touch})) \\
\text{num\_children} &\approx \left\lceil \frac{|\Delta q_{i,t}|}{\text{child\_size}} \right\rceil \\
o_{i,t,k} &\in \{\text{passive limit at best, passive inside, marketable}\}
\end{aligned}
$$

where $f(\cdot)$ scales child size with current depth.

In the rest of the section we treat this execution policy as a design object to be tested and modified using synthetic liquidity stress.

Limit Order Book Simulator and Generative Order Flow

To stress-test this strategy, we embed it into a limit order book simulator calibrated to historical data. Conceptually, the simulator has three layers:

- **Structural mechanics:** the matching engine implements continuous double-auction rules: limit orders, market orders, cancellations, time priority, and price-time queueing.
- **Statistical calibration:** typical arrival rates of orders, cancellations, and trades at different price levels and times of day, estimated from historical message data.
- **Generative perturbations:** a generative model that can produce order flow both in-sample-like and deliberately adversarial, controlling liquidity states as explicit variables.

Calibrating Depth and Queue Dynamics

We start by summarizing, for each stock and time-of-day bucket:

- Average and distribution of *depth-at-touch*, i.e. total standing volume at best bid and best ask.

- Typical shape of the first few levels of the book (volume as a function of distance from midprice).
- Arrival intensities of limit orders, market orders, and cancellations at each level.

These are modeled using simple stochastic processes. For example, we may use Poisson or Hawkes processes with time-of-day varying intensities for order arrivals, and parametric or non-parametric distributions for order sizes. The key point is not the exact choice of model, but that it reproduces the typical intraday evolution of spread and depth that the strategy would face in reality.

Generative Order-Flow Model

On top of this calibration, we introduce a generative model that treats *liquidity state* as a latent or explicit variable. Intuitively, we want the model to:

- Produce realistic order flow most of the time.
- Allow us to steer the system into "bad" but plausible states: dry liquidity, toxic flow, fragmented depth across venues.

One convenient abstraction is to introduce a discrete state variable $L_t \in \{\text{normal}, \text{stressed}\}$ and have the generative model condition order-flow parameters on L_t. In the stressed state, we reduce standing depth, increase cancellation rates, and tilt the probabilities so that trades against our orders are more informative (more likely to be followed by adverse price moves).

In practice, L_t can be driven by a separate process—for example, a Markov chain triggered by specific events (e.g. a synthetic macro announcement) or by the strategy's own activity (creating *endogenous* stress when we trade too aggressively).

Designing Adversarial Liquidity Scenarios

With the LOB simulator in place, we design a set of stress scenarios to expose the fragility of our execution rules. Each scenario is implemented as a controlled path of liquidity states L_t and order-flow parameters.

We focus on three families of stress:

Endogenous Liquidity Dry-Ups

In an endogenous dry-up, the market appears normal at the open. Depth-at-touch and spread follow their calibrated intraday profiles. As our strategy begins to execute, we gradually:

- Reduce depth-at-touch in the direction of our trading (e.g. when we buy, offer depth thins).
- Increase the cancellation rate of resting orders just ahead of our queue position.
- Slow down the replenishment of the top-of-book after trades.

Intuitively, the market becomes less willing to absorb our flow. This tests how our participation caps and reliance on passive orders behave when liquidity vanishes *because of* our presence.

Hidden Toxicity Spikes

A *toxic* period is one where the counterparties who trade with us tend to be informed; trades we execute are followed by adverse price moves. In the simulator, we create this by conditioning the midprice dynamics on our executed trades:

- During toxicity spikes, aggressive orders we send are more likely to be followed by immediate price reversion (we "buy the high, sell the low").
- Passive orders that get filled during such periods are assumed to have been picked off by informed flow—the price moves against us shortly after the fill.

This scenario probes our tendency to "lean on the book" (placing passive orders heavily at the touch) and our rules for switching between passive and aggressive execution when fills appear cheap but are actually information-laden.

Cross-Venue Fragmentation Shocks

Finally, we simulate a fragmentation shock: liquidity splits across multiple venues, some of which our baseline strategy does not access or monitors only coarsely. Depth-at-touch on our primary venue thins, while total market depth (across all venues) is closer to normal.

To instantiate this, we:

- Create venue-specific LOBs with correlated but distinct depth dynamics.
- Restrict the strategy to trading on a subset of venues.
- Allow large child orders to move prices more aggressively on the venues we do use.

This scenario stresses our assumptions about "available" liquidity: naive depth measures from a single venue may overstate how much we can trade without moving the market.

Measuring Slippage, Fill Risk, and Drawdowns

For each synthetic trading day and scenario, we track a small but informative set of metrics:

- **Slippage:** The difference between the realized execution price and a reference price (midquote at order submission or a short-horizon VWAP). We consider both instantaneous slippage and cumulative intraday slippage.
- **Realized spread:** For passive orders, the difference between the execution price and the midprice a short time after the trade; this captures adverse selection.

- **Queue position risk:** The probability that a passive order of given size at a given queue position fills within a time window. High queue risk means relying on passive fills is dangerous because we may not get filled before the price moves away.
- **Short-term drawdowns:** The distribution of peak-to-trough P&L over rolling windows (e.g. 15, 30, 60 minutes) within the day, rather than only end-of-day P&L.

We run two sets of synthetic experiments:

- **Baseline:** LOB dynamics drawn from the calibrated "typical" regime.
- **Stressed:** LOB dynamics replaced or interspersed with the adversarial scenarios just described, with the same alpha signals and portfolio targets.

The comparison between these two is what matters; it quantifies *fragility* of performance to liquidity conditions.

Impact of Stress Scenarios on Execution and P&L

When we overlay our strategy on the synthetic stressed markets, several patterns emerge:

- **Slippage spikes in clustered intervals:** Under endogenous dry-ups and toxicity spikes, average slippage remains modest for most of the day but exhibits sharp peaks around specific intervals (e.g. just after macro releases, or when our inventory hits caps and we are forced to trade).
- **Erosion of realized spread:** The strategy's apparent edge from passive execution disappears in stressed scenarios: realized spreads shrink or even turn negative, indicating that we are being picked off by informed flow.
- **Path-dependent inventory build-ups:** Participation caps that appear safe under baseline flow allow the inventory to drift

towards one side when liquidity evaporates; the lack of fills on the opposite side prevents timely rebalancing, leading to larger drawdowns when prices swing.

- **Nonlinear cost of crossing the spread:** In fragmented markets, bursts of aggressive orders, especially when child orders are too large relative to local depth, generate disproportionate price impact and slippage.

These effects are easiest to interpret visually, by comparing intraday profiles of P&L, slippage, and depth under baseline and stressed conditions.

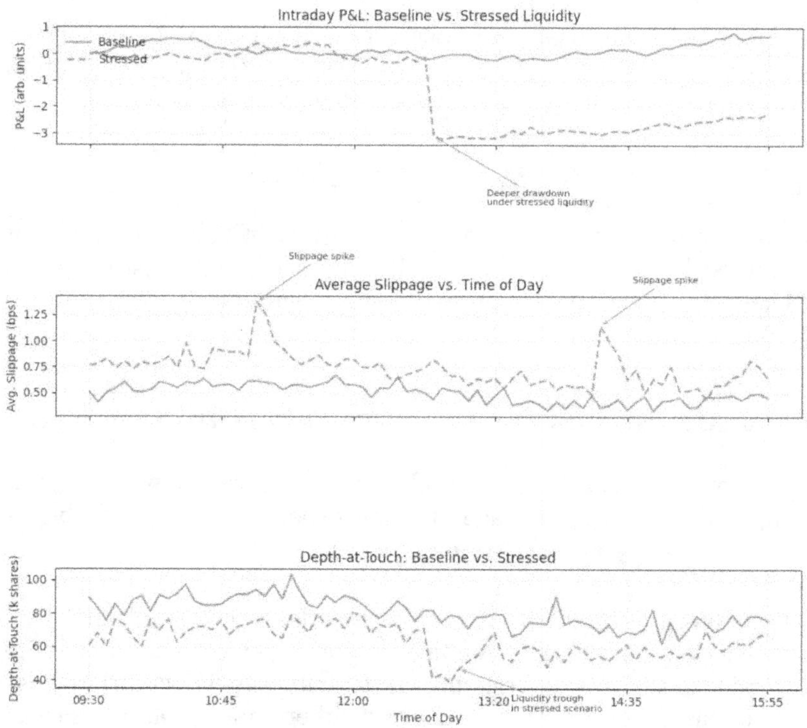

The three panels jointly show how, under stressed synthetic liquidity, P&L experiences deeper intra-day drawdowns, slippage spikes at specific times, and a clear trough in available depth. These shapes are not imposed by design but emerge from the interaction between the strategy and the adversarial order flow.

From Diagnostics to Execution and Risk Changes

The real value of synthetic markets lies in what we do after seeing these diagnostics. We translate the observed vulnerabilities into modifications of our execution policy and risk governance.

Tightening Participation Caps in Stressed States

Under endogenous dry-ups, we observed that a fixed participation cap (e.g. $\rho = 10\%$ of volume) was too aggressive once liquidity began to thin. To address this, we introduce a *state-dependent* cap:

$$\rho_t = \rho_{base} \times g(\text{depth\_score}_t),$$

where depth_score_t is a synthetic "volatility-of-liquidity" indicator computed from recent depth, spread, and cancellation rates, and $g(\cdot)$ is a decreasing function. In words: when the synthetic market indicates that liquidity is fragile, we automatically trade less.

Rebalancing Passive vs. Aggressive Child Orders

In the toxicity scenarios, we found that passive orders, which looked cheap under historical averages, became expensive because of adverse selection. Our response is twofold:

- **Adverse-selection filter:** before leaning on the book, we check a short-horizon predictor of toxicity (e.g. recent imbalance of trades and price response). If toxicity is high, we curb the use of passive orders at the touch and either improve our price (post deeper in the book) or reduce size.
- **Dynamic mix:** the ratio of passive to aggressive orders becomes a function not only of schedule urgency but also of the estimated

toxicity. Aggressive orders are not always bad; when depth is thin but toxicity is low, it may be cheaper to cross the spread in smaller clips than to expose ourselves to being picked off.

The synthetic market lets us backtest these more nuanced rules under replayed stress, rather than relying on intuition alone.

Adjusting Child Order Sizing and Throttles

Fragmentation shocks revealed that our child orders were sometimes too large relative to local depth, producing nonlinear price impact. Two concrete changes follow:

- We tie maximum child size to a *multi-venue* estimate of tradeable depth, when available, and to synthetic worst-case depth when not.
- We introduce throttles on sequences of aggressive orders: if slippage over the past N child orders exceeds a threshold, we automatically pause or reduce size, effectively implementing a micro-level stop-out.

These throttles are calibrated not to never trigger, but to trigger rarely under baseline flow and more frequently under stressed flow—exactly what we want in a risk control.

Revising Intraday Stop-Out Logic and Limits

Finally, short-term drawdown profiles from synthetic stresses inform intraday risk limits. Instead of a simple end-of-day loss limit, we define:

- A set of rolling-window P&L bands (e.g. 30-minute drawdown thresholds) derived from the tail of the synthetic stressed P&L distribution.
- Conditional actions: reduce participation caps, narrow the set of traded names, or freeze new risk-taking when these bands are breached.

Because the synthetic scenarios are constructed to be adversarial but plausible, these limits are neither overly conservative (as they might be if we used extreme heuristic scenarios) nor naively optimistic (as they might be if we used only historical backtests).

Validation and Production Integration

Before promoting any changes to production, we must validate that our synthetic LOB is not a fantasy world. We therefore perform two layers of validation:

- **Out-of-sample replay:** We simulate the strategy on historical days not used for calibration, with the generative model restricted to typical regimes. We compare simulated and actual realized metrics (slippage, fill rates, depth usage) to ensure the simulator reproduces baseline behavior.
- **Stress realism checks:** For stress scenarios, we compare synthetic extremes of depth, spread, and volatility to documented historical stress events (e.g. known flash crashes, macro event days). The synthetic stresses should be in the same ballpark, possibly somewhat more severe to guard against future surprises.

Finally, we integrate synthetic-stress outputs into production monitoring:

- The same indicators used in synthetic scenarios (volatility-of-liquidity, toxicity scores) are computed live from market data.
- Execution and risk controls learned in the synthetic environment (state-dependent participation caps, dynamic passive/aggressive mix, throttles) are wired to these live indicators.
- Periodic re-runs of the synthetic stress suite—for example weekly or monthly—are scheduled as part of risk governance, with changes tracked and documented.

In this way, the synthetic LOB environment is not a one-off research experiment. It becomes a recurring instrument for probing and hardening the strategy against liquidity stress. The next section will mirror this approach in the options world, where volatility spikes and surface dislocations replace liquidity dry-ups as the primary stress drivers.

7.2 Options Portfolio in a Volatility Spike

In the previous case study, we stressed an intraday equity strategy by deforming the *liquidity* environment in a synthetic limit order book. There, prices were relatively well-behaved, but the cost and reliability of execution changed in adverse ways. We now turn to a different axis of market stress: a sudden and persistent spike in volatility.

Our focus here is an options portfolio that is roughly delta-hedged but carries meaningful exposure to *vega* (sensitivity to implied volatility) and *gamma* (curvature with respect to the underlying price). We will:

- Describe the baseline portfolio and hedging policy.
- Build a synthetic volatility environment using regime-conditioned diffusions with extreme-value tails.
- Run stress experiments—front-end vol explosions, cross-tenor dislocations, and prolonged high-vol regimes.
- Use the resulting P&L and risk decompositions to reveal where vega and gamma are truly concentrated.
- Translate these findings into dynamic hedging, sizing, and risk-governance changes.

The overarching message mirrors the LOB case: synthetic markets are not just about testing level shifts (e.g. higher vol), but about exploring *paths* and *configurations* that strain the portfolio in ways historical data has only hinted at.

Portfolio and Baseline Hedging Policy

Consider an options desk trading index and large-cap single-name options. The book mixes three intents:

- **Directional trades:** long-call overlays, put spreads, and collars expressing medium-term bullish or bearish views on the underlying.
- **Relative-value trades:** calendar spreads (long one tenor, short another), vertical spreads across strikes, and dispersion trades (index options vs. single-name options).
- **Flow-driven positions:** residual inventory arising from client facilitation, partially hedged but not completely neutral.

Maturities range from weekly options to 6-month tenors. Strikes cover out-of-the-money (OTM) puts and calls as well as near-the-money options. The net book is managed under a simple, textbook-style hedging policy:

- **Delta hedging:** The desk rebalances delta to near zero several times per day. When aggregated over the book, delta is kept within a narrow band, for example
$$|\Delta_{net}| \leq \Delta_{max}.$$
- **Vega targets:** Net vega (sensitivity of portfolio value to a parallel shift in the implied vol surface) is monitored but typically allowed to fluctuate within quite wide bounds. The desk might have soft internal guidelines (e.g. "avoid being extremely short front vega"), but no hard limits tied to specific stress outcomes.
- **Margin usage:** Initial and variation margins are monitored against a limit; as long as margin utilization stays below, say, 60–70%, the desk is comfortable adding positions.

Under calm conditions, this policy *appears* adequate: daily P&L is dominated by realized theta and modest gamma scalping, while volatility quietly drifts within historic ranges. But this view hides two issues:

- The portfolio may be heavily exposed to *volatility of volatility* (how fast and far implied vol moves).
- Vega and gamma may be highly concentrated in particular strike/tenor regions, which become problematic in a spike.

To reveal these, we insert the portfolio into a synthetic environment specifically designed to stress volatility.

Synthetic Volatility Environment

We need a model that can generate entire paths for:

- The underlying price S_t.
- The implied volatility surface $\sigma_{impl}(t; K, T)$ across strikes K and maturities T.

The key design principle is the same as in the LOB case: *separate calibration fidelity from scenario creativity*. We first fit a regime-aware model to historical returns and implied vols, then augment it with extreme tails to explore volatility spikes.

Regime-Conditioned Diffusion

We assume that markets switch between regimes, such as:

- Calm regime: low realized volatility, stable or drifting-down implied vols.
- Stressed regime: elevated realized volatility, implied vols rising and surface shapes changing (e.g. steeper skew).

Let R_t be a hidden (or observable) regime variable taking values in $\{\text{calm}, \text{stressed}\}$. Conditional on R_t, underlying log-returns follow a diffusion,

$$d \log S_t = \mu_{R_t}\, dt + \sigma_{R_t}\, dW_t,$$

with $\sigma_{stressed} \gg \sigma_{calm}$. The regime itself follows, for instance, a Markov chain with transition probabilities estimated from historical episodes.

For the implied volatility surface, we represent log-implied vols at a grid of strikes and maturities as a low-dimensional factor model:

$$\log \sigma_{impl}(t; K, T) = a_0(t) + a_1(t)\, \phi_1(K, T) + a_2(t)\, \phi_2(K, T) + \cdots ,$$

where the ϕ_j capture typical shapes (parallel shifts, term structure steepening, skew changes) and the factors $a_j(t)$ follow regime-conditioned diffusions. In the stressed regime, factor volatilities and drifts are larger, embedding the idea that both levels and shapes of the surface move more aggressively.

Extreme-Value Tails for Volatility Shocks

Empirically, volatility spikes are not well described by Gaussian increments. To capture "big jumps" in vol, we enrich the factor dynamics with extreme-value-theory (EVT) tails:

- We fit the distribution of large changes in implied vol factors using an EVT model (e.g. Generalized Pareto) above a high threshold.
- During simulation, when a factor increment exceeds this threshold, we sample the tail from the EVT model instead of from a Gaussian.

Informally, this means that 1–2 day moves of +15–30 volatility points in the front of the surface—rare in history but possible—are represented with realistic frequency and magnitude. By conditioning these jumps more often in the stressed regime, we create synthetic paths with convincing volatility spikes.

Stress Experiments

With the synthetic environment in place, we design scenarios that specifically probe the portfolio's gamma and vega exposures. We use the same philosophy as in the LOB case: ask clear stress questions first, then construct scenarios that answer them.

Front-End Vol Explosion with Surface Steepening

The first scenario addresses the classic risk for short-vol portfolios: a sudden front-end spike in implied vols, especially in downside puts. We define:

- At $t = 0$, the market is in a calm regime with vols near historical medians.
- Over the next 1–2 days, we force a regime switch to stressed and trigger EVT tail events for short-tenor volatility factors.
- The surface steepens: short-dated OTM puts see larger vol jumps than long-dated or at-the-money options.

In this scenario, we are asking: *If we suddenly revisit a "mini-crisis" level of front-end vol, how bad does it get for our current vega positions and gamma-heavy structures?*

Cross-Tenor Dislocation

The second scenario focuses on relative-value risk along the tenor dimension. Calendar spreads, which are structurally long one tenor and short another, are sensitive to *non-parallel* moves in the surface. We construct:

- A synthetic path where medium- to long-dated vols rise modestly, while front-end vols spike much more, then partially mean-revert.
- A later phase where the medium tenors catch up or even overshoot, while the front-end normalizes.

This pattern represents a dislocation: the usual term-structure relationships break temporarily before re-aligning. It tests whether our book is effectively short vega in one segment and long in another in a way that could suffer large mark-to-market swings before convergence.

Prolonged High-Volatility Regime

Finally, we consider not just a spike, but a *plateau*: after an initial shock, implied and realized vol stay elevated for weeks. This can be especially challenging for structures that earn theta in calm times by being short vol but rely on short holding periods.

In the simulator, we:

- Switch to the stressed regime at $t = 0$ and keep $R_t =$ stressed for an extended period.
- Generate frequent but not catastrophic EVT tail events, representing repeated "aftershocks".

Here we ask: *Does our book assume that spikes are brief? Do our dynamic hedging and re-striking rules cope with a world where elevated vol is the new normal?*

Metrics and P&L Decomposition

For each synthetic path and scenario, we compute a detailed P&L decomposition. Let Π_t denote portfolio value at time t. Over a short interval Δt, we approximate:

$$\Delta\Pi_t \approx \Delta\Pi_t^{(\Delta)} + \Delta\Pi_t^{(\Gamma)} + \Delta\Pi_t^{(\mathcal{V})} + \Delta\Pi_t^{(\Theta)} + \Delta\Pi_t^{(\text{cross})},$$

where:

- $\Delta\Pi_t^{(\Delta)}$ is delta-related P&L (hedged close to zero by design).
- $\Delta\Pi_t^{(\Gamma)}$ is gamma P&L from curvature in S_t.
- $\Delta\Pi_t^{(\mathcal{V})}$ is vega P&L from changes in implied vols.
- $\Delta\Pi_t^{(\Theta)}$ is time decay (theta).
- $\Delta\Pi_t^{(\text{cross})}$ collects higher-order and cross-greek terms.

We also track:

- **Portfolio drawdown:** time series of running maximum minus current Π_t.
- **Margin utilization:** margin requirements over time divided by the allowed limit.
- **Greek concentration:** aggregated vega and gamma by strike and maturity before and during stress.

The Greek concentration is best visualized as a heatmap over a strike–maturity grid, which we will show after describing the key qualitative findings.

Findings: Where Gamma and Vega Really Live

Running the portfolio through the synthetic volatility spike reveals several patterns that are not apparent from simple snapshot reports.

Gamma Clusters Around Particular Tenors and Strikes.

Even though the aggregate gamma of the book may appear moderate, it is often concentrated in:

- Near-the-money options in the front 1–2 expiries (from short-dated directional trades and client hedges).
- Specific strikes involved in tight spreads (e.g. short verticals that add large local curvature).

In a front-vol explosion, the underlying becomes more volatile just as these gamma clusters come alive, amplifying intra-day P&L swings and the cost of frequent delta rebalancing.

Hidden Vega Concentration in Correlated Underlyings.

On the vega side, nominal vega by ticker may look diversified, but when we consider correlation (e.g. 20 tech names that move almost as one), we see effective vega concentration:

- The book is effectively short vega on a few correlated sectors (e.g. tech growth) and long on others (e.g. defensives).
- When a systemic shock hits, sector vol surfaces move together, and short-vega sectors dominate P&L.

This concentration is accentuated in cross-tenor dislocations, where the misalignment of front and back vols in a single sector creates large calendar-spread P&L before eventual normalization.

Margin Utilization Jumps Before P&L Bottoms.

Under the synthetic spike, margin requirements typically rise quickly as vols spike, even before the portfolio hits its maximum drawdown. This has two consequences:

- **Forced de-risking:** The desk may be compelled to reduce positions or forgo hedges just when they are most needed.
- **Path-dependence:** Two paths with the same terminal vol level can have very different impacts depending on *when* margin peaks relative to P&L.

Visualizing these phenomena helps anchor the intuition, which we do next.

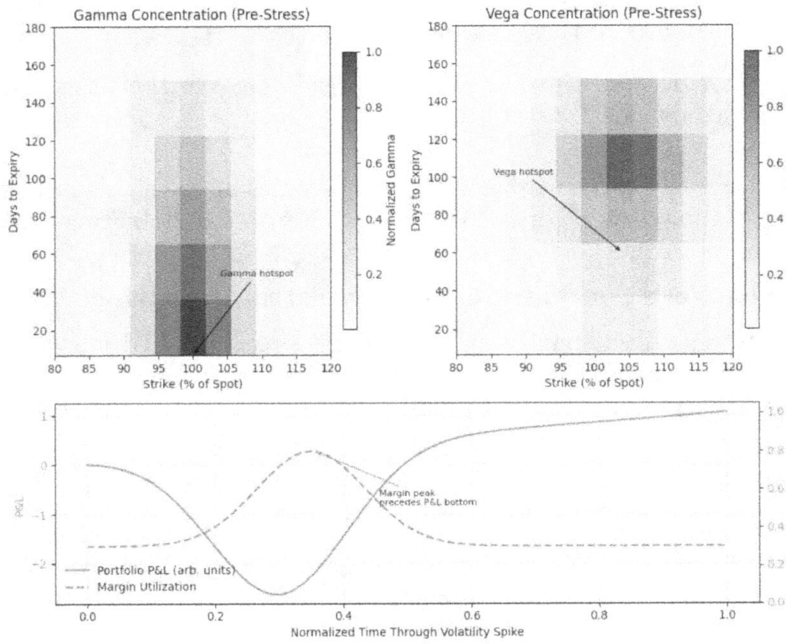

The top panels make visible what was previously a set of numbers in a risk report: gamma is tightly localized near the money at short maturities, and vega is concentrated slightly out-of-the-money in medium tenors. The bottom panel shows that under a synthetic volatility spike, margin usage peaks early, before the portfolio reaches its worst drawdown.

From Insights to Dynamic Hedging and Governance

Synthetic vol stress is only useful if it changes how we trade. Here we outline how the desk might respond to these findings in three areas: hedging policy, sizing limits, and governance.

Dynamic Vega Caps

Previously, the desk operated with a static notion of "acceptable" net vega, often tied to notions like "twice the average daily vega P&L." Using the synthetic spike results, we can instead define:

- **Scenario-consistent vega limits:** For each tenor bucket (e.g. 0–14 days, 14–45 days, 45–120 days), compute the distribution of vega-driven P&L under synthetic spikes. Choose limits so that the 99th percentile loss in each bucket is within an acceptable range.
- **State-dependent scaling:** Make caps a function of the current volatility regime. When live vol-of-vol indicators signal stress, allowed short vega per bucket is automatically reduced.

Formally, if $L_{\alpha}^{stress}(b)$ denotes the α-quantile loss in bucket b under synthetic stress, and $L^{max}(b)$ is the business tolerance, we require:

$$\text{VegaCap}(b) \propto \frac{L^{max}(b)}{L_{\alpha}^{stress}(b)}.$$

This anchors vega limits in a transparent stress metric rather than arbitrary heuristics.

Time-Varying Gamma Limits and Re-Striking Rules

Gamma concentration in short tenors suggests two adjustments:

- **Gamma-by-bucket limits:** Instead of a single global gamma limit, we define limits per maturity bucket, reflecting that short-dated gamma can be much more explosive under stress.
- **Automatic re-striking:** When short-dated gamma in a bucket exceeds its synthetic-stress-informed limit, the system suggests or enforces re-striking actions (e.g. rolling spreads further OTM, converting naked gamma into spreads).

The synthetic environment can be used to backtest such rules: we embed a simplified policy engine into the simulation and measure whether re-striking materially reduces worst-case intra-day P&L swings without unduly sacrificing normal times P&L.

Margin-Aware Position Sizing

The early peak in margin utilization indicates that margin should be treated as a *risk factor*, not just a constraint. We can:

- Generate synthetic time series of margin under volatility spikes across different portfolio configurations.
- Define a margin-stress metric: the maximum margin utilization over the stress horizon at a high quantile (e.g. 99th).
- Set position sizes and leverage such that this metric stays below a governance threshold (e.g. 80% of available margin).

This pre-emptively guards against forced de-risking in the middle of a spike, when liquidity and hedge effectiveness are poorest.

Embedding Synthetic Vol Stress into Ongoing Practice

As in the LOB case, the final step is to turn a one-off study into a recurring discipline.

- **Regular re-runs:** The synthetic volatility stress suite is re-run on the current book at regular intervals (e.g. weekly, or after large flows), generating updated vega/gamma concentration heatmaps and stress P&L distributions.
- **Pre-trade checks:** For large proposed trades or structural strategy changes, we can quickly project the new book into the synthetic environment to see how much worse stress outcomes become. If a single trade dramatically increases short front-vega exposure under spikes, it may require additional approval or hedging.
- **Risk committee integration:** Summaries of synthetic-stress results—including key visuals like those above—become standard agenda items in risk committees. This shifts the conversation from "What is our current vega?" to "How does our portfolio behave in a plausible but severe vol spike, and are we comfortable with that behavior?"

By combining regime-conditioned volatility models with extreme-value tails, and by focusing on intuitive Greek concentration visuals, the synthetic market for options helps bridge the gap between quantitative modeling and risk governance. The next, concluding section will synthesize lessons from both the equities LOB and options volatility case studies into general design principles and an implementation roadmap for synthetic markets in trading organizations.

7.3 Lessons Learned and Future Directions

The two case studies in this chapter—the intraday equities strategy in a synthetic limit order book and the options portfolio under a synthetic volatility spike—illustrate the same basic idea from different angles: generative synthetic markets are not just *models* of the world, they are *instruments* for asking structured questions about fragility.

This section distills what those examples teach us into three themes:

- Design principles for synthetic-market stress testing.
- Governance patterns and MLOps requirements to make synthetic markets sustainable.
- A roadmap for future research and production deployment.

We will take these in turn, always connecting abstract ideas back to the concrete LOB and options examples you have just seen.

Cross-Case Insights: What the Examples Really Showed

Before abstracting, it is useful to restate the main lessons from each case study in comparable language.

From the Equities LOB Strategy

The LOB case showed that:

- **Liquidity is a state variable, not a background constant.** By explicitly modeling depth-at-touch, queue dynamics, and order-flow toxicity, we saw that strategy performance depended as much on the *path* of liquidity as on price moves.
- **Execution logic can be structurally fragile.** Fixed participation caps, static passive/aggressive mixes, and rigid child-order sizing rules looked acceptable under typical conditions, but broke down under adversarial order flow.
- **Useful diagnostics are local and path-based.** Intraday slippage spikes, queue-fill probabilities, and short-horizon drawdown distributions revealed vulnerabilities that end-of-day P&L averages did not.
- **Stress results can be translated into specific rule changes.** Synthetic stresses led directly to state-dependent participation caps, improved passive/aggressive switching logic, throttles, and refined intraday stop-outs.

From the Options Volatility Spike

The options case highlighted complementary points:

- **Volatility-of-volatility and tails matter as much as level.** The regime-conditioned diffusion plus EVT tails produced plausible volatility spikes that are poorly approximated by Gaussian assumptions.
- **Greek concentration is multi-dimensional.** Risk lived not in a single "net vega" number but in gamma and vega clusters across strike, maturity, and correlated underlyings.
- **Margin is a path-dependent constraint.** Margin utilization often peaked before P&L bottomed, making margin an active driver of behavior under stress.
- **Stress metrics can anchor limits.** Synthetic-stress P&L distributions supported explicit, scenario-consistent vega caps, gamma buckets, and margin-aware sizing rules.

Across both examples, three meta-lessons stand out:

- You must choose *what* to stress before you decide *how* to generate synthetic data.
- It is critical to distinguish between replicating the past (*calibration*) and exploring plausible but different futures (*scenario creativity*).
- Synthetic results only matter if they close a loop back into strategy design, risk limits, and monitoring.

We now turn these into a more systematic set of design principles.

Design Principles for Synthetic-Market Stress Testing

Start with Clear Stress Questions

In both case studies, we began with explicit questions:

- *Equities LOB:* How does this intraday alpha behave when liquidity dries up because of our own flow, and how do execution rules cope with toxic order flow and fragmentation?
- *Options:* How does this roughly delta-hedged portfolio behave in a volatility spike, where the surface shape and vol-of-vol are adversarial, and where are vega and gamma really concentrated?

This may sound obvious, but in practice it is common to:

- Start with a complex model and generate generic scenarios.
- Then, after the fact, look for interesting patterns.

A better practice is:

- Write down 3–5 specific stress questions in plain language.
- For each, identify the key state variables (e.g. depth, toxicity, surface skew, vol-of-vol).
- Only then design generative mechanisms that can control those variables directly.

This question-first approach ensures that modeling effort is oriented toward decision-relevant aspects of the market.

Separate Calibration Fidelity from Scenario Creativity

Synthetic markets sit on a spectrum between two extremes:

- At one end, high-fidelity models that mimic historical distributions closely but do not readily explore unseen regimes.
- At the other end, ad hoc stress scenarios that are easy to imagine but may be unrealistic or incoherent (e.g. arbitrarily doubling vol everywhere).

The LOB and options examples illustrate a middle path:

- **Calibration layer:** Fit core dynamics (order arrivals, depth profiles, volatility regimes, surface factors) to history so that simulated "normal" days look like real ones.
- **Scenario layer:** On top of this, impose controlled deviations—adversarial order-flow states, forced regime switches, EVT-tail draws—to generate structured stresses.

Formally, you can think of this as having a base distribution P_θ, with parameters θ estimated from data, and a family of *stress measures* Q_ϕ obtained by deforming P_θ along a small number of interpretable directions ϕ (liquidity, volatility, correlation, etc.). Good practice includes:

- Keeping track of which components are data-driven and which are hand-crafted.
- Validating the base model against out-of-sample days to avoid building stress on a flawed foundation.
- Documenting scenario deformations clearly so they can be debated and refined.

Track a Minimal, Strategy-Specific Set of Stress Metrics

Across both case studies, we deliberately focused on a small number of metrics:

- LOB: slippage, realized spread, queue-fill probabilities, short-horizon drawdowns, liquidity-of-liquidity indicators.
- Options: P&L decomposed by Greeks, drawdown paths, margin utilization, gamma and vega concentration heatmaps.

The pattern is:

- Identify the limited set of quantities that actually drive decisions (execution parameters, risk limits, capital allocation).
- Design synthetic experiments and reporting around those quantities.

This avoids drowning stakeholders in high-dimensional plots while still honoring the richness of the simulated environment.

Design for Interventions, Not Just Diagnostics

A synthetic market that only produces interesting graphs is an academic toy. In both cases, we emphasized *interventions*:

- Adjusting participation caps, passive/aggressive mixes, child-order sizes, throttles, and intraday stop-outs in the LOB case.
- Redefining vega and gamma limits, re-striking rules, and margin-aware sizing in the options case.

A practical guideline is:

> For every stress metric you track, sketch in advance what you would do if that metric looked "bad" under synthetic scenarios.

If you cannot articulate such an action, reconsider whether the metric is truly necessary.

Governance Patterns for Synthetic Markets

Once synthetic markets start influencing trading and risk decisions, they themselves become objects of governance. Three patterns are particularly important: ownership, validation, and transparency.

Clear Ownership and Change Control

Synthetic environments live at the intersection of quant research, trading, risk, and technology. Without clear ownership, they drift. Effective organizations:

- Assign explicit owners for each major synthetic module (LOB engine, volatility engine, correlation engine, etc.).
- Maintain versioned configurations for both calibration and stress scenarios.

- Require structured review (e.g. change advisory boards, model risk committees) for significant updates.

This is especially important when stress outputs feed into hard constraints like risk limits or capital allocation. Changing the synthetic engine is, in effect, changing the lens through which you see risk.

Validation and Back-Testing of Stress Tools

Stress tools themselves need to be validated. In the LOB case, we:

- Replayed historical days with the strategy plugged into the simulator.
- Checked that simulated slippage, fill rates, and depth usage matched realized values reasonably well.

In the options case, we:

- Compared the distribution of simulated vol moves and surface shape changes against known historical episodes.
- Checked that improved and stressed paths were believable extensions rather than arbitrary distortions.

A structured validation framework might include:

- **Benchmark fit:** Does the base model reproduce key empirical moments (vol smiles, depth profiles, etc.)?
- **Historical replay:** Do strategies behave similarly in simulated and real environments on known days?
- **Stress realism:** Are synthetic extremes roughly in line with documented crises, allowing for deliberately conservative extensions?

Validation does not seek perfection; it seeks to rule out gross misspecification and to calibrate trust in the tool.

Transparency and Explainability for Stakeholders

Risk committees and senior management must be able to understand, at least qualitatively, what synthetic markets are doing. Good practice includes:

- Using intuitive state variables in narratives: "thin depth," "toxic flow," "front-end vol spike," "vega hotspot," instead of opaque model parameters.
- Presenting visuals such as intraday P&L under stress, Greek concentration heatmaps, and margin paths, each linked to clear explanatory text.
- Distinguishing clearly between model-derived insights and judgment calls (e.g. how conservative a stress to adopt).

The goal is that non-quant stakeholders can challenge assumptions, question scenario design, and understand the implications of stress results for business decisions.

MLOps Requirements: Making Synthetic Markets a Living System

From an engineering perspective, synthetic markets are complex machine-learning and simulation systems. To remain useful, they need MLOps support analogous to that for predictive models.

Reproducible Pipelines and Scheduling

Both case studies benefited from the idea of regularly re-running the stress suite on the current portfolio. To achieve this at scale, you need:

- Automated pipelines that:
  - Ingest positions and configurations.
  - Run calibrated base simulations.
  - Apply defined stress deformations.
  - Produce standardized metrics and reports.
- Parameterized scenario definitions (e.g. YAML or database-driven) that can be version-controlled.

- Scheduler integration so that stresses run on a schedule (e.g. overnight) and on-demand (e.g. when a large trade is proposed).

Reproducibility is critical: you must be able to re-run last quarter's stress with the then-current book and model version to audit past decisions.

Monitoring Data and Model Drift

Synthetic environments depend on real-world data and modeling assumptions that may drift over time. Examples include:

- Changes in market microstructure (new venues, fee structures) that affect LOB dynamics.
- Shifts in volatility regimes after structural macro changes or crises.

MLOps practices should include:

- Drift detection for key summary statistics (e.g. spreads, depth, implied vol levels and correlations).
- Alerts when the base calibration no longer matches recent data within tolerance.
- Controlled retraining or recalibration procedures, with backtests to ensure continuity and avoid cliff effects.

Model Registry and Audit Trails

Given that synthetic-stress outputs can affect limits and capital, regulators and internal audit functions will expect traceability. A minimal setup includes:

- A model registry recording versions of core simulation engines, their calibration data windows, and validation results.
- Logging of all stress runs with timestamps, input portfolios, scenario definitions, and summary outputs.

- The ability to reconstruct, months later, which model and scenario versions underpinned a particular decision (e.g. tightening vega caps).

These practices align synthetic markets with broader model risk management standards.

Roadmap for Future Research and Deployment

Finally, we sketch a roadmap for expanding synthetic-market usage from the two isolated case studies to a more comprehensive infrastructure.

Richer Multi-Asset Synthetic Markets

Real portfolios span asset classes. Natural research directions include:

- Joint LOB and volatility environments: e.g. equity options where liquidity and volatility stresses interact.
- Cross-asset correlation and contagion: synthetic scenarios where equity, credit, rates, and FX markets co-move in crisis-like patterns.
- Funding and collateral dynamics: integrating synthetic stresses on repo markets, haircuts, and funding spreads.

This requires carefully coordinating multiple simulation engines and designing consistent cross-asset scenarios.

Agent-Based Adversaries and Co-Evolution

In both case studies, the synthetic environment reacted in stylized ways to our strategies. A more advanced direction is to populate synthetic markets with explicit adversarial agents:

- Liquidity providers that adapt spreads and depth based on our flow patterns.
- Informed traders whose activity clusters around our executions or hedges.

- Competing volatility sellers or buyers whose presence shapes surface dynamics.

Using reinforcement learning or game-theoretic setups, one can explore co-evolution: our strategy adapts to the synthetic market, which in turn adapts to our strategy. This can reveal equilibria and failure modes that static stress scenarios miss.

Stress-on-Demand in Research and Production Tools

In mature setups, synthetic markets become a *service* available to researchers and traders directly from their existing tools:

- In research IDEs, a quant can write a new strategy, click "stress-test," and receive synthetic P&L and risk reports within minutes.
- In trading dashboards, a portfolio manager can preview the impact of a proposed position change under standard stress suites before approving it.

Implementing this requires:

- Well-defined APIs around the simulation engines.
- Scalable compute infrastructure (e.g. distributed execution, GPU acceleration where relevant).
- Thoughtful UX so that stress results are understandable and actionable, not just data dumps.

Continuous Validation Against Emerging Regimes

Finally, synthetic markets must stay in touch with reality. As new regimes emerge—pandemics, new monetary policies, structural market reforms—the models and scenarios must be updated. A forward-looking roadmap includes:

- Periodically back-testing the synthetic engines on recent stress episodes they were not trained on.

- Adding new scenario families inspired by those episodes (e.g. negative rates, persistent inflation, regulatory-driven liquidity shifts).
- Retiring or down-weighting obsolete scenarios whose underlying market structures no longer exist.

In this way, synthetic markets become a living representation of "what could happen next," constantly informed by what has actually happened but not limited to it.

www.ingramcontent.com/pod-product-compliance
Lightning Source LLC
LaVergne TN
LVHW010917300926
849194LV00025B/257
* 9 7 9 8 8 9 6 6 5 2 3 7 3 *